Memories

of

Magical Waters

Memories
of
Magical Waters

Gord Deval

Foreword by Paul Quarrington

NATURAL HERITAGE BOOKS
TORONTO

Published by Natural Heritage / Natural History Inc.
P.O. Box 95, Station O, Toronto, Ontario M4A 2M8
www.naturalheritagebooks.com

Library and Archives Canada Cataloguing in Publication

Deval, Gord, 1930-
Memories of magical waters / Gord Deval ; foreword by Paul Quarrington.
Includes bibliographical references and index.

ISBN 1-897045-12-3

1. Deval, Gord, 1930-. 2. Fly fishing—Ontario. 3. Trout fishing—Ontario. 4. Fly fishing—Québec (Province). 5. Trout fishing—Québec (Province). I. Title.

SH415.D88A3 2006   799.1'2'092   C2006-900881-7

All visuals unless otherwise identified are courtesy of the author.
Cover and text design by Neil Thorne
Edited by Jane Gibson

Natural Heritage / Natural History Inc. acknowledges the financial support of the Canada Council for the Arts and the Ontario Arts Council for our publishing program. We acknowledge the support of the Government of Ontario through the Ontario Media Development Corporation's Ontario Book Initiative. We also acknowledge the financial support of the Government of Canada through the Book Publishing Industry Development Program (BPIDP) and the Association for the Export of Canadian Books.

I would like to dedicate this book to my best fishin' buddy, my lovely wife, Sheila.

Table of Contents

Acknowledgements

There have been hundreds of folks with whom I have wet a line, or practised casting at targets or for distance in competition over the years—and many others who in different ways certainly influenced my life's direction. Although a number of them are no longer with us to help me celebrate this, my sixth book to be published, I would like to thank and recognize as many of them as I can recall here.

My father, Roy Ward Dickson, an extremely intelligent man who unfortunately never passed those particular genes on to his son, nevertheless set me on my career path prescribing courses I took and giving me a pocket allowance based on a weekly essay I had to write for him, and monitored it accordingly as long as he was able to do so. My parents were separated when I was seventeen.

My dear mother, Helen, although having few opportunities to wet a line herself, had a love of the outdoors and made the most of every chance she had to go fishing or take a stroll in the countryside. Bob Wilcox, my uncle, loved fishing, especially for trout. His ardent pursuit of trout and different places to go after them was possibly the greatest influence on my love of fishing during my early years.

I owe much appreciation to my children, Connie, Wendy, Randy and Ronnie, all of whom enjoyed fishing with me during their own early years, I have vivid recollections of my daughters' times on the water with their old man, while my sons both became experts with rod and reel, learning how to read and appreciate whatever they discovered in the outdoors. Another huge influence in my fishing and casting pursuits was my first wife and the mother of my children, Joan, a fine fisherman in her own right.

I wish to thank Jim Gifford who suggested I write this book and Bill and Jamie Gairdner who sponsored me for years at the Fitness Institute and to the World Casting Champions, and Clive Caldwell and Steve Roest of the Fitness Institute who also assisted me in this respect. Most importantly, I owe my life to Dr. Khoa Le, who made it his personal goal to bring me back from the dead when I was critically struck down with a near-fatal case of pancreatitis.

Several of my earliest fishin' buddies, who were kind and interested enough to join me on quite a few of my early forays into the angling wars, were Kenny Dorsey, Carl Wilkinson and, of course, Tom Wells. During my later teenage years, relationships with Art Walker and Ron Duncan developed to the point where we competed with each other in tournament casting, fished together all over the place and exchanged knowledge freely as long as health permitted. Unfortunately, in later years Ron became ill and Art, twice my best man, passed away.

Also, during those early years, I began reading every book and magazine I could get my hands on that dealt with angling—or competitive tournament casting. Earl Osten, a gentleman whom I never actually had the pleasure of meeting, wrote a book, *Tournament Fly and Bait Casting*, that was my early bible on the subject until the pages yellowed and wore thin. Perhaps the person who was the most influential in my life's direction was that wonderful fisherman and outdoorsman Lee Wulff.

One of the finest tournament casters who ever graced the casting docks was Myron Gregory. His assistance and expertise, freely given was of tremendous help to me in that endeavour. Other tournament casters whom I would like to recognize here, all of whom also helped me in many ways with any casting prowess that I was able to develop over the years include: Jim Chapralis, Allan Ehrhardt, Dick Fujita, Rene Gillibert, Chris Korich, Steve Rajeff, John (Zero) Seroczynski, Jim Venable, Zack Willson and Stan Yonge.

This book, based on my memories of the incredible experiences gained in fishing, predominantly trout, would not have been feasible without the friendship of my "fishin' buddies" and their influence on me, commencing in my youth. I wish to thank them for going along on the ride: Brad Allen, Don Allen, Paul Becker, Gary Benson, Don Burd, Roger Cannon, Ray Cockburn, Dave Collins, Paulo Conceicao, Len Connelly, Mike Dinner, Christopher Eckart, John Finnegan, Jimmy Folkes, Hans Gulde, Oliver Johnston, Ashok Kalle, Paul Kennedy, Italo Labignan, Fred Leibl, Jim Lloyd, Ken Lusk, Rick Matusiak, Pete McGillen, Don Petican, Pete Pokulok, Scott Purcell, Paul Quarrington, Mike Roskopf, Doug Ryder, Steve Ryder, Leon Schwartz, Larry Sykes, Bill Taylor, Paul Voisin, King Whyte and Jack Wilkings.

I also wish to thank my publisher, Barry Penhale, for his belief in me and for having some fine fishing tales himself, and Jane Gibson, editor for Natural Heritage Books, whose patience was thoroughly tested in editing the text.

Foreword

Gordon Deval is made of different stuff than I. His senses seem more acute. On our fishing trips, he sees things long before I do. Little things: mushrooms, insects, the flora decorating the riverside, big brown trout sitting in muddy holes. He not only sees things before I do, he sees things I just plain don't. Gordon points them out helpfully, but I don't have his eyes. He sees the world in a special way. He sees both the details and the big picture. Gordon can spy the natural world that lies beneath our human artifice.

Gordon's memory is different than mine, too. Mostly because he has one, I mean, a remarkable one. I think he can remember every fish he ever caught. Gordon can remember the excitement that accompanied each of them.

Gord Deval and Paul Quarrington on the Ganaraska River.

I may have to work harder than Gordon does, but I can summon many memories of the man I affectionately call "The Old Guy." I can remember the first time I saw him, for example. It was in a school gymnasium, and Gordon was demonstrating a fly-casting technique known as the "double haul." It's a beautiful thing when executed properly, a way to shoot great lengths of line. It involves a combination of grace and strength, and I'm still working on it twenty-odd years later.

I can remember the first time we went fishing together. This is actually quite a vivid memory, because of the presence of a ferocious dog and a nasty-looking gentleman who felt we shouldn't have been fishing a particular section of the Ganaraska River. But that gets back to what I was saying before, about Gordon seeing the world differently than I do. He often misses things like fences and "No Trespassing" signs.

One of my fondest memories—at least, the one that makes me chuckle the most—involves the two of us driving into the heart of the United States of America. Every time we passed a field, Gordon would say, "There's a nice field." There was frequently some other reason for praising the field—perhaps there were puffballs sprouting in its middle, perhaps a fox was running along its perimeter—which Gordon would note, although I never saw any of that stuff. I would simply nod, having managed to spot the field. One of the reasons fields are so beloved of Gordon is that they give him space to practise his distance casting; he reigned as Canadian champion for many years. He would also praise any river, rivulet or rill we passed by. "There's a beautiful stream," Gordon would grin, no doubt imagining all the beautiful fish that lived in the beautiful stream. So for hundreds of miles, these were his most frequent observations, a proclivity I finally pointed out with a slight tinge of irritation. Gordon was quiet for a long moment. "I like fields, and I like streams," he acknowledged. "And by god, I love that magazine."

It is that kind of good spirited liveliness—as well as his memory, and a quick, clean writing style—that make this book by Gordon Deval so delightful.

Enjoy it.

Paul Quarrington
Toronto, 2006

Prologue

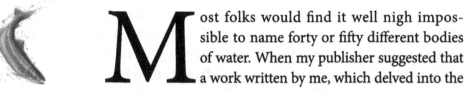

Most folks would find it well nigh impossible to name forty or fifty different bodies of water. When my publisher suggested that a work written by me, which delved into the charm and mystique of the many streams, rivers and lakes that I have been fortunate enough to have wet a line on or in during my more than sixty-five years of fishing, would appeal to anglers past and present, I sat down with a pencil, then slapped on my thinking cap. Amazingly, the list of waters that tested my angling skills over all those years totalled *more* than one hundred and seventy. If it had not been for this exercise, I would not have believed it.

Although a few of these waters provide me with only a faint and or mundane recollection, many others are indelibly etched in my memory bank. As often as not, big fish have little to do with it. Each and every brook, stream, river and lake that tested my mettle as an angler over all those years left its mark—several, pleasantly and a few not so pleasantly—while countless others provided magnificently vivid and detailed reminiscences. It is these wonderfully magical waters and the wonderful hours enjoyed fishing them that created all these magical memories.

Allow me to share a few of these moments with you.

Here are the "magical waters" listed alphabetically:
12 Mile Lake, 30 Island Lake, A/B Lake,* Allen Lake, Bald Lake, Balsam Lake, Baltimore Creek,† Bateaux River, Bay of Quinte, Beanpole Lake,* Beaver River,* Beaverkill River (NY), Benson Lake, Bighead River, Birchy Lake, Bitter Lake, Bivouac Lake, Black Lake, Blue Lake,*Bowmanville Creek, Boyne River, Broadback River,* Brooks Lake,† Brule Lake, Buckhorn Lake, Burdoch Lake, Butternut Lake, Cache Lake, Canoe Lake, Cavan Stream, Centreton Creek, Charleston Lake, Clear (Clean) Lake, Clement Lake, Coldwater Creek, Desert Lake, Devil Lake, Duck Lake, Duffins Creek, East Lake, East River, Echo Creek,* Fishtail Lake, Fleetwood Creek, Frenchman's

Bay, Georgian Bay,† Golden Lake, Grace Lake, Grand River, Grants Lake, Green Lake, Green Lake (2), Grenadier Pond, Gull Lake, Gull River, Hall's Lake, Harburn Lake, Castleton Creek, Indian Brook, "Itsy Bitsy" Brook,* Janetville Stream, Jessops Creek, Jocko River, Kashagawigamog Lake, Kashawakamac (Long) Lake, Kawagama (Hollow) Lake, Kennesis Lake, Kiefers Creek, Kingscott Lake, Lady Evelyn Lake, Lake Huron, Lake Nippising, Lake of Bays, Lake Ontario, Lake Simcoe,† Limit Lake,* Little Birchy Lake, Little East River, Little Jocko River, Little Kennesis Lake, Little Mackie Lake, Little Redstone Lake, Long Mallory Lake, Long Schooner Lake, Loughborough Lake,* Lucky Lake,* Mackie Lake, Mad River, Madawaska River, Magnetwawan River, Mazinaw Lake, Mill Creek, Moore Lake, Moose Lake, Mosque Lake,* Muskoka Lake,* Noisy River, Nonquon River, North Lake, North Quinn Lake, North River (P.E.I.), Nottawasaga River, Oshawa Creek, Otonabee River, Ouse River, Papineau Creek, Peach (Miskwabi) Lake, Pefferlaw River, Pigeon Lake, Pigeon River, Pine Lake, Pine River, "Piss" (Trout) Creek,* Pottawatami Lake, Pretty River, Quinn Lake, Redstone Lake, Reinl Lake,† Rice Lake, Rideau Lake, Rock Lake, Rocky Saugeen Stream, Rouge River, Round Schooner Lake, Rupert River, Saugeen River,* Scugog Lake, Severn River, Sharpes Creek, Sheldon Creek,† Shelter Valley Stream, Silver Creek, Silver Lake, Skootamata Lake, Sludge Lake,† South Quinn Lake, Sturgeon Lake, Sturgeon River, Sullivan Lake,† Sydenham River, Tedious Lake,* Temagami Lake, Toronto Islands, Trent River, Trout Creek (Pennsylvania), Trout Lake, Willemoc River (NY).*

The asterisk (*) in the above list indicates the greatest of all locations for the memories pertinent to these waters, and the symbol (†) marks those I also consider superb, thus their inclusion in this work. This book will, of course, deal with the most powerful and interesting recollections. The other waters listed here should still be considered as excellent sites, well worth a visit for the enterprising fisherman.

Chapter 1
The Waters of Uxbridge

Founded by Dutch settlers in the late 1800s, Uxbridge is a delightful little town resting in a cleft between the hills and forests on the north side of the Oak Ridges Moraine, an esker running some eighty to a hundred kilometres from west to east, about half an hour's drive north of Toronto. The moraine is home to a myriad of cold-water springs that become the headwaters of most of the brooks, creeks, streams and rivers, flowing southwards towards Lake Ontario while a number of others originating on the other side of the moraine flow in a northerly direction.

Many of these waters emerge from their underground reservoirs in minuscule fashion, bubbling out amongst the roots of the trees that form the nucleus of the swamps and forests in the area. Hiking through these areas, one can hear the springs gurgling as they escape their secret hiding places and emerge into the open then bubble along a few feet, only to retreat beneath the roots and mantle of sphagnum moss carpeting the forest floor. With the decayed leaves from the few hardwoods that manage to exist in the saturated swamps and bush in the area adding to the moss and accumulated humus on the ground, one gets the sensation of walking on six inches of the plushest broadloom imaginable. The only thing missing from this unique ambience is the presence of tiny dryads perched provocatively on their fungal saddles.

Pick your way a little further along through the sudden silence, broken only by whispers of the breezes in the treetops, and suddenly the lilting music of the bubbling springs, materializing as a tiny sparkling brook, once again dominates the character of the bush. This then is the environment that I recall most fondly from my earliest exposures to the pleasures of these magical waters that are the origin of all our lakes and streams.

Before I had reached the ripe old age of ten, I had become fairly proficient at collecting dew worms. When I was a kid they were called "night-crawlers," as they emerge after dark. Bob Wilcox, my uncle, often conscripted me into collecting a supply of dew worms for him and Curly, his fishing buddy. When he wasn't fishing, Curly raced motorbikes on dirt tracks.

My reward was a promise to take me with them to sample the fishing delights in the brooks below the Town of Uxbridge, if my parents would give their permission. My mother wasn't entirely pleased with her brother-in-law's somewhat devious scheme to avoid the backbreaking chore of having to pick his own dews. Of course, my pleading with her to be allowed to stay up late enough to gather the bait so I could accompany them on the fishing excursions usually prevailed.

These outings were never in the spring, however, as least as far as my participation was concerned. I suppose, unable to avail themselves of my services during that time, they bought their bait. It wasn't until the summer months with school out that I would find myself crawling around the neighbourhood lawns an hour or so after sunset with my moss-filled pail, flashlight beam zigzagging back and forth, while my eyes strained for the momentary glimpses of the shiny dews before they instantly drew themselves back into their burrows.

I soon discovered that if the flashlight beam was not shone directly on the worms, or the batteries weakened, the elusive critters were far less likely to be spooked into retreating, and I was able to collect enough to satisfy Curly and Uncle Bob. I seldom fished with the worms myself, preferring to manoeuvre artificial trout flies into the holes between the roots and overhanging grass alongside the tiny brooks.

On the odd occasion though, I would dangle a dew worm behind a fluttering lure, a Colorado spinner,[1] and work it along the edges of the watercress beds that bordered all the brooks in the area. I had read in one of the fishing magazines Mom had bought for me that brook trout preferred to dwell in the shady shelter of the watercress, (a delectable green growing in spring-fed brooks) emerging only to pluck appetizingly appearing morsels from the flow for their snacks. Actually, Uncle Bob had taught me to just use the fat end of the dew worm and completely thread the hook through it, leaving only the barb exposed.

I can close my eyes while I write this now and effortlessly visualize that first wonderfully magical moment when a magnificently bejewelled seven-inch speckled trout darted from nowhere and seized my Parmachene Belle trout fly.[2] Although I had accompanied the men on a couple of earlier trips to the Uxbridge brooks, this was the first "speck" (another of the many monikers applied to speckled trout) that I was able to seduce into having

The young Gordon Deval at the Uxbridge Pond, 1947.

a go at my fly. Unceremoniously, the tiny trout was jerked out of the water into the branches of a tree behind me. Tossing aside my steel rod, I pounced on the catch before it could escape.

Nevertheless, I remember admiring the vividly coloured trout for only a moment before carefully detaching the hook as my uncle had shown me when he put undersized trout back into the swim. It, too, was gingerly placed back into the beckoning brook.

This is definitively my earliest memory of what today is still a magical place for me—Uxbridge Brook.

Although the Uxbridge area produced my earliest memory of the countless waters I have fished, it also produced several others worthy of mention. The springs and brooks escaping from the underground aquifers in the ridge to the south of the town are not the only Uxbridge waters to have tested my angling abilities. The brooks feed a large pond, intersected by a road and bridge with a few lovely homes along its shores. With its feeder springs and brooks, the pond forms the headwaters of the main Uxbridge Brook which flows northwards towards Lake Simcoe after it pours over the small dam in the heart of town. The stream, still fairly small at this stage of its development, produced a couple of other exceptional memories easily recalled in full detail as follows.

The affable citizens of this lovely town whose backyards front on the meandering brook have never become terribly upset at my fishing my way downstream while working the many enticing pools with their log-laced cover. That is, other than the occasional emergence of someone either reminding me to, "Please be careful going around my flower beds, son," or simply questioning our luck with, "Catching anything," or that most oft-asked question of fishermen, "How are they biting?" Almost sixty years of fishing this particular section of waters has never resulted in my being asked or told by one of the owners to get off his land.

There are small, gorgeously coloured speckled trout in the brook. Unfortunately they have to share their territory with an occasional tire or old stove tossed in by some thoughtless person, most likely a non-resident. No longer pristine as they were many moons ago, these icy cold waters still provide an interesting, if not necessarily aesthetic, fishery for the "brookies,"[3] some of which had actually departed their cover in the beds of watercress to take up residence in, or beneath, the debris.

A short distance beyond the town's main street where the stream emerges from its subterranean course below several buildings, it travels beneath another bridge before flowing alongside a row of ancient willow trees with many of their gnarled and enormous branches suspended low over the water. The roots of these massive trees, many of which extend into the stream, provide excellent cover for its fishy inhabitants. However, on one occasion when travelling through the village and taking a minute to see what I could raise from the undercut bank and willow roots, I experienced another magical moment.

I studied the stream looking for the most promising target for the first cast. It appeared probable that the place with the most potential to provide a brookie, worthy of being kept for the pan, would also be the most awkward spot in the area to fish. A huge branch, jutting out from the main trunk of the biggest willow tree on the bank, guarded the likely holding spot for a decent-sized trout—an entanglement of the willow's tentacle-like, underwater roots. It would require a perfect and flat cast in order to propel the spinner far enough beneath the branch that a trout, holding court in the cover, would catch a glimpse of its flashing blades, exit the hole and strike.

The branch, more like a twin to the tree's main trunk, was probably a foot or so in diameter and suspended only another foot or so above the water. It was a challenge I could not refuse, although the likelihood of donating my spinner to one part of the willow or another was considerable. Flexing the rod tip with wrist movement a couple of times, while keeping it close to the surface of the stream and holding my breath for a brief moment, I fired a sharp cast towards the selected target. As luck would have it the lure shot over the branch, not under as intended.

"Damn!"

Then came the memorable moment! After crossing above the big branch, the silver spinner did not have enough momentum remaining in the cast to even reach the water on its far side. It hung there enticingly, its blade flashing six or eight inches above the surface of the stream and a few inches beneath the branch, while I contemplated the best way to extricate it—but only for a split-second.

Before I could repeat the cuss word, a seventeen-inch brook trout shot out from the hole's nether regions and acrobatically managed to latch on to the still fluttering spinner. This was easily the largest and most beautiful brookie I had ever seen in any stream, anywhere, and I somehow knew that I had to have it—but how?

Fortunately, reflex action had immediately taken over on my part. I had already loosened the clutch to the point where the weight and struggling of the trout was sufficient to pull the line smoothly down off the branch without its hanging up. With the fish now in the water, at least now its weight alone would not suffice to free it from the lure's treble hook. Without pausing and wearing only my regular clothes and street shoes, I leapt into the pool, splashed my way furiously towards the branch and awkwardly passed the rod over the top to a spot where I could reach beneath and grab it before it dropped into the stream, all the while attempting to maintain sufficient tension on the line so that the hook wouldn't simply fall out of the trout's mouth.

Soaking wet from stem to stern, only a few minutes more remained before the battle was over, including one heart-stopping session where I had to extricate the brookie that had retreated into its underwater tangle of roots under the bank. My luck held and, stumbling backwards towards the bank, I carefully worked my prize into the shallows then pounced on it on all fours. I thought for just a brief moment about placing it back in the swim, but the fish appeared to be as exhausted as I, so it was kept for showing off to my fishing buddies at home and for the frying pan the next day.

My plans for that day were of course completely derailed by the experience as I sloshed my way back to the car and headed home, grinning all the way back to Toronto. Even the scolding I endured from my wife for ruining my clothes and shoes didn't dampen my enthusiasm. Easily, this is one of my most incredible memories ever and it occurred in what has always been for me—the magic of the waters of Uxbridge!

The waters in and around Uxbridge didn't become the fodder for the opening of this book merely by chance, or just because of the earliest magical memory factor, but because there is a wealth of these wonderful recollections pertinent to the area in my mind's hard drive. There is probably enough material stored there to actually write an entire book on the memories created over all those years by its springs, brooks, the pond and the river.

A couple of other reminiscences occurring at the pond deserve reporting here. Although the principals in the first anecdote do not include me, the Uxbridge Pond and I were sufficiently involved to create this next recollection. The Scarborough Fly and Bait Casting Association, launched by me and a few cronies in 1984, has from its outset been a club comprised of fishermen, skilled anglers and expert fly and bait casters along, of course, with others wishing, practising and learning to become skilled in the art of angling themselves. A few years ago we were approached on the last evening of the summer season at our outdoor practice venue, the reflecting pool behind the Scarborough Civic Centre and City Hall, by a couple of curious and interested spectators while we practised our presentation and accuracy on the floating targets.

Instead of the usual and dumb, "How're they biting?" remarks, they inquired about the club's activities and what were the requirements to join. Although their names have escaped me, I do remember that they were recently retired senior citizens who had moved to Ontario from Newfoundland a few years before our meeting them. They mentioned several times though that it was unlikely that they would become long-term club members, as their plans were to return to the island province within a year or so. But initially their stated objective was to become as proficient with their fly rods and casting prowess as were the club's expert anglers. Both became eager students when we moved our operations indoors for the fall and winter season, working diligently on their fly tying and casting fundamentals. Their thoughts on the island and its excellent trout and salmon fishing were never far from their minds though. We were frequently entertained throughout that winter in the gym with tales of the wonderful trout fishing to be had in their home province.

I distinctly remember one of the chaps addressing us around the fly-tying table one evening, "You know, boys," he stated unequivocally, "it's got the finest trout fishin' in the world, the island has, you know."

He continued, "We've caught speckled trout there as long as your arm and as thick as your leg. At least eighteen inches and a couple of pounds on the scales."

We all glanced at our arms then our legs then each other. His buddy, not quite as loquacious as he, then inquired, "You got any trout like them in these parts, boys?"

Not wishing to be impolite, we merely nodded back and forth, before someone spoke up, "Well, yes, occasionally we hear tell of trout that big caught not too far from here."

Another added, "Usually a brown, but the odd big brook trout does show up, too."

By the May 1 opening of the trout season and our exiting the gym for the outdoor practice pool, both of the club's Newfoundlanders had become quite competent with their fly rods and eager to test their new skills on the real thing. I was asked, "We've got a twelve-foot canoe we would like to use for fishing if you know someplace not too far away where we can catch trout? Neither of us have got good enough legs to do a lot of walking up and down streams."

Uxbridge Pond immediately came to mind. "There's a spot," I said, "actually a fair-sized pond, not much more than a half an hour's drive from here that has an assortment of fish in it that you can catch on a fly; specks [speckled trout], perch and 'bows [rainbow trout]. The trout are smallish, maybe nine or ten inches tops, but they do smack flies there pretty good and you should have a bit of fun. You can test your new fly-casting skills by trying to lay your presentations right on top of the rises. Get on top of them quickly enough, and they'll strike every time."

They left indicating they'd give it a try on the weekend.

Saturday afternoon, the opening day of the trout season, the phone rang as I was cleaning my own morning's catch of a half-dozen stream brook trout. The call was from one of the gentlemen who had taken our advice to test the Uxbridge Pond waters.

Occasionally when Newfoundlanders talk quickly, because of their dialect it can be difficult to interpret what they are saying. What at first sounded like exuberant gibberish was quickly determined to simply be the excited voice of one of the islanders. Finally calming down, he explained that they had enjoyed their outing, canoeing and fly fishing on the pond, caught a dozen or so small trout, but just before leaving had the thrill of their lives when a trout, much bigger than any of the others sucked in one of their dry flies.

"Bloody thing towed our little canoe around that pond for fifteen minutes, eh, before we even saw him," he swore. "Never saw anything like it," he continued, "except one time thirty miles from shore back home when I hooked and landed a fifty-five pound halibut after it towed me out in the Atlantic, half-way to England."

Dying to know about the Uxbridge adventure, I interjected, "Did you land it, or what? What was it? How big?"

"Yeah we got it all right...it's a 23-inch brown trout, almost four pounds and it's going to the taxidermist this afternoon," he replied. "I'm taking this baby home with me when we go back!"

After he finished profusely thanking me for the assistance and instruction he had received in the club, along with the suggestion to fish the pond at Uxbridge, he asked if I would like to have a look at his trophy before he took it to be mounted, which I was delighted to do and at the same time snap a picture for the club album.

A few weeks later I learned that the Department of Lands and Forests had previously placed a couple of their retired brood stock of hatchery browns in the town pond in the hopes that one of the local kids in the town's annual "Fishing Derby for Kids Day"[4] would experience the excitement and adventure that my two friends from Newfoundland had enjoyed.

Another recollection also concerning the Uxbridge area, is a story I have told many times when reminiscing about my earlier days working over the brooks south of the town. I had just recovered from a terribly debilitating bout of poison ivy that covered me from head to foot. The noxious stuff was contacted on a previous trip to another stream a little west of Uxbridge after taking my girlfriend, Mona, with me to introduce her to my *second* favourite love, trout fishing. We had paused for a bite of lunch later in the morning and as it often does when it's springtime and you're eighteen years old, one thing led to another. I was too engrossed in the moment to notice that we were stretched out on a large bed of poison ivy until it was too late.

It took several weeks for the rash and pustules to fade and, having been on my back completely coated with lotion to soothe the itch for that long, it was a relief to get out of the house to wet a line once again. This time—on my own! Nevertheless, I still chose to head to my favourite brooks below Uxbridge for the hour or so that I had at my disposal, but kept well away from the poison ivy patch.

Most memories do fade somewhat after more than fifty years, but we are dealing here with magical memories, those that never wane or diminish. As it developed that day though, I was not the only one who had awakened in the morning with an urge to do a spot of fishing for a few brookies to bring home for supper. For some reason or another, the old Ford parked on the side of the gravel road had failed to catch my attention. Slipping on my hip boots a little way down the road from where I had parked my own car, I decided to avoid the more heavily fished area where the creek crossed beneath the road and access it instead a hundred yards downstream. In most of these places the trails disappear rather quickly when one works a little further on from the easiest access, normally where the brook crosses the road.

Hiking a few yards into the bush I could hear the brook gurgling seductively inviting me forward through a dense growth of six-feet-tall ostrich ferns. Suddenly I almost fell over a fisherman sitting by the edge of the creek—my mother! Comfortably ensconced in a bend of a huge, curling, tree root, she held a pocketbook in one hand with her fishing rod in the other, while her line disappeared through the grassy blanket topping the

Gord's mother, Helen, at The Beach in Toronto near the Fallingbrook neighbourhood; photo taken in the mid-1940s.

little brook. Mum was so engrossed in her book, probably a Harlequin romance novel, that she was completely unaware of both her son's presence and the gentle twitching of her rod tip.

Trying not to unduly alarm her, I gently said, "Mother, I think you've got one on...using worms, eh?"

Without batting an eye she replied, "Of course I'm using worms. How else can you fish here? Oh! It's you, Gordon! How did you know I was here?"

I explained while she reeled in another plump eight-incher, efficiently dispatching it before threading a fresh dew worm onto her hook, that I hadn't known that she was fishing there—or even realized that she knew about the waters of the Uxbridge area. Undeniably, a very special memory indeed!

Chapter 2
Fishing on the Ganny

The Ganaraska watershed, an hour's drive east of Toronto is comprised of a great number of springs, brooks and streams, all merging at one point or another into the main southerly flow, the Ganaraska River, providing all in all well over a hundred miles of exceptional and varied trout fishing for its aficionados. The "Ganny," as most of us prefer to call it, is home to resident brown, speckled and rainbow trout all year. It also hosts spring and fall runs of steelhead trout and chinook salmon entering the river from Lake Ontario on their annual spawning rituals to supplement one's angling prospects for success.

If there is one river with its magical waters that has created more memories than any other during my sixty-five years of trout fishing it is the Ganny. Only the mighty Broadback River in northern Quebec, with its huge brook trout, takes up as much space in the part of my brain that stores these recollections.

Over my many years of working over the Ganny, we have learned that the numerous and varied sections of the watershed with their complexions switch abruptly from shallow and fast, clay and meadow waters, to heavily tangled bush-bordered pothole sections. Such variations have led to our creating a range of nicknames[1] for specific locations, names such as the "Red River stretch," "Picnic Grounds," "Nudie stretch," "Used Car Lot," "Fly-fishing stretch" and the infamous "Allan Hepburn stretch."

The "Allan Hepburn stretch"[2] of the Ganny has been responsible for several situations that will be forever etched in my memory—there certainly are a couple of lessons to be absorbed from recounting our adventures on this section of the river. The almost three-mile Hepburn portion is a veritable minefield of awkward and potentially dangerous stream, bush and swamp conditions that one must negotiate in order to fish its relatively untouched, therefore magical waters. Between the masses of jungle-like vines and enormous multi-trunk trees are tangles of six-feet-tall grass, ferns and goldenrod, much of which extends right over the stream bank. Beneath them are unseen, underfoot rotten logs and branches, interspersed with holes, just waiting to trip you up or break your ankle. If one survives those niceties there are always others with which to contend, such as the poison ivy, stinging nettles and needle-laced hawthorn trees and raspberry canes designed by Mother Nature to rip at, or pierce your skin. I haven't even touched on the seasonal mosquito, blackfly and deer fly infestations. My fishing buddies and I are seldom concerned about overfishing or finding other folks plying these difficult to negotiate waters.

Nevertheless, some anglers such as my fishing buddies and I covet the challenge in being able conquer the diversities and complexities in waters such as these in order to capture a few trout for the pan. Some would say we are foolish, and they may be right, but merely sitting in a boat or on a dock while drowning a worm or minnow beneath a red and white plastic float, is and always has been, far too mundane a pursuit, fishing-wise, for us to even contemplate. The reality is that we consider ourselves to be anglers—not simply fishermen

Several years ago, at a pre-arranged location—a truck stop on the highway, near Bowmanville on Highway 401. I met good buddy Roger Cannon at five o'clock in the morning and after grabbing a couple of coffees we continued on in my car towards the Ganny. Previously we had fished a number of lakes, rivers and streams together and worked over several sections of the Ganny, usually with moderate success. Roger is an excellent angler, competent with both spinning and fly-fishing gear.

As we drove towards the river, I recall asking if he would like to try the Hepburn stretch? I didn't think he had fished it before.

Pausing to contemplate the questions, he answered hesitatingly, "No. Don't think I have. Isn't that the spot where you've been trying to get that six-pound brown that you've been after for a while now? Yeah, I don't mind trying something different. I think you once told me that it's too difficult to fly fish so I guess we'd be throwing tin.[3] Maybe you'll get another shot at your big brownie."

I warned him that it was not only a tough stretch of water to fish but just getting through the bush alongside the stream was extremely difficult. He was not deterred and although it was still early with very little daylight to assist us we were soon parked and getting ready to do battle. As is our custom when fishing most streams, we booted up, grabbed our fishing gear and headed downstream. Although with our adrenaline flowing we were

Find Gord making his way through the dense growth of ferns on the Hepburn stretch of the Ganaraska.

eager and fresh, our tackle would remain unassembled until we reached the spot where we had decided we would begin, depending on the amount of time we had at our disposal. This would serve two purposes. One, we would be fishing in the much preferred upstream direction and two, when we finish and are obviously tired, we would emerge from the bush right at the car. This is a much better system than fishing for several hours then having to struggle back through the bush to the car with little strength left in your legs.

Roger, younger and stronger than I, however, took the lead in picking our way through the dense tangle of bush and underbrush. It was still rather dark and we hadn't penetrated the bush more than a hundred yards when an unseen log beneath the profusion of ferns and grasses seemed to reach up and grab my foot, effectively poleaxing me. In an attempt to avoid the fall, I tried to throw my left leg up and over the log, but failed. With my hands protecting my face, I crashed to the ground on the other side, legs askew on top and my right foot snagged on something or another. Fortunately the dense grass cushioned the fall somewhat. But I was even more shaken up when Roger, racing back to assist me after hearing me yell and swear, pointed out that my face had just missed striking a three-inch tree stump obscured by the ferns and grasses. It had been sharpened to a point by the teeth of a beaver gnawing a tree to knock it down for its dam. After Roger had helped me to my feet, and I had partially regained my composure, I refused his suggestion that perhaps we should wait a while longer so more daylight would make it easier to see where we were going. Actually, we usually feel our way through dense cover such as this, with careful and rather slow leg movements that allow you to locate the pitfalls before they locate you. However, on that day Roger was out in front, eager to get going, and I had to move much faster than my normal pace to keep up with him.

"Let's just keep going," I said, "but maybe a little more slowly, okay?"

I stretched, took a step forward then discovered I had pulled the hamstring muscle in my right thigh. Lifting the leg, which suddenly seemed to weigh about two hundred pounds, became quite painful. Nevertheless, completely forgetting that the Hepburn stretch of the Ganny was fraught with many other impediments to progress through the bush, I mistakenly theorized that struggling through to our destination would provide enough exercise to work out the strain. Moving more slowly might allow my leg to loosen up, so I thought, but as a precaution I suggested that perhaps my taking the lead would allow me to set the pace.

With little strength in the sore leg I went down once more when I couldn't force my way through a stand of willow. By the time, a good half-hour later, we reached the end of the Hepburn section where we had planned to begin fishing our way back upstream, I had stepped into a hole, slid off a grass-covered embankment dropping a couple of feet into the water, and tripped several more times over unseen logs. If my memory of that day is correct, Roger managed to remain in a vertical stance throughout the entire exercise, only having to stoop occasionally to assist me to my feet while commiserating almost continuously. Being a very busy chap, Roger was not able to get out and go fishing with us as often as he wished so I stubbornly refused to cut short the outing. We soldiered on.

What makes the recollection of that particular day exceptional was not simply my getting hurt, or catching a big trout, but the total picture of the day's results. One might be inclined to think that after conquering such adversity that I would have had difficulty keeping fish off the hook. *Lots of them and big ones, too!* However it was not to be. I was completely skunked! Couldn't even catch a tiddler, while Roger had one of his best days on the Ganny ever, landing several brown trout in the eighteen-inch class and a host of smaller ones that he released. It is most unusual to be totally fishless on the Ganny. There are always countless little fellows willing to test one's presentation with flies or spinners. For me, that day on the Hepburn stretch is forever etched on my mind.

But there are other memories. Many others! Here are a couple of incidents on the same stretch of river. Although these are comparatively recent incidences, both having occurred in 2003, I know they will be easily recalled on any future occasion. They took place on opposite ends of the season, the opening weekend[4] and the final weekend.

The first took place on opening day of the trout season, a day that my good friend and fine fisherman, Paul Kennedy, and I have traditionally shared for the past six or seven years on one stream or another. Whereas we had normally worked brook trout waters on opening day, Paul suggested that this year he would like to try a stretch of the Ganny for browns and steelhead.

"Sounds good to me," I concurred, "but there'll be a mob scene on the lower reaches, you know. This time of year when the big 'bows move upriver from the lake everybody wants a go at 'em. Most of these guys will be gone once the pike and pickerel seasons open in a couple of weeks."

I reminded him, however, that most folks stick to the more open waters rather than the tougher parts of the river like the Hepburn stretch. He agreed and off we went.

Opening day that year was April 27, and it was colder than Hades when we stepped out of the Jeep at the bridge below the village of Kendal, our starting point for the walk downstream to the upper-end of the Ed Till stretch where we would begin fishing the three miles of Ganaraska River back to the vehicle. The thermometer in the Jeep had recorded the external air temperature at minus 2 degrees Celsius.

The spring-fed water in the river, cold even in mid-summer, would have been only a degree or two warmer than the air. Although the ferns, grasses and willows had not yet emerged from their winter's sleep, the bush was still a daunting challenge with the swamps, vines and holes providing their own tests of our agility and patience. The half-hour hike was made without any of the traumatic incidents or undue stress, the likes of which I had experienced on the Hepburn stretch many times previously.

Although we were a long way from Lake Ontario, there were a number of big rainbow trout that had already migrated that far upriver seeking their ancestral spawning grounds in order to perform their own spawning rituals. The fruits of their labours, the eggs deposited by the females on the redds (those shallow depressions in gravel or sand created by the hens

Gord with his fiddleheads, wild leeks and brown trout, his harvest from the Ganny, Spring 2002.

using their tails to scoop them out where they deposit their eggs), provide a feast for the resident browns of the Ganny. I have actually witnessed some of these brown trout boldly bumping the big 'bows in the belly attempting to hasten the discharge of their eggs.

Within rather short order, both Paul and I had caught and released several big 'bows and a few small browns. A couple of the larger browns taken from one of the deepest pools on the Hepburn stretch were kept for the pan. Those deep pools can be an enigma. Most often, even when fished correctly, they produce only minimal results, six to ten-inch trout, while on occasion absolutely nothing gives our flies or lures a look-see. We have always believed that when a likely looking pool or bit of cover generates zilch then it probably contains a boss fish, one suffering from lockjaw.

These big fellows do most of their feeding at night. The Ganny is a small river with an average depth seldom exceeding three or four feet in the waters that we fish, however, holes where the current has gouged out depths of a metre or so do occur. Larger trout seek out cover adjoining these pools where they can take up residence.

It is our custom to alternate when fishing these streams in pairs, with one working the pool while the other observes. There is just as much pleasure in watching someone else expertly read and work the water as there is in attempting to do so oneself. It was Paul's turn to fish the next hole, the big pool around the bend in the river. Trees and heavy bush bordered the side of the stream that we were on, with some of them actually extending over the water and the three-foot high bank.

Carefully going ahead and working through the heavy cover towards a vantage point where he could assess the pool and properly cast and fish it, Paul paused while I attempted to follow in his footsteps and catch up to him. My back was turned towards the water as I edged backwards along the embankment, spinning rod in my left hand while clutching a branch with the other hand for stability. The branch, older than I had thought, snapped and I plunged backwards into the water, shoulders striking first, and totally sinking to the bottom. Fortunately, the shock and bitter temperature took my breath away, preventing my swallowing any water as I popped up a few feet away, carried there by the current. I will never forget the sensation of momentarily lying in freezing water on the bottom of the Ganaraska River on that April day, and through its surface being able to see the warped image of my buddy, Paul Kennedy, helplessly staring down at the scary scene below him.

The entire sequence was over in a matter of seconds. Paul was somehow able to haul my soggy carcass back up the bank at the foot of the pool where

Fishing the Hepburn stretch in 2005.

I had been deposited by the current. My heavy cold-weather fishing clothes were, of course, completely drenched and my hip boots full to their tops. It was far too cold to even contemplate pulling the boots off to drain them. They would have been almost impossible to don again and we were still miles away from the Jeep. Instead while I lay on one of the few patches of ground available for the purpose, Paul simply hoisted and held my legs up for a minute or two until most of the water escaped the boots. What we didn't realize was that although much of the water had been temporarily removed and squeezed out, with so much moisture in the rest of my duff, it would continue to drip and drain down, and refill the boots. The struggle through the bush back to the Jeep was tremendously difficult. Within minutes, the sopping wet clothes were sheathed in ice while the boots were once again full of water.

Although initially not feeling the cold, dragging my sorry, iced-up carcass with what seemed like five hundred pounds of water in my clothes and boots was an experience I would never wish on my worst enemy. Somewhat hypothermic, I soon began shaking. Even though my body temperature had been increased by the excessive exertion, it was contained by the iced-up clothing. Nevertheless, with Paul's hovering over me all the way back and assisting me over obstacles, we eventually reached the Jeep. With the heater going full blast, I stripped and warmed up while he drove home.

That will certainly always be one of my most indelible memories, one that could have been a "tragical" memory if it had not occurred in one of the deepest pools on the Ganny. In shallower water I could have suffered a fractured skull, a dislocated shoulder, or possibly even worse, broken my neck and been paralysed. As it developed, nothing was broken, not even my fishing rod—I just had to nurse a rather sore shoulder for several months.

Although the two episodes described here might give one the idea that I am the sole klutz to have succumbed to the Hepburn stretch's difficulties, I would like to state emphatically here that I am not the only victim to have fallen prey to the entrapments of this section of the Ganny. It seems a little bizarre, but even with my doing the backflip into the river on opening day of the trout fishing season that April day, we did manage to fish it with several different fellows over the summer. There was very little difficulty until closing day when fishing there with another buddy, Jim Lloyd.

Jim Lloyd of the mighty leap, still living dangerously.

Not far from where I performed my graceless backflip into the icy spring flow in April, Jim was attempting to negotiate a similar high bank around an awkwardly placed tree stump on its edge. He, too, while leaning over the river, used another large log for his support and balance. Fortunately, although that is seldom the case in these situations, his feet were firmly planted. The log broke the instant he leaned on it and he was faced with an instantaneous decision. He could either fall straight down into the river as he protected his face with one hand and his nether region with the other, or he could attempt to leap across to the other side of the stream over whatever perils lay below. There, he knew, the water was shallow and the landing if he was successful, would be comparatively gentle—on a muddy bank.

Standing a few feet away from him, surrounded by six feet of grassy cover, I witnessed a feat of athletic endeavour that I doubt had ever before been achieved. When the log gave way, Jim, without a pause didn't simply jump, he launched himself powerfully across the water and landed on all fours on the opposite stream bank with nothing bruised but his ego. Still clenching his rod like a baton throughout the episode, he looked like he had been shot from one of those ridiculous circus cannons. I swear that as he passed over the middle of the stream, the apogee of his flight was at a higher plane than when he pushed off. With that kind of athletic and acrobatic ability, I suggested afterwards that he hire himself and his act out to the Cirque de Soleil. This Hepburn stretch of the Ganny has produced countless and unforgettable memories for us over many years.

Another favourite section of the Ganny for my fishing buddies and me is the "Picnic Grounds" stretch, a three- or four-mile section of magical waters that has also produced innumerable memories. But the first thing to come to mind would be why—and when—this section was first labelled the Picnic Grounds. Perhaps the easiest stretch of the Ganaraska River to fish and negotiate, this is where I have taken dozens of neophyte fishermen on their initial wand-waving pursuits to help them learn the intricacies of the beautiful sport of fly fishing. It is also the place where I introduced my two sons to trout fishing.

My sons, Randy and Ronnie, were eleven and twelve years old respectively when I first surrendered to their pleas to take them stream fishing. Although they had already fished with their old man for several years and become proficient casters with their spinning tackle in the process, they had not experienced the trials and tribulations—and yes—the pleasures, of stream fishing for trout. The lads' previous angling experiences had been restricted to fishing on lakes, either in our car-top boat or from a variety of piers and docks where it was easier for the youngsters to learn how to use their light-weight fishing tackle than on the tight quarters to be found on the streams that their father fished.

Prior to their initial exposure to stream fishing with their own equipment, they had accompanied me on numerous sorties to more easily negotiated streams such as the headwaters of Duffins Creek, a few miles east of Toronto. Duffins is in an area with well-defined stream-side trails due its proximity to Ontario Ministry of Natural Resources conservation area at Claremont.

Their patience was sorely tested that summer as they tagged along with me on those occasions, not to fish, but simply to observe and learn. If they were going to be able to enjoy their fishing on streams, decidedly more difficult than fishing out of a boat on lakes, then reading the current, determining the holding spots and how to fish them and simply getting through the bush, were lessons that I deemed necessary.

Although they were eager to prove that the lessons had been absorbed, they both patiently awaited the word from the teacher and consoled themselves with cleaning some of the brookies that I flipped over my shoulder towards them. By the end of that summer they were allowed to bring their rods with them and fish some of the more accessible pools on successive trips. It soon became obvious that I would have to begin cleaning my own fish again as both boys proved that they had become excellent students and were ready for a more exciting and difficult test of their recently acquired skills—fishing the magical waters of the Ganaraska River.

The season was almost over, but after managing to fish the Ganny on a couple of short, problem-free outings and their having caught a few small trout in the process, I was being bombarded on the one-hour trip home with pleas to go again and be allowed to stay over and camp on the riverside. There is a little copse where I normally parked the car and where we had taken luncheon breaks on these trips to devour the goodies their mother had packed in the picnic baskets for us. That was the spot they had in mind.

I can remember every detail of the conversation and what followed on the way home after our second visit to the Ganny. Although it was more than forty years ago, it is such a startlingly vivid recollection that it must be considered my number one truly magical memory of fishing the waters of the Ganaraska River.

As we drove back to Scarborough, Ronnie asked, "Dad, why don't we ever fish until dark, or early in the morning like you do when you go with the *other guys*? You're always telling us that that's the best time to catch the big ones."

Before I could answer his question, Randy fired one of his own at me as well, "Yeah, Dad, can we bring our tent the next time we come? We could set it up in that clearing right beside the spot where you park the car. You know, the "Picnic Grounds.""

Still contemplating their surprising requests, I had yet to respond when Ronnie suggested, "You could help us set up the tent before you leave then Randy and I would be able to fish until dark before we got into our sleeping bags. Then we would get to fish early in the morning, too, before you come back to pick us up. What do you think, Dad? Could we, please? Please?"

"I don't know about that, guys. What about food? And there are animals there, too, you know. I doubt if Mom would ever give you permission to stay overnight in the bush and right beside a river—all by yourselves."

"Ah, Dad! Please. You can tell Mom that we'll be okay, won't you, please? We're not little kids now, you know!"

They moaned in unison. I told them I would think about it for while. By the time we arrived home I had pretty well made up my mind to consent to their wishes, but only if their mother could be convinced that they were capable of surviving the mini-adventure.

The final weekend of the trout season was approaching and Ron and Randy had both been on their best behaviour since our last outing. Their exemplary conduct, along with my assurance that I believed they would be able to stay out of trouble eventually led to their mother's acquiescence. We agreed that providing they packed their gear and Mom made lunches for them the night before, that I would pick them up from school and they could change their clothes in the car. In that way we could reach the Picnic Grounds with time to set up their tent and still get in an hour or two of fishing before dark.

Arriving at the edge of the stream, they chattered with exhilaration as their sleeping bags, picnic basket, tackle and tent were unloaded. They refused to let me assist them in setting up and could hardly wait to say goodbye to their old man. My final words to them before departing were that there was to be no campfire and that they had to be in their sleeping bags before dark. The boys had a couple of reliable flashlights with them to ease any fears of the dark after they zipped up the door to the tent. Trying not to display my anxiety at leaving them there on their own, I swallowed my concerns, smiled and hugged them both before hopping into the car and waving until I was out of sight. As I glanced in the rear view mirror I could see they were paying no attention to my departure and already busying themselves in setting up their little camp.

I slept fitfully that night, skipped breakfast in the morning and had to suppress my urge to set a speed record for the drive to the Ganny. We had agreed that I wouldn't come for them until at least ten o'clock so that they could have a little time to fish by themselves in the morning. As I bounced down the trail towards the Picnic Grounds, I could see by the grins on their faces as they greeted me by the tent, each displaying a fat fifteen-inch brown trout for my approval, that my concerns had been completely unwarranted.

After the hugs, I admired their catch and asked if they had stayed up talking all night or managed to get in a little sleep because I had another treat in store for them. They had slept alright, or so they said, but a big fish splashing around in the pool right in front of the tent had awakened them a couple of times.

"Yeah," Ronnie added, "and there was a bear or something poking around outside the tent, too. But when we shone the light through the side of the tent we could hear it scramble away."

"Probably just a big racoon after your fish or the picnic basket," I said. "After all, you were trespassing on its night-hunting territory, you know."

Things had gone so well for them that I thought we would spend an hour fishing another piece of the Ganaraska watershed. Obviously it was no problem getting them to agree to the proposition. I was thinking of a big pool below a dam some distance upriver from where we were, the section of the river we referred to as the "Used Car Lot" stretch. The owner of the land there sells used-car parts from wrecks that he buys and stores on his property, hence the name.

I sweetened the suggestion, "It doesn't look as nice as the Picnic Grounds, but if nobody else has fished there yet this morning you'd have a chance at catching a big brown, even bigger than the ones you've already got. Sound okay to you?"

The smiles that had not left their faces since my arrival, broadened even further as we threw everything in the car and drove the back roads for twenty minutes until we came to the lane leading between the wrecks and derelict cars strewn around the property which led directly to the pool below the dam. Pointing the way down the lane to the dam, I said, "You guys can fish from shore there while I go back down the road to the bridge and fish the stream near it for a bit. Okay? I'll come back and meet you right here on the main road in an hour. All right?"

We synchronized our watches as I dropped them off and wished them good luck. The hour flew by, and while I was standing on the bridge a couple of hundred yards away from the lane leading to the Used Car Lot pool, no fish in my creel, I could see the lads emerge on to the main road and head in my direction. I have lousy hearing but have always had excellent vision. Even at that distance I could see that although they were soaking wet they were both smiling excitedly, while Randy was making a futile attempt to disguise the fact that he had a huge fish strung on a length of cord and hanging over his shoulder down his back. The problem was its tail was easily visible between his legs, swinging back and forth in unison with his footsteps. Not wishing to spoil the surprise that they were hoping to lay on their old man, I feigned ignorance and awaited their arrival.

"Okay guys," I said, "What's with the grins? Catch a 'biggie,' or something?"

Randy heaved the big brown trout off his shoulder and when I could see how big the thing really was, I no longer was able to hide my own enthusiasm. "Where in hell and how in hell did you catch that? It's got to weigh over eight—maybe even nine pounds!"

With Ron speaking first, their story spilled out excitedly, "Randy got it, Dad, right below the dam. It almost broke his rod charging all over the pool trying to get away."

"I wasn't going to let it break my rod," Randy interjected, "so I slid down the bank into the water to keep it from trying to get under a bunch of logs. Ronnie jumped in near the logs, too, to help me steer it in the other direction where the water was shallower."

Ron explained the rest of the struggle and eventual capture. Seemingly, when Randy finally got the fish into the shallow water at the bottom of the pool, they both jumped on top of it and dragged it up on shore. Their pleasure was somewhat marred for fear I would be angry at them for getting their shoes and clothes soaking wet.

"Are you kidding," I said, "I'd jump in myself if I ever caught a trout as big as that one! It's way bigger than any brown I've ever caught."

As a matter of fact, to this day my son's big brownie is still larger than any I have caught ever since that episode thirty-five years ago.

Randy Deval at ten years of age: his first overnight camping trip and his first large brown trout.

According to Gord, his will stipulates that his ashes are to be spread on this pool of the Ganny.

There is a rather inconspicuous pool on this Picnic Grounds stretch, about half a mile upstream from where we leave the car and just around the corner from the swimming hole, the deepest spot in this entire section of the Ganny. It, too, has provided me with several wonderful memories.

A four-and a-half-pound male brownie sporting a huge kipe (an extension of the lower jaw of a male fish that occurs during spawning) fell to one of my fly-fishing efforts on the river there while filming a show for the CBC television network. The same hole provided me with one of the biggest thrills I have ever experienced in all my years of fishing for trout. It was the largest rainbow trout, actually a steelhead, to have ever tested my tackle and patience—and lost!

Weighing almost twenty pounds and thirty-seven inches in length, the trout took over half an hour of my splashing up and down the stream, while first it charged in one direction then another, frantically attempting to break free, before finally being brought to captured. Really big rainbows rarely break the surface, normally preferring to fight their battles in the depths, however that fellow hadn't read the "rainbow trout manual." With its head shaking violently from side to side, it was airborne in exhilarating leaps and cartwheels at least six or seven times. It rests majestically now on a plaque above the piano in our dining room. The Picnic Grounds stretch of the Ganny has unquestionably earned its inclusion in my list of magical waters.

Chapter 3

Land O' Lakes and Land O' Fish

In a four-hour drive from Toronto into eastern Ontario, lying almost halfway between Kingston and Ottawa, lies an area comprised of hundreds of lakes and ponds, many of which still do not have access roads. Shank's mare,[1] float planes, all-terrain vehicles, or snowmobiles remain the only methods of reaching these off-road waters. Remarkably, a few of the best lakes in the area, that is, best from a fisherman's point of view, were accessible by automobile as far back as the thirties and forties, providing one was not overly concerned about the condition of the vehicle after the adventure.

I have probably fished twenty-five or thirty of these, but only a few could be legitimately described in my recollections as truly magical. A few of the more memorable appear here beginning with Brooks Lake near Plevna, north of Kingston, Ontario.

In 1949 at the age of nineteen, I had yet to fish for speckled trout in any body of water larger than a stream, river or pond, with my largest catch, a seventeen-incher. My Uncle Bob, also a small-stream trout fisherman, owned a used-car business and had an ancient army truck advertised for sale. A phone call from a gentleman in the Land O' Lakes forever changed that status quo for both of us. The man's name was Bev Woolnough and he operated Birch Lodge on Buckshot Lake, halfway between the villages of Plevna and Vennacher Junction located in the general vicinity northeast of Kaladar on Highway 7.

As I subsequently fished with Mr. Woolnough for more than twenty years, using his lodge and cabins as a base for our explorations of many of the nearby and not so nearby Land O' Lakes waters, I feel free to refer to him here as he preferred to be called, by his first name Bev. Visiting relatives in Toronto for Christmas that year, he had discovered the advertisement my uncle had been running for the old army truck. After a lengthy discussion he agreed to purchase the vehicle, but because he had his own car with him, only if my Uncle Bob would drive it up to his lodge on Buckshot Lake. As incentive he suggested that he would take my uncle ice-fishing for brook trout on a small body of nearby water, appropriately named Brooks Lake, and not charge him for a night's lodging. The lake was named after an old fellow whose family had homesteaded the area, not for the fish.

An avid fisherman especially when brookies were the intended goal, my uncle struck the deal. Realizing he would be a couple of hundred miles from home with no way of getting back to Toronto, Uncle Bob easily convinced Curly, his fishing buddy, to follow them to the Land O' Lakes in his own car, with the ice fishing for speckled trout proving to be the catalyst in the discussion.

The day after they returned I was summoned to see what they had brought home—their limit of big speckled trout, which back then was *fifteen pounds plus one*. The sight was mind boggling to say the least, seven or eight brookies between three and four pounds each. I could hardly wait to test the lake for myself, however, with the *legal* trout fishing running from the first of May until the thirtieth of September, we had more than three months to dream and plan our own assault on Brooks Lake.

Like many of the thousands of lakes in Ontario, the lake was also known in some quarters by a second name, in this case, Burns Lake. However, there was an old gentleman, Les Brooks, living on a clearing carved out of the bush at one end of the lake. Apparently his folks had homesteaded the area many years earlier and Old Lessie, as he was known to all, simply carried on the family tradition. As the last of the Brooks family, and living the life of a hermit with only a couple of horses and an old goat that appeared as old as he for company, Lessie existed with only his tiny vegetable garden supplying food for sustenance. That, along with the few staples that Bev, the owner of Birch Lodge, would occasionally bring him, were all he had going for him.

When we phoned ahead to the lodge to inquire about fishing and renting a cabin by the lake, we were advised to take a couple of cans of "chews" for

Birch LODGE

ON
BUCKSHOT LAKE IN
THE LAND O' LAKES DISTRICT

Come early in May for Speckled Trout or bring the family for summer vacation. Wonderful Bass, Trout and Walleye fishing, sandy beach. Modern cabins with running water. Excellent meals.

Rates — American Plan.
Make reservations early.
Write or Phone

J. B. Woolnough

BIRCH LODGE, PLEVNA, ONTARIO
PHONE 1-ring 2.

This advertisement for Birch Lodge ran in The Outdoorsman: Ontario's Voice of the Outdoors, *Vol. 2, No. 1 (1963). Courtesy of Barry Penhale.*

Gord and Johnny Finnegan making their way along the treacherous shoreline of Brooks Lake.

the old fellow who lives there. Later, when for the first time we met him, we discovered the truth of the suggestion as his eyes searched our pockets, looking hopefully for the tell-tale bulge of a couple of tins of tobacco. We were fortunate that Bev had previously warned us about Lessie's predilection for the "chew," otherwise we would never have located the old trapper's boat near the end of the trail. Originally Bev had told us that it was pulled up on shore under a couple of fallen cedar trees, right beside a big dead birch. Uh huh! It turned out that the shoreline of the mile-long lake was totally layered with fallen cedars and dead birches.

My fishing buddies back in the forties were Art Walker, Bill Taylor and Johnny Finnegan. Because Art had carelessly chosen the May 1, the first "opening day" weekend, on which to get married, the *odious* task of exploring Brooks Lake and its wondrous brook trout fishery was left to Bill, Johnny and myself. With my uncle's scribbled directions clutched in Bill's hand, an Ontario Highway map in John's and mine firmly affixed to the steering wheel of my ten-year-old Buick, we left Toronto in the wee hours of the morning. The plan was to get to Brooks Lake in time to wet a line before dark. Uncle Bob had also suggested that it would be in our best interests if we were to drop in and introduce ourselves to Bev Woolnough and take a look at the lodge. We had previously planned on just finding the lake, fishing until dark, then going back to Birch Lodge to spend the night in one of their cabins or whatever.

Much later, after half a day of travelling and negotiating an unbelievingly hilly and twisting twenty-five miles of back road, which culminated in another ridiculously difficult eight miles of corduroy road (logs laid across the muck, supposedly to allow for automobile travel), we pulled up beside Birch Lodge. Having heard the old Buick approaching, Bev Woolnough was waiting outside to greet us. He gave us the final directions to the trail a few miles up the road that would lead us to our anticipated "pot of gold," along with the instructions for finding the boat.

Several hours later, and already pooped after getting lost several times while attempting to stick to the semblance of a trail supposedly leading to the lake, we struggled through the tangles of shoreline brush, swamp and dead trees for another hour or so in a fruitless search for the, "old trapper's boat under a couple of cedars, right beside a dead birch." With the sun approaching the horizon, we were almost ready to throw in the towel, and get an early start the next day when we heard a voice emanating from somewhere in the bush behind us,

"You boys looking for the boat?"

It was Lessie, looking exactly as one might imagine a toothless old hermit living in the bush should look. We introduced ourselves, offered him his chews and thanked him for the instructions tossed idly over his shoulder as he retreated into the bush,

"It's just back there a bit you know, beside the dead birch. You must have almost tripped over the old scow."

Johnny was the first to report that he had found it as he hoisted an assortment of flotsam and jetsam to reveal the outline of the ancient trapper's scow almost buried in the water and shoreline muck. Bill's truly appropriate comment as we wrestled with the hulk to free it from the suction of the swamp and scoop out handfuls of mud and weeds broke the tension of our disappointment, "I think the goddamn thing's taken root!"

Once the laughter subsided we were finally able to wrench the thing out of its temporary grave, then set about trying to make it seaworthy, at least sufficiently seaworthy enough to launch. The boat was necessary, as there appeared to only be one or two places where one could fish from shore and they were on the opposite side of the lake. Fly fishing would be almost impossible unless we could make the boat workable. There was only an hour or so of daylight left when we finally pushed off to the lyrical sounds of Johnny's belting out, "Rub-a-dub-dub, three men..."

With our butts glued to the rickety seats, our fingers crossed and our weight centred in the tipsy craft, we used a couple of trimmed branches to pole the thing around while the fly rods were being quickly strung and flies fastened. The old waterlogged wooden floorboards were so slippery that we dared not stand, so our casting prowess was about to be thoroughly tested.

Nevertheless our feathered attractions hardly hit the water when we were fast to a couple of fine brookies, larger than any of us had seen before, at least on the end of our lines. Previously I had helped my uncle clean the catch he and Curly had brought back from their earlier ice-fishing trip to Brooks Lake. After the furious initial excitement, tallying three or four trout in the twenty-inch class and losing at least the same number, the action suddenly tailed off. Darkness was approaching anyhow and the possibility of our losing our way again on the trail weighed heavily on our minds. It was time to call it a day.

Later, back at our compact cabin with its upper and lower bunks, the trout were cleaned, then stashed on ice beneath the sawdust in the ice house. After a quick snack, our tired but happy crew hit the sack, all with grins on their faces in anticipation of the excitement lying in store for us on our next day of fishing Brooks Lake.

We were not to be disappointed. Within moments of pushing off in the sodden wooden hulk passing for the trapper's boat, Bill had raised and lost two fabulous brook trout, both of which would have easily topped four pounds. Then, like the day before, as quickly as it began, the trout seemed to develop lockjaw. Once the three of us lost confidence in our favourite, feathered creations, our fly boxes were all being scoured, searching for a winning pattern—all to no avail.

Finally fishing on Brooks Lake: Gord (left) and Johnny Finnegan in 1950.

A proud Gord displays his first big trout on Brooks Lake.

Between sips of hot coffee from his Thermos bottle, Johnny blurted out, "Dammit all anyhow, Deval, I told you we should have brought worms! Trout love worms, you know. This must be the first time I ever went fishing without them." Then remembering the new spinning equipment I had obtained, he said, "Why don't you set up that crazy outfit you bought? You've got some little spoons and spinners and stuff there that you showed us. Maybe that's just what the doctor ordered."

Other than an hour or so of practice in the park to see how the thing worked, the new tackle had yet to be put to the use for which it was intended. Nevertheless, I agreed immediately. While Bill and Johnny continued to flail away with their fly rods, mine was soon put away and the spinning tackle set up. One of the half-dozen lures that I had bought, the Halfwave, a tiny Swiss-made wabler,[2] was fastened to the line and we were ready to do battle.

The day before, just locating and seeing Brooks Lake for the first time was definitely an unforgettable moment for all of us, but what transpired in the next couple of hours may be one of the most magical memories I have ever experienced in my lifetime working over all those streams and lakes. Although an entire book could be written detailing the thrills and excitement the three of us enjoyed on that tiny trout lake before we had to pack up, with so many other memories to relate I will only touch on the highlights of that memorable morning.

The brass Halfwave, hardly any larger than the Despairs and bucktail streamer flies[3] with which we had been attempting to entice the brookies earlier, was flung out with little ceremony. I had barely begun the retrieve

The results of the exceptional fishing at the "Hatchery" on Brooks Lake.

when the water boiled beneath the lure, followed by the line being fiercely ripped off the spinning reel. While Bill and Johnny were furiously snapping pictures, the battle see-sawed back and forth with the trout tearing off fifteen feet of line, then my managing to gain ten or twelve back. Eventually, the power of the cane spinning rod, together with the security of the slipping clutch on the reel, overcame the brookie's resistance.

More photos—then the spinning rod was again put to work. As before, the Halfwave was attacked as soon as it broke the surface and the tackle was once again put to the test. Bill spotted it first—a strange phenomenon and one I have never seen since. He yelled, "Good God! Look at that, guys! There's at least another dozen trout charging around the one hooked on your spoon—probably trying to wrest it away from him."

"Somebody grab a picture. Quick! Before they spot the boat and disappear." I yelled, "If we don't have any pictures nobody will ever believe this."

I needn't have worried as the trout were not the least bit timid. They continued to follow and harass the gorgeously appointed speckled trout furiously trying to shed the annoying chunk of metal stuck in its lip. One after another was hooked, with most being released, but my buddies were still unable to seduce a single trout with their feathered offerings, so the spinning outfit was soon being shared among the three of us, with everyone participating in the fantastic action. Hardly a cast was made without a response from the fish, all with exactly the same result, a posse of others alongside the unlucky one with the lure in its mouth.

There were a few moments of panic, however, when the seemingly deadly Halfwave was almost surrendered to one of the many underwater obstructions near shore. Mostly trees that had been felled by beavers, they provided the cover where the trout seemed to disappear to when they were not chasing the lure or one of their hooked brethren. Luckily, we had been able to work the lure free each time when we discovered that the hook would straighten with a slow pull on the spinning line.

The frenetic fishing continued until noon hour when we decided to give the lake and our arms a rest, and eat the cheese sandwiches that had been thrown together in the wee hours of the morning before leaving the cabin. The spinning outfit was retired for the day when we agreed that perhaps the challenge of trying to entice and hook one of these so obviously plentiful brook trout with fly tackle would present a more interesting way to wind up one of the most fantastic days of fishing any of us had ever experienced anywhere, anytime. A couple more trout were taken, including the largest of the trip, a twenty-four-inch-long beauty that tipped the pocket scale at almost six pounds. Bill caught it on a Despair fly that he had tied, rather than on one of the fancy creations he had purchased back in Toronto.

As much as we would have liked to stay, there was much to be done before the long drive back to Toronto. I think it was Johnny who on the way home from that exceptional day on the magical waters of Brooks Lake, referred to the little bay where those few hours of frenzied action occurred as the "Hatchery." I suppose it was truly like fishing in a hatchery and when recounting this story, as I am sure each of us has often done during the many years since, I usually begin with a question, "Heh, have you ever fished in a hatchery?"

The second most prominent memory of moments in the Land O' Lakes area occurred on Mosque Lake. Originally called Mosquito Lake, Mosque was renamed by Russell Wells, a veteran of the Second World War who used his veteran's grant to buy a piece of property on the lake then build a fishing lodge and several small cabins. Feeling that the existing name of the lake, would not be conducive to an operation that was dependent on attracting guests, he successfully applied to have the lake's name altered and his camp became Mosque Lake Lodge.

During one of our earlier trips to fish Brooks Lake, we met Fred Day, an officer with the old Department of Lands and Forests. In those days,

Don Petican, another fishing buddy, had a cottage on Mosque Lake.

they were simply called game wardens. Subsequently, in those early years of fishing the Land O' Lakes we ran into Fred a number of times, occasionally when being checked by him in his official capacity and once or twice at Birch Lodge. All the while making notes, Fred would pick our brains for details on our fishing in Brooks, Grants and one or two other lakes in the area. It was he who introduced us to Mosque when he inquired if we had ever fished there in our search for big speckled trout. He added, "If you boys want big specks then that's the place to get 'em. Greys up to twenty pounds there, too!" Grey trout was the prevalent moniker applied to lake trout in southern Ontario in the forties and fifties.

He was absolutely correct. Our first visit to Mosque Lake with old buddy, Art Walker, was indeed memorable, from the trials of negotiating the trail recently carved out of the bush and barely adequate to drive a car on, to a couple of magnificent seven-pound beauties that fell to our offerings. EGBs,[4] those superb little spoons made in Switzerland, were, along with the aforementioned Halfwave, our lures of choice and still are these days, right up there with the Crocodile wabler.

A rather imposing figure, tall and lanky with what looked like a permanent scowl etched on his countenance, Russ Wells strode down the hill toward his dock where we were unloading our outboard motor and fishing gear.

"Don't you boys think you should get permission before you unload that stuff?" he barked at us from halfway down the hill. "This place is private you know—for our guests."

I mustered my best smile and scrambled up to meet him before he reached the bottom, trying to mollify his hostility by apologizing for not having gone to meet him first. Justifying our actions by attributing our excitement at the possibility of doing a little fishing after the long drive up, I commented on the desperate state of the road, "Boy, that last couple of miles is sure one hell of a drive—at least in my old jalopy anyhow."

Seeing him grimace even more threateningly, I realized, too late, that he probably had built the bloody road himself. Then, attempting to extricate myself from the predicament, I put my foot in my mouth once again by commenting on the adventure the drive on the road had given us, acknowledging that it must have been pretty tough building the last couple miles.

"Built it myself. Built this whole damn place myself," he replied curtly.

His entire demeanour, however, suddenly changed when he saw us both reaching for our wallets, "Yeah, I'm Wells. Guess you want to rent a boat, right. It'll cost you a couple of bucks. That okay? You need minnows? Got some for sale in that box in the water by the dock. A buck, a dozen. Worms don't work worth a damn here if you're after big trout. They'll just catch you a bunch of little ones."

After we introduced ourselves and thanked him for the live bait instructions, Art explained that we just fished with artificial flies and lures except when ice-fishing where minnows definitely seemed superior.

Chuckling heartily, Russell pointed to the dock and indicated the boat we should take. "The less leaky one," he said, explaining that the boats had only been in the water a couple of weeks because the ice was late going out.

As a parting shot, he added, "Gotta soak up a little before they tighten up, you know. You'll be back for minnows in a little while. Just help yourselves. There's a couple of pails on the dock you can use. We'll settle up when you come in. Just come up to the lodge. Okay?"

Don Petican holding a 1980 Mosque Lake beauty.

We carried on unloading our duff as he tromped back up the hill, pausing for a moment to look over his shoulder and yell, "I'll have Eva whip up some scones for you to knock down with a pot of hot tea when you come in. The wife makes her own jam, too."

We did not have to go back to the dock and help ourselves to Russell's minnows. As a matter of fact the next few hours produced one of the most incredible memories of all time—all my time, anyhow. Because fly fishing is always our preferred attack when trout fishing, that tackle was quickly strung together with the resulting wand-waving providing a variety of thrills involving specks in the three to four-pound class. Most were released in the hope that even larger trout would fall to our charms.

With our arms tiring and still hoping to find and do battle with one of the huge brook trout that the game warden, Fred Day, had alluded to, we had eventually switched to our new spinning gear with EGBs replacing our feathered offerings. The results were truly phenomenal and when we returned to shore a little later and casually flopped a six pound and a couple of seven-pounders onto the dock, Russell, who was busying himself filling paint cans with cement to serve as anchors for his "fleet," dropped everything and came running with a yelp, "Holy Jesus! Mother of God! Bloody good, boy! Were you using worms, or what? You didn't get them on goddamn flies, did you?" The two big ones gotta be about eight pounds!"

Art spoke first, explaining the actual size showing the lures we had used.

"On what!" he exclaimed.

"E.G.B.," I spelled out for him, "They're little spinning lures, made in Switzerland." I left it at that for the moment while I placed our tackle on the dock and Art carted the trout to what was obviously a fish-cleaning table on shore near the foot of the dock. Then pointing to the spinning rods, I said, to the apparently still befuddled chap, "Heh, Russ, have a look for yourself. They're still on both the spinning rods."

He examined the two tiny Swiss spinning lures and said, "Pretty bloody small! What the hell does 'EBL' mean anyhow, Deval?"

This time I spelled it out determinedly, "They're EGBs and damned if I know what the letters stand for, probably the name of the outfit in Switzerland that makes them or something. All I can tell you is that they sure work great on trout. All trout!"

When I asked if he would like to try the lures for himself, it became evident that he did not have a spinning rod. Luckily I had another inexpensive spinning outfit in the car as a spare in case one of our regular outfits broke down or something. We gave Russell a quick lesson on how to use the tackle as we had done previously with Old Lessie at Brooks Lake. After he made a few casts to get the feel of the strange equipment, he seemed to believe that he could use it well enough and offered to pay for it. When we said the rod was on us, he refused to charge us the regular five bucks for the privilege of fishing on his territory and even said our boat would be free too, the next time we came back.

Of course his prognosis was dead on. We have fished Mosque Lake hundreds of times since that splendid initial visit to one of the most magical waters I have ever wet a line in. The lake has created dozens of special memories for me and my fishing buddies. The fruits of several of those delightful labours now hang resplendently on my walls at home.

Grants Lake is one of the tiniest speckled trout waters that I've fished and deserves a place here, but for an entirely different reason. Only a half a mile long and at its widest, a spit in width if one possessed good lungs, Grants produced excellent fly-fishing catches over a couple years for us until a devastating winterkill[5] applied the *coup de gras* to its fishery. Deemed unsuitable for natural reproduction, the Ministry of Natural Resources (formerly the Department of Lands and Forests) subsequently refused to stock it again after learning about the destructive exposure.

The lake is four or five miles off the beaten path, about ten miles north of Buckshot Lake where we used to stay at Bev Woolnough's Birch Lodge near Plevna. There had been successive years of fine spring and summer fishing on Grants when, along with a couple of buddies, we decided to try a little hard-water fishing there one winter weekend. Al Jones and Norm Wallachy were invited to join me for what was expected to be a pleasant jaunt, with two of us on the Skidoo and the third in the attached sled with all the fishing and shore lunch gear.

It began snowing rather heavily during the four-hour trip from Toronto and had not yet ceased when we arose the next morning to pack and head off to the lake. Skidoos are vehicles designed to negotiate most snow conditions, but even the best of them quickly lose their efficiency if heavily loaded down and faced with extreme snow depths. Today's more modern snowmobiles are better equipped to deal with those conditions than the narrow-tracked machines produced in the sport's infancy.

Mrs. Woolnough of Birch Lodge was well-known for her culinary skills. From The Outdoorsman: Ontario's Voice of the Outdoors, *1963. Courtesy of Barry Penhale.*

With one and sometimes two of the fellows baling out every so often to lighten the load on hills, we managed to negotiate the seven-mile trip up the bush road. This was followed by a three-mile trail across an ancient farm and several frozen swamps that lead right to the edge of the lake. As is our custom when ice fishing, the first objective is to get the holes cut and the tackle set up. While important, but secondary, a spot has to be cleared for the ever-present dinner fire on shore and, accordingly, enough wood gathered to last the day.

On Grants there is a swamp several hundred yards down one side of the lake with a nice stand of dead birch and cedar where enough can easily be knocked down with the Swedish saw to serve our purpose. I had to pay my respects to the bush for a few moments and, by the time I struggled back through the deep snow, the fellows had the holes and tackle organized. It was left up to me to unhook the sled from the Skidoo to lighten the load, then head on down the lake, fell a couple of dead trees, rope them and drag them back to where we were set up on shore.

The holes were cut and the ice-fishing buzzers (Fish O' Buzzer) were set up in short order. I eased the old Skidoo off shore and onto the deep snow on the lake, moving cautiously because occasionally the combination of a severe load of snow with little ice thickness actually depresses the ice, forcing water up through various cracks in the ice. When this happens, the water and snow become slush, a sloppy mess as much as a foot or two thick. A peculiar spinoff of these conditions occurs when there is more water on the lake's surface than the snow can actually absorb, at which time gravity enables it to locate the lowest point on the surface where a crack has occurred and it trickles back through the ice into the lake. As the water increases and the hole enlarges, like the water in your bathtub or sink back home, it swirls in clockwise fashion while continuing to drain. The swirling action of the water gradually creates an enlarged hole with a continuous whirlpool action as the eddy and hole constantly enlarge.

I'm not certain why, but most ice fisherman refer to these lake surface winter abnormalities as "sump holes" and treat them with the utmost respect as the swirling waters polish and narrow the edges making them precarious should one approach too closely for a better look. As the Skidoo forged its way through and across the deep snow down the side of the lake towards the swamp and dead trees, I could easily see several places where sump holes occurred. These were partially covered with newly fallen snow, which had appropriately darkened as it absorbed the swirling water.

Hearing a whoop of success from the lads back at the end of the lake spurred me into a "haste makes waste" mode. As I scrambled through the deep snow towards the first dead birch, an unseen branch buried in the drifts grabbed my foot, pitching me headfirst into three feet of snow. Shaking it off, I forced a laugh at my carelessness and carefully took down the birch and two slightly smaller dead cedars. The birch has better staying power, but the cedar is great for getting things underway by establishing a good bed of coals for building a fire. One end of the load was fastened with a couple of slip knots to the tow bar. Because the snow is almost always substantially deeper near shore and the machine now also had to contend with a couple of hundred pounds of dead trees to drag, I headed towards the middle of the lake. Oops! A huge mistake!

A rather large and ominous dark spot out there clearly indicated the presence of a sump hole, with the shading emanating from its epicentre four or five feet in all directions, clearly one to be treated with caution. However, the drag of the trees made jockeying the snowmobile from side to side, with my weight on the rear to prevent the skis from digging in, a necessity to avoid becoming bogged down in the deep snow. While wrestling with the machine I kept one eye on the threatening shadow in the centre of the lake.

Progress was slow, but steady until I suddenly discovered that the snow that I had been riding on was only a veneer on top of a foot or two of deep slush. The big machine bogged down. I had cautiously maintained what I felt was a respectful distance from the sump hole in the middle, only to learn that I was now very near to another nasty one, which because of a freshly driven snowdrift was previously undetectable. I slid off the seat and promptly found that the slush and water were well over my boot tops and rapidly wicking their way into my upper clothing.

There are various ploys that can be used to extricate oneself from this situation, such as elevating the skis then rocking the machine gently while pushing from the rear with mild track acceleration, or pulling from the front while another operates the throttle. The suspension, however, was so clogged up with the heavy, now-compacted slush that progress seemed impossible. I ignored the yells from the distant shore, not wishing for them to get completely soaked as well, and believing that somehow I could free myself from the mess without their assistance.

Eventually, after tilting the machine and scooping out handfuls of the heavy slush from the track, I was able to advance a few feet when suddenly I found myself going from the frying pan into the fire. Apparently the movement of the machine disturbed the snow surface sufficiently to cause it to be sucked in to the slush mass as well. The machine and I were helplessly sliding towards another, gaping, newly exposed sump hole. The thing appeared large enough to swallow both the Skidoo and me along with it. Soaked to the skin with freezing water that was rapidly forming a coat of ice on my sopping wet clothing, I could see the guys beginning to head towards me as inextricably I was being drawn towards an unpleasant dunking and, perhaps, worse! Much worse! I screamed at them to follow my initial trail near shore then approach me from the rear where the trees that had been felled were now suddenly serving as anchors, having been sufficiently jammed up in the slush to arrest my forward movement.

Although they could easily see the entire situation and the mess I was in as they approached, because it was the first time that either of the fellows had been up north in these conditions, it seemed necessary to scream to watch out for the sump holes. The Skidoo had come to a halt with the nose of the machine partly underwater, with the tips of the skis resting a foot beneath the surface. It appeared that only the trees anchoring its forward progress were preventing a disaster. The skis, fortunately, had not gone entirely under, or extricating the machine would have been impossible with their being caught beneath the edge of the ice.

By the time Al and Norman made their way to where I was hanging on to the back of the Skidoo, they, too, were soaking wet. Finally, the three of us, using the well-anchored trees for support, managed to drag the machine from the sump hole and a potential watery grave. The suspension was "de-slushed" and when we were safely clear, the trees were unfastened then placed on the fresh undisturbed surface in front of the machine to serve as rails to allow for a quick start. The Skidoo was revved up and we made our escape to shore without further incident.

On shore, the Ski-boose was rehooked and all the gear unceremoniously tossed inside, along with the nice brookie that Al had taken earlier. The three of us now completely ensconced in a layer of ice squeezed onto the Skidoo to begin the trip back to Birch Lodge. Although it sounds ridiculous to say it now, other than our faces and fingertips that were nipped with frostbite, our bodies were warm. The ice that encased us obviously allowed us to retain the substantial body heat that had been generated by all the exertion required in escaping from the sump hole.

However, we were still faced with the forty-five minute ride through the bush and down the back route to our cabin at the lodge. By the time we reached the road the temperature had plummeted to near zero Fahrenheit and, combined with the wind chill factor created by the speed of the Skidoo, we were close to passing out by the time we reached the cabin. Hypothermia had obviously overtaken our bodies and brains and only the innate sense of survival drove us beyond that point where our systems would have shut down.

With each of us concentrating on his own personal survival mode, hardly a word was spoken during the trip back. No one had enough strength left anyhow to shout loud enough to be heard above the roar of the old Skidoo's engine. When we finally arrived back at camp it took the last vestiges of our willpower to disengage ourselves from the machine. To any observer we would have appeared to be walking like zombies but looking like King Arthur's Knights of Old as the thick layer of frozen armour almost entirely prevented any movement.

After an hour or so of chopping and hacking off the ice and discarding our soaking wet boots and clothing, we began to shiver in earnest. We were not without a few tears, some of relief and some in response to the pain from the frostbite, as our bodies warmed in the heat of the cabin. Luckily, no permanent physical problems resulted from that trip to Grants Lake, but for some reason or another it turned out to be our last to those waters with its absolutely unforgettable outcome.

Butternut is another small lake with a difficult approach in the Land O' Lakes. In order to partake of its brook trout fishing, one must access a hydro road leading north from the village of Ompah, then drive another five or six miles before branching off on a bush road for several miles, then finally hiking the last mile or so to the lake. As must be evident by now, we brook trout anglers, often seeking the most distant and inaccessible waters to ply our craft, are a stubbornly persistent lot whom most other fishermen would deem foolish. Nevertheless, having heard rumours that Butternut had been deliberately poisoned by the Department of Lands and Forests to kill the existing unwanted fish species, then subsequently stocked with yearling speckled trout, its allure became irresistible.

Another fishing buddy of mine, Bill Taylor, was recruited to join me for our initial attempt to find the trail to Butternut and check out the fishing. I happen to have a lousy sense of direction, even getting completely disoriented on occasion in large malls like the Eaton Centre in Toronto, whereas Bill always seems to know which way is out of the bush and back to our car when he and I are partridge (ruffed grouse) hunting. Tagging along behind him when we began the hike to the lake, after having located the trail with little trouble, was easy and the entire exercise rewarding.

It proved to be a lovely little trout lake with a great vantage point about half-way down the shore, a rocky promontory from which we were able to hurl our lures in three directions. A half-dozen sixteen to eighteen-inch brookies were landed in short order before the bite went off for the day. All were released to do battle on another occasion. Keeping them would have been foolish anyhow as the temperature had soared and the trout's edibility might not have survived the hike back to the car in the oppressive heat.

My two sons, Randy and the older lad Ronnie, not yet teenagers, had become quite proficient with their own tackle and fished numerous streams and bigger, more easily accessible waters with me ever since they were able to flex a spinning rod. However, neither had been on one of our more exploratory junkets. After hearing the many tales about some of these escapades, the boys pleaded with me to be taken with us on the next "mission impossible" excursion, hoping to experience some of the adventures they had been hearing from their old man since, as they put it, they were kids. After much discussion, among the boys, myself and their mother, it was decided that they were now old enough, strong enough and big enough to endure a lengthy trip to Butternut Lake in the Land O' Lakes where Bill and I had enjoyed a fine, not too difficult to reach, day's fishing. When the lads were told that we had put back a half a dozen fat brookies their excitement grew even more. Seldom had they been on trips where we had actually caught more trout than we wished to keep for the pan.

The following weekend saw us heading once again for the Land O' Lakes and while I tried hard to not display my trepidation, the boys were bursting with anticipation. I didn't have old buddy, Bill Taylor, with us to help locate the final trail to the lake and thus keep us from straying. Although spotting where the bush trail branched off the Hydro Road proved to be no problem, with Ronnie interpreting the topographical map, my concern proved to have been justified shortly after we parked and struck out on foot in the direction of the lake. Every little game trail branching off our chosen course caused a momentary pause and discussion timeout concerning which path to pursue. After a couple of hours of fruitless wandering, it became apparent that if not lost, we were certainly well off course. After my third attempt at reassuring the boys that we were indeed moving in the proper direction, I noticed the surreptitious glances between them interspersed with disbelieving looks in my direction.

I finally had to swallow my pride, admit defeat and call for a "sit down" with a chance to study the top maps and discuss the situation before we continued any further. We broke out the sandwiches that had been prepared for our shore lunch at the lake. With our appetites appeased, the alternative strategies were kicked around: Should we call it a day and try to find our way back before we end up spending the night in the bush? Continue in the direction that the compass dictated for us? Or back up until we located a more likely trail branching off in the same general direction?

Ronnie finally came up with the winner. According to the topographical map, the esker[6] we could see fairly close to our position in the bush was the highest spot in the area. He suggested that we head in that direction and climb the tallest tree on the hill, hoping to see the lake and our proximity to it. With two eager and athletic youngsters vying for the privilege of climbing the tree and the honour of discovering it, we agreed that Ronnie, whose idea it was in the first place, be given the opportunity.

We worked our way up the hill, selected the tallest tree and with a boost from us, Ron began to negotiate the difficult climb. At least, it looked rather formidable to me with little space between the branches, but he scrambled up as easily as climbing a fight of stairs. Even before he reached the uppermost branches he let out a yell,

"I see it! I see it, Dad!" Pointing back in the direction from whence we had just come, he hollered, "It's just back there a little. We must have walked right by it without seeing it."

That is exactly what had happened. The bush is so dense in those never-logged hills that we had actually passed within a couple of hundred yards of the lake. We were probably sidetracked by another game trail, plenty of which criss-cross the bush in all directions forming a lacy network that can easily lead to disorientation.

Ron and Randy Deval fishing at Butternut Lake in the early 1970s.

Fifteen minutes later after my having to endure a number of snide remarks from the "cheap seats" about their old man's sense of direction, we stumbled out of the bush directly onto the rocky promontory which had been our intended target all along. While I sat for a few moments to collect my thoughts and recharge my batteries, the boys set their tackle up and were in action before I was even back up on my feet. Randy was the first to score—and he scored big time with a lovely twenty-incher.

Capping the day and the memories of the trip with my sons to Grants Lake was the thrill and excitement of limit catches of specks for the boys. None was kept, other than Randy's first, which, as it developed, turned out to be the day's largest. The old man was skunked—but did achieve a small victory nevertheless. We made it back to the car with only a bare minimum of miscalculated trail decisions.

Bearing the name of Lucky Lake there is no way that it could escape being included in this compendium of magical waters and memories. Lucky is a lake trout and a bass lake and has produced quite a few lakers for us, some weighing as much as eleven pounds, exceptionally large for a comparatively small lake, less than three miles long and a half-mile wide. Lucky is truly magical as it also produces some of the largest smallmouth bass to be found in the province—trophy fish, twenty-six inches long and eight pounds.

A particular memory comes to mind of a morning on Lucky when we were fly fishing the edge of a weed bed, searching for one of the lake's behemoth bass but attracting only perch after perch to our feathered offerings.

It was near the end of June with bass season open, but the spring-fed lake was still quite cold. We had not given any thought to the possibility of the lakers, normally a cold and deep water fish, still cruising the shallows that late in the season as they do shortly after ice-out.

My old buddy, Art Walker, and I were tossing Mickey Finn streamer flies[7] into the weed lines, attempting to entice one of the lake's big bass into believing these lures were the lake's predominant minnows, golden shiners. Just as I hooked another perch, Art thought he saw a leviathan boil just beneath the surface behind his fly. He had barely mentioned it when the water erupted under my little perch and Mickey Finn. I was fast to a racing locomotive of a fish streaking for the deep water in the centre of the small lake. Fortunately it hadn't chosen the weed bed area to dive into, or we might never have had a chance to determine what it was.

"Gotta be a big trout!" Art yelled, as my reel screamed. "Bass never run like that and almost always head for cover, not deep water."

Too excited to respond, I merely grinned and nodded in agreement while holding the rod high and upright to cushion the fish's antics as it was now shaking its head violently in attempts to remove the constant pressure being applied by the rod, line and me. A meal of a small perch had never created this kind of a problem for the big trout before—only the odd foreign object stuck in its jaw, when it had once upon a time carelessly mistaken a fishing lure for a minnow. (The trout still wore a scar in its lip where a hook had penetrated before being torn out when another angler had applied too much pressure on that occasion).

"Whoa there, fish," I pleaded, easing the pressure on the line in the sudden realization that the trout or whatever probably was not fast to my fly, but simply hanging on to and refusing to forfeit its meal. If I had had my wits about me when the fish struck, I would have given it enough slack to swallow the perch, but after all its contortions, if slack were applied to the line now the fish might simply let go and release the perch. I maintained a slight pressure and crossed my fingers, toes and eyes for luck.

The foolish fish, apparently not wishing to release its "catch," hung on until fifteen or twenty minutes later we were able to work it alongside the boat and carefully slide the landing net under it—a thirty-three-inch-long, eleven-pound lake trout. To this day it remains the largest I have landed on a fly—pardon me, on a fly rod!

An earlier section involving Grants Lake, recounted a tale of horrendous conditions during a winter ice-fishing trip. Exceptionally deep snow, heavy slush and dangerous sump holes, all combined with Arctic-like freezing temperatures, were the nemeses on that occasion. Similar situations occurred several times and in a number of areas. A few that come to mind occurred on A/B, Limit and Beanpole lakes in Haliburton, but without doubt the most memorable and possibly most dangerous incident in my sixty-plus years of ice fishing and snowmobiling occurred on little Lucky Lake in the Land O' Lakes.

That year, as well, was a winter with an exceptional snow load on the frozen waters of the Land O' Lakes, with temperatures below zero on many of the weekends that were chosen by us to test our hard-water fishing skills on the various trout lakes in that area. Lucky Lake was selected for a couple of reasons: gorgeous, large and plentiful lake trout and an interesting and challenging cross-country and cross-lake Skidoo trip to get there from our cabin on Buckshot Lake. Conquering adversity on these trips is for us half the pleasure in a sort of masochistic manner. We were supplied with a great deal of that "pleasure" after a memorable winter day on Lucky Lake.

Getting to Lucky from Birch Lodge in the winter required either a lengthy, time-consuming drive trailering the machines, two of them and the Ski-boose, around a number of country back roads, or snowmobiling three or four miles across Buckshot. From there we would pick up a trail at the far end of the lake that leads to Brule Lake, then it's a good mile and a half run across Brule to another trail and, finally, a half-mile run through the bush to Lucky. Disregarding the challenging conditions, of course, we chose the latter.

On trips of this nature it always behooves one to leave word with others of the intended destination and course of action in case of difficulties. Having experienced several of these winter ice-fishing junkets that bordered on the brink of extreme peril, word was left with Bev Woolnough, the proprietor of Birch Lodge, that we would be heading out in the wee hours the following morning (Saturday) and crossing both Buckshot and Brule in order to get to Lucky to fish for lakers. Bev told us what we already knew, that the ice and snow conditions were rotten and suggested fishing Brooks Lake, smaller and much closer by, for specks. But our minds were made up and Lucky it was to be. After all, we surmised, our experience with these conditions would stand us in good stead and actually we were looking forward to the difficult snowmobiling as much as we were the fishing. We left instructions that even if we were not back by dark, not to send a search and rescue party as we felt quite confident in our own ability to look after ourselves, no matter what the situation. It would have been dangerous and foolish for others to head out in darkness looking for us in those conditions.

"However," I did suggest, "heh, if we're not back by morning, then maybe help would be appropriate."

We began the trek across Buckshot in the wee hours just as the sun was creeping above the horizon. There was a decent crust on top of the snow and few watery areas, but with the prospect of the slushy conditions on the lakes, we had wisely decided to use backpacks instead of the heavy sled, so both Skidoos travelled the length of the lake only kicking up slush in two or three areas. The crust that had formed overnight stood us in good stead, providing support for the machines in all but the worst places. Occasionally we would break through, but only momentarily, as our momentum carried us on without our becoming stuck.

On this trip I was partnered by another old fishing buddy (who shall remain nameless for reasons that will become obvious later in this story) and my Brittany Spaniel, Jamie, who loved to tag along with us whenever possible. Where appropriate, Jamie would run behind us on the track the machines created in the snow, or if not, he would sit on the seat in front of me with my arms around him while I steered the machine.

There was a swamp to negotiate leading to a large ridge that we had to climb before working down the other side to Brule Lake. Unfortunately no one else had recently crossed between the two lakes so it was left to us to break trail in the deep snow. On another earlier trip through there, my Skidoo's track, the rubber belt driven by the motor that propels the machine, had been torn up by an unseen sharpened base of a tree trunk, whittled into a weapon by a beaver. Beneath the snow, it had lain there just waiting to inflict its nastiness on a wayward snowshoe or carelessly steered snowmobile. Remembering that incident when we were forced to limp all the way back to camp with the snowmobile track barely able to function, we proceeded cautiously with Jamie leading the way this time and seemingly able to determine the trail's correct path beneath the snow. Other than once again breaking through the surface several times in low, wet areas where the suspensions took in a load of slush, we made it through the swamp. Up the hill we sped and down the other side to Brule, passing Jamie who leaped out of the way.

Before striking out across the next lake, the machines were tipped on their sides and as much slush as possible was scooped out of the tracks. Then, with the dog firmly seated in front of me, we raced across the lake towards the final lap, the trail leading through a half mile of bush to our goal, Lucky Lake. The lake appeared virginal, untouched by other snowmobiles. Startlingly beautiful in the bright sunshine now creating the illusion of a million diamonds sparkling on its unblemished, pure white surface, the lake was inviting. But unbeknownst to us, a trap lay in store, one which I know will never be forgotten by either of us.

The shoals where we wanted to set up were three-quarters of the way down the lake. Driving the more powerful and heavier machine, I volunteered to lead the way in order to compress the track. That was the second mistake (the first was getting out of bed that morning and planning to go and fish Lucky Lake). Because of the deep snow, Jamie would ride with my buddy a cautious distance behind my machine, in case I bogged down or whatever.

In very short order I realized that we were in rather serious trouble! Less than a quarter mile from shore my track was no longer riding on top, but digging in to an awesome layer of slush. Knowing that I was about to become completely bogged in, with one hand I waved furiously attempting to halt the second machine's progress before it, too, fell into the trap. Too late! The roostertail of slush it was discharging out its rear was proof that we both were in dire straits. When the Skidoo sputtered to a stop, Jamie jumped off and damn near disappeared in the depth of snow and slush. My buddy, now enmeshed like me (our lower bodies rapidly soaking up the freezing water), picked the terrified dog up and sat him on his Skidoo where he seemed quite content to wait until we extricated the machines. I looked at my watch. It was not yet nine o'clock.

Looking beyond our position, further down the lake, we felt that if we had had a good head of steam we would probably not have bogged down. Also the remainder of the lake looked so inviting it didn't seem possible that there would be other areas as precarious as the one we were stuck in. We set about freeing the machines from the clutches of the slush. The first thing to do in these situations is to get the machine up on to a firm, higher base of packed-down slush and snow, then allow it to drain its excess water and scoop the slush from the suspension.

This sounds easy enough but calls for much patience and hard work. The machine is left where it is until a ramp is constructed as moving it out too soon exposes it to the freezing air causing the compacted mess in the suspension to freeze, whereas if kept down in the water it won't solidify. The ramp is constructed by shovelling (we always have a small collapsible one strapped onto the side of the Skidoo), then kicking the snow and slush into a pile before stomping it into submission. The process is repeated many times until we have constructed a launching ramp of at least twenty, but preferably thirty feet, high enough to clear the snow-covered lake surface. Such a ramp would normally supply one with sufficient room to accelerate smoothly, but rapidly to escape the slushy area.

A couple of hours later, both machines were draining on their newly constructed ramps, Jamie was de-iced to the best of our ability and the lead machine, mine, revved up for the launch. Avoiding the temptation to apply full throttle, otherwise the track would simply dig right in and we would be back to square one, I got it moving smoothly and firmly accelerated until it shot ahead off the launch pad. Triumphantly I raised one fist in the air as I shot at least a hundred feet down the lake—then bogged down once again.

Impatiently, my buddy had already begun his own launch and, driving the lighter machine, he roared past me for a few feet then also bogged down. Jamie somehow fought his way up to us and desperately attempted to climb up on the seat of my Skidoo on his own. All three of us looked at each other in disgust, before the freezing temperature spurred us into action once again. A formidable layer of ice had already begun to form on our exterior clothing and we chipped the ice that had built up between Jamie's toes. His incessant licking in attempts to warm them only made matters worse for him as it melted the accumulated snow and slush that promptly froze in place.

A glance at the watch showed we were now well past noon hour and approaching two o'clock. Needless to say the three of us were not happy campers! Throughout the ordeal there had been a dearth of conversation with the concern, pain, extreme effort and exertion all taking its toll on our brains and bodies. Finally we agreed to call it a day, forget the fishing, the thoughts of which for all intents and purposes had already been shelved, and get our asses out of there while we still could and before darkness overtook us. At that time of year, the sun sets around five.

Forcing our sore and tired muscles into action, we once again almost drained the last bit of energy left in our systems, but before the exhaustion completely overwhelmed us we had both machines up and draining on new rapidly freezing compacted slush ramps and pointing in the direction of the trail that had brought us to this frightful situation. Sore, tired, half-frozen and probably already hypothermic, we had taken until darkness to complete this last set of launching pads.

On these trips I almost always wear a down jacket over top of a down vest, a heavy, woollen Jack Shirt and insulated underwear. Of course I was still cold, but only my face, hands and head were worrisome. Hence it was an easy decision, when my buddy pointed out that Jamie, scrunched up in a fetal position on my Skidoo seat seemed to be in big trouble—bigger than we were. We chipped the ice off his feet and wrapped him snugly in my big down jacket.

It was then that we realized that the lake was so badly chewed up by all our machinations and efforts to overcome the slush that, in reality, all we had done was draw more of the surface water off the lake and into the area that we had already butchered. We were now faced with more than two feet of water and another foot or so of slush that would have to be conquered if we were to escape the clutches of "Lucky" Lake. Just walking in the mess was scary, but with darkness and the temperature now plummeting, a solid crust was gradually forming over the entire football-field-size mess. It would have been impossible to negotiate the quarter mile or so that was still left to us to get off the lake, and then there would still be the sections we had chewed up just getting there from Buckshot Lake. With nothing left with which to build more ramps, even if we were somehow able to muster the necessary strength and energy to do so, there were absolutely no alternatives if we were to survive until morning when a group of machines would be coming out to look for us. We had to remain in the area until they arrived.

While I only briefly pondered this situation, my buddy, his brain now befuddled and his body hypothermic, began to plough through the crusty surfaced water and slush towards the distant shore. I yelled at him as forcefully as I could, "For Christ sake, hold on—where do you think you're going, man?"

He turned, looked at me quizzically and paused, while as quickly as I could, I caught up to him. More frightened than I have ever been in my life, I said through chattering teeth, "I don't know what you had in mind, old fellow, but whatever it is, forget it. We have to stay together if we are going to beat this thing.

"You do what you want, Gordon," he muttered, "but I'm walking back to the cabin. I've had it with this shit! Gotta get outta here! Do you read me?"

Grabbing his arm as he turned, I yelled, "Forget it! You'll never make it. It's going down below zero and you're already half-frozen and completely exhausted." I repeated my words, this time shouting every one.

His eyes were glassy.

"Do you hear me, old buddy! For God's sake, and yours—and mine and Jamie's, listen carefully!"

Barely able to talk, he whispered as I still held on to his arm, "Never mind. I'm going—gotta get outta here…"

There were tears in my eyes as I realized what I had to do. I slapped him on the face hard. Once, twice then as he winced and shook his head, once again. He, too, then took a deep breath and placed both arms around me and shook violently for a moment or two before taking another couple of deep breaths then with a tear or two in his own eyes backed off a little and said,"Okay, okay, I'm fine now. What do you have in mind, Deval? We build an igloo or something?"

I knew then that we were all right and would make it out together all right. "Not a bad idea," I replied, "but I've got a much better one." Continuing quickly, because simply standing still was causing the cold to permeate my inner core, I said, "Listen carefully, please. The ramps and all this water will freeze up solid overnight. We leave the machines right where they are, up on their ramps. They're both starting and working well, so we will easily be able to drive off when the slush freezes over and get the hell out of here in the morning. Remember where we picked up the trail to here back at Brule?" I asked. Continuing, I said, "There's a big cottage right there—you probably didn't see it because it was pretty well buried in snowdrifts. Getting there's going to be tough slogging, but I know we can make it if we get going and don't stop. We'll take turns carrying Jamie."

I figured that once we got there, we'd find a way to get in, jimmy a window if necessary. Once inside, we would get a fire going in the fireplace, thaw out and hang in until the sun came up the next day. With luck there might even be some food.

That is exactly what we did. After we pried open a boarded window, my buddy crawled through and I passed Jamie through next. There was a stack of firewood buried beneath the snow outside the cottage. A couple of dozen split logs were dug out then tossed through for the big fireplace, matches were located, along with a candle or two, a can of beans and even a can of dog food, all frozen of course. Both were opened with my Swiss Army knife and, without waiting for them to completely thaw by the fire, they were devoured by man and beast.

We had no money with us to leave for the owner, but found a notepad and pencil. An apologetic thank-you note with my name, address, phone number and explanation was written and secured with masking tape on the kitchen cupboard. Although we were utterly exhausted and managed to nod off briefly several times, only Jamie actually slept.

At first light, still soaking wet and not looking forward to the cold trip back to the cabin at Buckshot, we nevertheless struck out for the now tightened-up Lucky Lake. Without further incident and with no problems at all, we got the machines underway and left the lake with only a momentary pause to look back over our shoulders at its ridiculously chewed up surface. It was no longer the magnificent pristine view we had been treated to almost twenty-four hours earlier. We got as far as Brule Lake when a convoy of about fifteen machines, following our now frozen tracks from the day before, were spotted heading towards us. Wisely they had brought blankets and extra, dry clothing. Luckily, there were no permanent ill effects suffered by either Jamie and or ourselves. Now thoroughly bundled up, we drove back along with our escort to the cabin at Birch Lodge.

Several months later I made a special trip to Brule Lake, not just to fish for its plentiful lakers, but hoping that the cottage's owners would be there so I could thank them personally, pay for the damage to the window sill and recount the story of our escapade. They were wonderful and refused to take any money, even for the beans and dog food, completely understanding the necessity of our actions. Their generosity of spirit is now also part of this particular memory on the frozen water of Lucky Lake.

Chapter 4
Muskoka Magic

Several wonderful fishing experiences in the Muskoka Lakes district immediately come to mind when I think of this region. Two in particular occurred at the mouth of the Muskoka River where it enters the huge Muskoka Lake, several miles downstream from Santa's Village near Bracebridge, Ontario.

The first, I'll refer to as "Good Friday" as it took place on Easter Weekend, traditionally one of the finest fishing weekends for my buddies and me over the years. The days preceding this particular weekend had been blessed with a rising barometer and beautiful weather, a combination that creates an itch under the skin of most fishermen after a winter of freezing weather and ice-fishing outings.

A couple of days earlier, my Uncle Bob, one of my favourite fishing compatriots, phoned to ask if I would like to join him for a couple of hours of fishing on Good Friday morning.

Responding without hesitation, I agreed, and, mentioning Muskoka Lake in particular, I reminded him that the smelts should be running in the river mouth. Often some of the lake's bigger fish come right into the shallows for a feed while the water is still in the low forties. With most of the lake still ice-covered, the conditions should be just about perfect. He liked the suggestion, but he reminded me of having to be home by mid-afternoon to be with the family. I figured that if we could leave early, then fish till noon hour, we could get home well before three. By taking sandwiches with us, we would eliminate the need to stop anywhere for a bite of lunch.

At that time, I hadn't done much fishing there before but had heard stories of thirty- and forty-pounders taken out of the big lake. People don't really talk about it much, trying to keep the great fishing to themselves, I guess. Although I'd been up there a couple of times previously, I had only managed to catch a seven-pound whitefish, but the year before "Good Friday," about the same time, I told him, I had hooked into the lake's granddaddy lake trout. The thing just grabbed my plug and swam away rather leisurely, feeling like a Mack truck in low gear. About twenty-five seconds later it simply let go, never once giving me a chance to set the hook. After my speech, he was raring to go.

Good Friday arrived, still with the promise of great weather. We left at our appointed hour of five a.m. and after a three-hour drive to Bracebridge and its famous Santa's Village, the car-top aluminum boat was lifted off its rack. We slid it across some remaining crusty snow and launched it into the chilly Muskoka River, littered with chunks of floating, honeycombed ice heading for their destiny downstream at the lake mouth. The frozen flotsam and jetsam, including the odd willow tree carved from the bank by the spring floods and ice floes would swirl around, also clogging the mouth of the river before piling up against the remaining ice canopy covering the lake.

We had to work our way through it all quite cautiously so as not to damage the outboard motor's propeller. Fortunately for us—and the propeller—at the point where the river entered the lake and where we had been hoping to fish, that part of the bay was being kept free of the ice floes and debris by a stiff westerly breeze. Feeling that perhaps the waters were too super-chilled by the drifting blocks of ice to draw the smelts from the deep waters into their spawning areas where the big lakers forage on them (smelts require at least 42 degrees Fahrenheit temperatures before becoming randy enough to complete their mission), we decided to fish with shiny wabling spoons[1] rather than plugs such as the Rapalas that we would normally use when the smelts are in abundance. The flashing spoons, it was reasoned, would possibly attract the attention of any trout attempting to get a jump on the feeding frenzies that occur when hordes of the tasty little smelts moved into the shallows. With the river still in a spring-flood mode from the melting ponds and lakes upstream, its clarity suffered too, but the shiny spoons would pick up and reflect whatever available light managed to penetrate the roiled water. That and the vibrations emitted by the undulating wabler had often proved successful in similar conditions elsewhere. My uncle was a patient and fine fisherman, but that particular day belonged to me. It was destined to become another of my all-time magical memories.

After snagging my Swiss Halfwave wabler on an enormous underwater stump and hoisting the anchor to paddle over and free the lure, I made a casual cast in the direction of the piled-up pack ice, placed the rod firmly behind my knee, then began the paddle back to our previous location. My uncle was continuing to cast while I stroked us backwards, away from the swirling ice debris.

"Damn, stuck again!" I swore as my rod tip bent sharply, but when I raised the rod from its clenched position behind my knee and passed the paddle to my uncle to paddle us back, it became obvious that the lure was stuck all right—but not on bottom. It was slowly moving in the opposite direction, towards the ice pack. The Halfwave, only an inch long with a single but very sharp treble hook, was instantly reefed by me, not only to set the hook but it was hoped, to spur the beast on the other end to change its direction away from the threatening ice pack. A metal lure is also much less likely to be held on to by a fish than a wooden or plastic plug, therefore I knew one must always react immediately by striking back to a hit or suspected hit from a fish. I struck back once or twice more, as hard as I could with the light-action spinning rod and four-pound test line to make sure the hook was set.

The ploy worked. The fish, now apparently well-hooked and puzzled by the pervasive knocks on him caused by the striking, minuscule tackle, casually reversed direction and swam directly towards the boat. Gathering line as it approached, I got ready for the expected reaction when the trout saw the boat looming above it. Expecting the fish, which was still unseen by either of us, to take off like a scared jackrabbit when it caught sight of the boat or its shadow, we were startled when it loomed out of the murky depths and were momentarily mesmerized by its enormity.

Looking stunned, Uncle Bob muttered, "Oh, my God, Gordon, that thing's at least five feet long and more than fifty pounds!"

Gord with his 38-pound laker, his biggest fish ever, caught on Good Friday, 1969. Uncle Bob (Wilcox) is in the background

Not prone to such exaggeration (although most of my buddies would beg to differ) I rejected the speculation, but still thought that it had to be more than a yard long and at least forty pounds. The fish was so big that it seemed to take an eternity for it to pass out of view. It calmly kept right on cruising towards the only slightly deeper water, apparently unconcerned about the pressure I was now applying with the tackle. Glancing at my watch, I laughed then remarked, "This is going to take awhile, Uncle Bob. You might not get home in time after all. It just turned nine o'clock, but with this little outfit and only a four-pound test line we could be here all day before we get this "sucker" into the boat. I can only put so much pressure on it before the monofilament breaks, you know. Hopefully it'll be enough to control the trout and keep it away from the ice pack. It's game over, if it manages to get under the ice—the line will hang up for sure and break."

A series of "give and goes"[2] commenced, with the huge laker taking eighty, ninety, a hundred feet of line. With the anchor pulled, my uncle paddled furiously to keep up to it before it stripped the spool of all its line and backing. Then when the big trout did pause for a moment, I carefully avoided creating any slack in the line, keeping the rod bowed and reeling in as the monofilament was regained.

Long before that wondrous Good Friday I had learned that to successfully land large fish with light, almost fragile terminal tackle, a couple of things must be religiously observed: a constant pressure on the fish with the rod tip (as much as the line and rod can endure without breakage) must be maintained; secondly, the clutch must be properly adjusted, just beneath the breaking point of the line when tested. That should be performed, not by pulling it off the reel, but from the rod tip as the fish does. As well, a little prayer or two probably can't hurt, either.

Of course, it goes without saying that patience must be observed and the desire that sometimes overtakes the fishermen to rush the fish to the net should be disregarded. Many a trophy fish has been lost due to a lack of discipline in observance of that rule. With my uncle maintaining the pursuit and my attempting to adhere to the above cardinal stratagems, an hour or so passed in what seemed like an eternity with the monster trout not tiring in the least. I was feeling the strain, with my arms becoming sore and nerves frazzled. It literally towed us around the entire bay, several times perilously close to the ice pack, before I sensed that its runs were finally becoming shorter and less persistent.

Feeling that I was getting the upper hand in the battle, I suggested, "Maybe we should head in the direction of that bit of beach over on the other side. Could you try to work us over that way? The water should be shallow enough there to get out of the boat and play the fish from shore."

I thought I would have a better chance to land the thing that way. By now I really did want this one for the wall. If I could work it into the shallows, I could get behind it and just walk the brute right in until it beached.

"You land this trout, young man," my uncle said, "and, yeah, you'll have it for the wall all right—and I'll pay the taxidermist, too!"

Now with only a begrudging, weakening resistance from the trophy trout, now, he was able to pole the boat into the shallow water off the slip of sand. Misjudging, but unconcerned about its depth, I leapt out into two feet of water, filling my boots and getting completely soaked. Still holding the rod tip high to cushion any last minute contortions from the big bruiser, I looked at my fortunately waterproof watch. It was just short of two hours since I first hooked the leviathan.

Suddenly, after the constant pressure of the little spinning rod had worked it in near my position in the shallow water, the huge lake trout made a last minute desperation surge for freedom when its belly touched the sandy bottom. Unfortunately for the fish, but fortunately for us, it lunged in the wrong direction and finally I could breathe easily as the giant beached itself in about a foot of water, belly on the bottom and dorsal fin sticking straight up in the air.

My uncle shouted, "Do you want the net?"

With a grin on my face a yard wide, I replied, "No thanks, he's all mine. Watch."

And I simply escorted him the rest of the way until it was all over—other than a half a roll of film being used for pictures—two hours and eight minutes after the battle began. The laker was taken to town to be officially weighed and measured—thirty-eight pounds and forty-one inches and, yes, it is now on the wall in my recreation room, my largest catch ever!

Amazingly, we were back in Toronto at exactly three in the afternoon. Good Friday, indeed!

The next Muskoka reminiscence serving as a special memory of these magical waters should be entitled "Lady" not for my wife or daughter, but for my first Brittany Spaniel. Although we have been fortunate to have owned three very different Brittanies over the years, Lady, our first, was my favourite. She was much more than a pet and hunting companion—she was family.

Other than on our many stream-fishing sojourns, where trying to keep her from spooking the fish and out of the water would have been a nuisance, there was seldom a hunting or fishing trip where we were not accompanied by her. On a couple of occasions she had leapt from the boat when a particularly feisty hooked rainbow trout jumped or cartwheeled just beneath the surface. As she had been trained to do with a crippled duck or goose, she would go after the splashing fish and timing its next appearance on the surface perfectly, grab it in her teeth, clutching it firmly but not enough to puncture the skin, then swim back to the boat with her prize.

It was my younger son, Randy's, first trip to the waters of Muskoka. Later, on his second venture, he would hook and land a twenty-six pound lake trout, the largest caught on that outing and to this day his biggest catch of any kind. However, his first exposure to Muskoka's fishing had come exactly a year after the memorable trip on which I captured my own record fish. We had no idea that Muskoka magic—or lightning—was about to strike again.

After an hour or so at the mouth of the river without a touch on our lines, we hoisted the anchor and moved over near the ice pack where the river current had piled up the drifting ice and debris against the remaining ice shield covering the main body of the lake. Lady was in the boat with us and once or twice made overtures to leave the boat and scramble on to the ice for a run. Although she had been dropped off on shore previously, I suppose we impatiently had not given her enough time. She knew she shouldn't relieve herself in the boat so, mistaking the ice for shore and dry land, would place a paw on the gunwale and look longingly at what she thought offered her relief, then have to be restrained.

During one of these moments, with the boat held fast to the ice pack by the current, another of Muskoka's giant lakers latched on to my Halfwave wabler. Although I struck back and set the hook hard, it casually began to swim away against the current. I held the rod up high with one hand and rather than allow the powerful fish to get too far away to be able to control, fired up the motor with the other and went after it. I passed the rod to Randy with instructions to keep a steady tension on the line and gather it in smoothly as we gained on the fleeing trout. Fleeing is probably too strong a descriptor, meandering away might be a better description.

Lady sensed our excitement but was ignored in the euphoria of the moment. When we felt that we were far enough away from the ice, the motor was cut. Randy passed me the rod and I resumed playing the fish that was now beginning to display signs of an awareness of its situation. Then the battle began in earnest with a powerful hundred-yard run which stripped enough monofilament off the tiny reel to reveal the backing underneath, followed by a series of violent, side to side head shakes as it attempted to dislodge the foreign object firmly implanted in its jaw.

As we had done a year earlier with my initial Muskoka monster, the time of the strike, almost eleven-thirty, had been recorded by my son, but it appeared that if we were able to hold on to this fellow, it would tire much more quickly with all the energy it was using trying to gain its freedom. However, the trout that we still had not seen, but nevertheless knew was huge, was using the river current to its advantage. Positioning the boat in a favourable location to apply the eventual *coup de gras* was proving difficult as the river current forced us back to the ice pack. The big fish seemed determined to head for and swim beneath the ice as if it understood that that manoeuvre represented its only salvation. Within moments our boat was rocking gently back and forth alongside the pack ice and debris that fronted the main ice shield as the giant laker continued to cavort back and forth slightly upstream from our position, although remaining fairly close to the boat.

The remainder of this tale sounds like an unbelievable fish story, but what happened next jolted us out of our concentration on the trout—and apparent neglect of Lady's situation. I wish I could simply report that she relieved herself in the boat, but, no, she would never have done that. Instead, while we were getting our first glimpses of the great fish on one side of the boat, there was a splash behind us on the other. Realizing immediately what had taken place, I almost tipped the boat as I threw down the spinning rod and lunged backwards just in time to grab a handful of Brittany Spaniel hair. Lady was being swept beneath the ice by the powerful current!

The drag on her little thirty-three pound body was tremendous and we thought we had lost her. Although we were both in tears, that Muskoka magic was working in our favour once again. Randy, too, now had a handful of Lady's rump hair, and even though we were both leaning over the same side, the boat somehow avoided being tipped. With all thought of the fish forgotten, we were able to resist the drag of the current sufficiently to get enough of her body to the surface where she was quickly held in place beside the boat then dragged, sopping wet, over the side and onto our laps.

We both cried like babies while Lady gave us a *"What in the hell was that all about?"* look and shook aggressively, spraying water in all directions. Already soaking wet from the exercise, Randy and I hugged each other and sobbed with tears of happiness. Then almost simultaneously we both suddenly yelled, "The fish!"

While Randy restrained and attempted to calm Lady who was now shivering profusely from her exposure to the icy water, I grabbed the rod which had been ignored and forgotten in the excitement, fully expecting that I would merely be reeling in slack line with nothing on its end but, I hoped, my unbroken Halfwave—a lure that was difficult to find and expensive to buy.

To my surprise, once I had reeled in fifty or sixty feet of loose line drifting aimlessly in the current, I became aware that the foolish fish had not taken advantage of the situation and was still firmly fastened. Although it had had time to get a second wind while Lady's rescue was underway, the magic returned and the big lake trout was soon brought to net without further incident. A glance at my watch indicated that almost two-and-a-quarter hours had passed since the fish had first struck. With approximately fifteen or twenty minutes of that time devoted to the rescue, this trout, too, had taken a couple of hours to subdue.

At home a few hours later, we weighed the trout in at thirty-six pounds and measured thirty-nine inches long, almost as big as the one already on the wall and a few pounds heavier than Lady—our other "catch" of the day. Although I could not really afford it, that trout now also sits proudly on the wall in my recreation room. A first-place magazine contest award of three hundred dollars certainly eased the cost of the mount.

The entire episode of Lady's rescue is recounted every time someone looking at these huge lake trout in their glass cases asks for the details of their capture.

The third part in this little Muskoka Lake trilogy should be called "Trout fishermen surely are a persistent breed—if not truly nuts!"

A dozen or so years after the glorious memories just described, we were once again fishing in Muskoka. This time, however, I was with new fishing buddies from our recently formed club, the Scarborough Fly and Bait Casting Association. We had not planned on testing our luck in Muskoka, but rather on the Saugeen River's rainbow trout in the Southampton area, nowhere near Muskoka.

The Saugeen is a huge river flowing in a northeasterly direction, meandering for many miles before eventually emptying into Lake Huron at Southampton. A superb run of rainbow trout collects at a particular area every year during the spring run a few miles upstream from the mouth of the river. Quite well known among the fishing fraternity, the spot is normally busy with fishermen seeking the majestic steelheads, the tag applied to the silver bows during their spring spawning run from the depths of Lake Huron. It was late in March, but two weeks of comparatively balmy weather and warm rains had tricked us into believing the fish would be making their runs sooner than usual.

The sun was just beginning to creep above the horizon when we completed the three-hour drive from Toronto, a great time to begin fishing anywhere. However, a shock lay in store for us as the car crept down the still ice-covered hill toward the river. Mountains of ice that had piled up on both shores alongside the river during the earlier ice break-up and resulting spring flood, prevented us from approaching the normal parking spots in the area. It also made it impossible to launch the car-top boat in which we had planned to go upriver to reach our favourite fishing locations. Fishing would have been impossible anyhow, even if we had been able to launch, as the river was still in flood condition way above the bank with the water hopelessly roiled and muddied. It was obvious that dry weather and many days would be required before the Saugeen would become fishable once again. It would have made an interesting picture: three eager, but frustrated anglers, Ashok Kalle, Paul Kennedy and I, standing there, perplexed looks pasted on our faces as we stared at the river and not a word being spoken for what seemed like an infinite moment.

Finally Paul cut through the impasse by saying, "Gord, you know those big momma lakers hanging in your rec room. You said they were caught around this time of year. Right? Didn't you say it was on Good Friday? Well, Good Friday's next week, isn't it? Let's go where you got 'em!"

Still in a quandary over the condition of the Saugeen River in front of us, his comments took a moment to gel in my bewildered state. By this time Ashok was pointing out that Muskoka was nowhere near the Saugeen River. I snapped out of my lethargy to consider the proposition and could sense their patience wearing thin as I finally broke the silence, "All right, then. "It's not seven yet. I think we could get to Muskoka in a couple of hours by using the back roads most of the way instead of having to take the highway all the way back to Orillia. It will be a long drive, but an interesting one.

I cautioned them that the fishing could be boring, with absolutely no guarantee that we would encounter one of those monster Muskoka lakers, and reminded them that it would cost each one of them almost twice as much for his share of the gas.

Three hours of driving and half an hour coffee stop later, that scene from the Saugeen River was repeated on the frozen shore of the Muskoka River in front of Santa's Village. The three of us perplexed, wannabe trout fishermen stared incredulously at another icy dilemma. An eternity seemed to pass before I disturbed the serenity of the lovely springtime scene by letting loose with a string of oaths.

Then, with a little of my frustration relieved, I said, "Heh, guys, this ain't the first time I've been faced with this predicament. Let's get the friggin' boat in the friggin' river and work it down to the river mouth where the current should have the bay reasonably clear of ice so we can get in a bit of fishing. There might be a trout or two there as crazy as we are and just as eager to get the season underway."

On this, his first ever trout fishing trip, Ashok wore a look of utter amazement at what we had suggested and were about to attempt. Nevertheless, in short order the aluminum car-top boat, motor fastened but raised, our

Breaking ice on the Muskoka River.

tackle and all the paraphernalia with which anglers are festooned and their boats cluttered stowed aboard, was being cautiously slid across the inshore ice towards the hoped-for negotiable current in the middle of the river. The three of us had death grips on the front and sides of the craft with all eyes studying the ice surface in anticipation of its cracking beneath our combined weight.

As the instigator of the precarious exercise, I had assumed the responsibility for the lead position and front of the boat while Paul and Ashok clutched its sides with steely determination. When we approached the middle, with the first sensation of the ice's cracking and possibly giving way, I yelled and we clambered aboard—just in the nick of time to avoid soakers all around.

Using the paddles, the guys broke up and shoved the pack ice away until we were able to lower and fire up the Evinrude, then point the boat downriver towards the river mouth a couple of miles away. Our labours were just beginning, however. Using the motor's propulsion, along with a continuous rocking of the boat from side to side, we were able to slowly move downstream. The rocking action forced waves beneath the ice edge, breaking it up and widening the open water path in order to facilitate our progress. Nevertheless, other tactics also had to be employed three or four times as we approached several of the wide areas of the serpentine river where it remained ice-bound. With the three of us as far back in the boat as was safe, we used the motor to run up on the hard ice then, like an Arctic ice breaker, as we shifted our weight forward the nose would break through, and we would begin the manoeuvre all over again, repeating until we reached open water once more.

Seemingly stuck for a few minutes in a particularly difficult and heavy ice sector, we became aware, while banging away at the ice with the paddles and shoving the detached floes away with our hands, of shouts from shore some fifty yards away, "What the Hell do you guys think you're doing out there, anyway! Are you stuck—or what?"

The shouts were coming from a couple of Ontario Provincial Police officers, a man and a woman, and it was obvious that they had become soaking wet while working their way down the shoreline in an attempt to intercept us. Probably they broke through some of the shallower areas of the river topped with deceptively thin ice that had formed during the night. Some distance behind them, a couple of women, apparently from the cottages strung along the shore, were also pointing and screaming at us. We were to learn a week later exactly what had preceded the cops' appearance.

However, we yelled back that we were okay, not in any difficulties and just trying to get down the river to do a spot of fishing. As they shook their heads in disgust then turned to retreat, it was easy to ascertain that none of them were properly clothed for the weather and circumstances. They were shivering and all four had to struggle through deep snow to get back from whence they had come.

It was mid-afternoon before we were finally able to free ourselves from the clutches of the river ice and move out into the open water of the river-mouth bay. When we finally dropped anchor and set up our tackle, Ashok broke Paul and me up with the following tongue in cheek comments, learned during his dozen years in Canada since he had left India to begin his successful computer business, "Gee, this is fun, Gord! Wonder what the poor people are doing for laughs today!"

Although we worked the water as thoroughly as we could in the time we had remaining no trout were caught, but we agreed that it certainly had been an adventure that would be remembered by all. I suppose the power up above who looks after such matters had decreed that we had not put sufficient effort into the day's activities to warrant a reward, but it was there anyhow—in the form of a very valued memory on a stretch of certainly memorable body of water, reached after a drive of almost five hundred miles.

One week later, an article appeared in the *Toronto Star* newspaper under this heading—"Three Idiots Risk Lives on Frozen Muskoka River." The story was apparently submitted to the paper by one of the women we saw from the cottages who must have summoned the OPP to our "rescue." The byline suggested that she was a regular contributor to the *Star* as a Muskoka correspondent. With little of interest there during that time of year, I guess she had to have something to write about, so after seeing us out in the river and believing us to be in trouble, called the police.

Chapter 5

Up Pefferlaw Way

After writing about the giant fish and huge waters of Muskoka Lake, it seems appropriate to attend to a delightful little waterway that is so small that it remains unnamed, except by my buddies and me. We call it "Itsy Bitsy."

This little brook, like many of the streams that we fish, originates on the upper slopes of the Oak Ridges Moraine and is one of the many tributaries in the headwaters of the Pefferlaw River that flows northerly into Lake Simcoe. It can be reached from where I live in Scarborough, Ontario, in less than half an hour. With such quick access, I can often find time to visit it for a wee spot of fishing.

Visiting Itsy Bitsy is like visiting a jewellery store. The brook trout swimming in this tiny stream always remind me of the finest and most colourful gem stones available. It is a nursery, producing and providing magnificently adorned speckled trout for the Pefferlaw River, the headwaters of which all produce specks with similar garnishments; the enchanting embellishments with which most brookies are festooned.

My beguiling admiration for these beautiful fish knows no boundaries. Brookies were bequeathed with the entire spectrum of the rainbow, while the colours were obviously applied by the hand of an ethereal master artisan.

Although similar in most respects, another intriguing feature with these fish is that, when laid side by side, as is often done by successful fishermen for comparison, it becomes apparent that no two are decorated in exactly the same fashion. Some have many spots, others few. Some will have large spots, others, small. On some the colours are startlingly pronounced and on others more subdued, almost pastel-like. On all, other than on the dorsal and tail, the fins are decorated in contrasting slashes of red, black and white. The spots will vary in brightness from indigo to azure, with a centrepiece dot in shades of vermilion or orange. The dots also fluctuate considerably in size and the intensity of their colour.[1]

Reading about the fascination created for us when one of these little jewels are lifted from the water, it should be easy to understand why fishing for brook trout—or specks—if you prefer—are often *numero uno* on fishermen's lists of angling pursuits. The brook trout of this minuscule waterway are among the most beautiful fish I have seen anywhere, including on many snorkelling trips to the coral reefs of the Caribbean Islands. I find it impossible, as I am sure you may have noticed, to overstate the charm of the little jewels of Itsy Bitsy's truly magical waters.

One might find it difficult to believe that we can obtain as much pleasure in fishing for trout that seldom exceed seven or eight inches in length as we do, for example, in fishing for wily browns and big steelheads in the Ganaraska and Saugeen rivers, or the giant lakers of the Muskoka area. In reality, probably more than fifty per cent of the hours I spend on the water in an average year are enjoyed on small trout streams like little Itsy Bitsy.

It is a rare day when we are skunked on any of the Pefferlaw River waters, but even more rare when on Itsy Bitsy, therefore I won't hesitate to take a trout or two home occasionally for a feed from the bigger waters. Itsy Bitsy's jewels, however, are seldom kept for the pan. But while treating myself to an hour or so of fishing its ice-cold, spring-fed waters one day a few years ago, a startlingly magical moment occurred as a flash of iridescence almost overpowered my Polaroid sunglasses. A brookie, looking far too big for these waters had darted out and back from a bed of watercress bordering the tiny brook in pursuit of my tiny spinner—but missed.

For most of the several miles that Itsy Bitsy meanders before spilling into the main flow of Pefferlaw Brook, it can easily be hopped across or simply straddled. After the shock of my seeing a speckled trout there that would not have looked out of place on the Broadback River in northern Quebec had settled somewhat, I eased my silhouette slowly into the background, waited for a few moments, then worked my way downstream from the bed of watercress and stepped across.

These mini trout streams almost always wend their way through heavily forested and bushy areas, far too small to be pleasantly worked with fly-fishing equipment, therefore the angler is forced to employ live bait, worms, etc., or use as we do, spinning tackle with artificial lures such as small spoons or spinners. If one is to enjoy using this type of tackle under these awkward and restricted conditions, it is necessary to achieve a considerable degree of proficiency and accuracy with one's equipment. If not, much time will be spent attempting to free their lure from all the traps lying in wait to steal them, such as underwater roots, logs, weeds, watercress and just about anything else one could think of. Then there is the shoreline cover, assorted bush and often willow and/or cedar with their branches overhanging and their roots interspersed under the bank, all hungry for a carelessly placed lure or incompetent retrieve. Some may think I am trying to discourage any thoughts they might entertain of fishing Itsy Bitsy, so be it. However I am merely trying to emphasise the fact that the correct use of spinning tackle is in no way inferior to that of employing fly-fishing equipment, as well as being every bit as much an art form. In the hands of an expert, such as my good buddy Jim Lloyd, who can beautifully work over a small trout stream, one can see and appreciate the skills required with this equipment.

Believing that enough time had passed to allow the brookie to settle down after missing its first attempt to snatch my spinner, I moved into a position, slightly downstream from its lair in the cress bed and studied the current carefully, plotting the correct approach for the second cast. I suppose that particular trout must have made an errant decision in Pefferlaw Brook near the mouth of Itsy Bitsy, then enjoying the cooler waters of the smaller stream gradually moved well up into its headwaters and stayed. Feeding there on the abundant caddis and stone-fly larvae in and around the watercress and gravel beds, it fattened and grew quickly.

Years ago there was a minimum legal size limit of seven inches on speck-led trout. The majority of Itsy Bitsy's specks seldom achieve this. Almost always, smaller waters produce smaller fish, but this fellow, although seem-ingly being the "exception that proves the rule," was obviously a refugee from the bigger stream, the Pefferlaw River, where the trout do grow large.

Because an overhanging branch lay just above its reassumed position and understanding that most brook trout, if not having actually touched the lure, will return to their cover, I made an underhand flip cast to keep the flight of the lure close to the surface. The spinner's blade had barely begun revolving when the speck dashed out once again and was immediately hooked. Being the boss fish in the area, it fortunately stayed in the little open water pool and deemed it unnecessary, as is their wont, to dig into the cress or roots beneath the bank so it was quickly brought to heel. The gorgeous brookie was cradled lovingly in the water while I only briefly debated keeping it to show it off back home later, thinking that without my camera to capture a picture of the spectacular catch, who would believe it.

Before I removed the hook from its lip, however, with the rod held in my left hand and the fish co-operating by holding still and finning gently by the bank, I spanned its length with my right hand. I play a little piano and can span an octave plus one key, nine inches. That magnificently coloured speckled trout measured eighteen inches, tip to stern. Only one other stream brookie in my memory, a seventeen-incher from Uxbridge Brook, ever came close to that fish, which coming from waters as minuscule as Itsy Bitsy with its visual six-, seven- and eight-inchers seemed even larger than its actuality. The magic of that moment as the cradled fish was lovingly eased back into the current returns every time I visit Itsy Bitsy.

Many of the streams and rivers that flow into the larger lakes in Southern Ontario can provide varied and interesting trout fishing. Pefferlaw Creek is no exception. Pefferlaw flows northerly emerging near the village of the same name at Lake Simcoe. Previously we talked about a wee brook, Itsy Bitsy, that flows into Pefferlaw River near its headwaters where it is often called Pefferlaw Brook, but there should have been a codicil about a morning I spent fishing Pefferlaw with another buddy, Paul Kennedy.

Together, Paul and I have done opening day fishing the small streams for brook trout within an hour or so of Toronto for the past six or seven years. Paul lives in Uxbridge, about a half an hour north of where I live in Scarborough and a stone's throw from where we planned to fish—Pefferlaw River. We planned to meet at a Tim Horton's for a coffee and discuss our planned assault on the stream. A couple of incidents occurred on that particular outing to make the day memorable and certainly the waters memorable as well. For one reason or another that has since escaped me, we had previously decided to forego our customary six in the morning start to our days on the streams for an eight o'clock beginning.

I arrived at the coffee shop about seven, shortly before Paul and was watching out the window when he drove up. He stepped out of his car with a disgusted look on his face, clutching several lengths of what appeared to be his broken spinning rod. Still brandishing the rod, now a three-piece wand instead of the former two-piece, he explained that it wasn't even his own but his brother's. It had broken in the trunk when the tire jack fell over on it. He knew that I carry a little kit in my haversack with bits and pieces, spare reel parts, epoxy glue and so on, and wondered if I could fix it.

When I rummaged around in my car and trunk there was no haversack to be found. Realizing I must have left it on my work bench, I suggested we head to a hardware store in town once the shops were open. All I needed was glue, a piece of coarse sandpaper and a clothes peg. A little monofilament from our reels could be used to wrap it once the repairs were made.

To kill a little time, we had some coffee and a doughnut, and discussed the merits of fishing Itsy Bitsy, perhaps starting there and making our way to the Pefferlaw River. We finished our breakfast and headed for the local hardware store.

"No I can't sell you just a single sheet of sandpaper and a single clothes peg," the surly storekeeper snarled. "Everything comes in packages nowadays you know. I've got the glue you asked for, though."

I was reluctant to buy a whole bundle of clothes pegs and a package of sandpaper, but Paul was impatient to get the stuff, get his rod repaired and go fishing. I decided to spell out for the gentleman what we required the items for and his whole demeanour changed when he learned that we were fishermen with a rather serious opening day problem—a broken fishing rod. Back in the coffee shop, which we opted for rather than tying up space in the small hardware store, we began the business of fixing Paul's rod. It was almost ten o'clock before we finished. There were no problems doing the repair, but we did have to deal with a number of other fishermen who had already finished their own opening days on the local trout pond and other streams in the area. They were fascinated with the procedure.

Repairing a broken fishing rod is simply a matter of first removing any loose material in the break. Next matching one-inch angled surfaces are fashioned on each side of the broken sections by firmly working the blanks with one hand on the coarse sandpaper, held in place with the other. When that is completed, a plug or dowel is shaped from the hardwood peg. It should provide a firm connection into each side of the refurbished break, while supplying additional surfaces for the epoxy cement to do its job of securing the carefully glued and aligned joint. Then, beginning half an inch from one end of the new joint, tightly wrap the monofilament or strong thread to the corresponding other end, then back over to finish where the wrap began. If this is done correctly, the finished product in that portion of the rod should be stronger than the original.

I think Paul and I probably established a fishing "first" with our opening day, broken rod repair in a Tim Horton's coffee shop. Nevertheless, we did eventually find ourselves on Itsy Bitsy working over a few of its larger holes, but sticking to the plan to skip most of the minuscule brook's holding spots in order to get to the big junction pool where it merges with the Pefferlaw River.

Before we could get there though we had to either go around, or work our way through a bog with floating mounds that, providing one did not hesitate before leaping to the next one, served as stepping-stones. It felt as if we were hiking in the Florida Everglades. Fortunately, it was too early in the season for the mosquitoes to be a problem, but if you were not careful, you could step into the quicksand-like areas between the boggy island mounds. And that is exactly what happened to me! Paul, long-legged and more than six-feet tall, had no trouble working his way through the swamp, but I, less than five foot seven, leaped a little short about halfway through, and immediately discovered that it was a huge mistake. Both legs quickly sank in the mire and the more I attempted to free one, the other sunk deeper. I remembered reading somewhere that the only way to extricate oneself from this sort of predicament is to throw your upper body forward and lie prostrate so that the weight is removed from your legs. Theoretically, you can then work your legs upwards and free of the quicksand's grip.

However, reluctant to impregnate my fishing vest and clothes with swamp muck, I continued to helplessly wiggle my legs until water began seeping over the hip-boot tops. I began yelling for my buddy who was about fifty yards beyond me. He detected the urgency in my screaming. With his long legs he got back quickly and immediately sized up the situation. Bracing himself on one of the few firm mounds, he passed a long branch towards me that he located on the swamp's perimeter.

"Grab it with both...hands and don't let go!" he ordered, "or we will both go base over apex into the muck."

With the water now completely over my boot tops it was almost impossible to wiggle anything other than my toes, but Paul is a very, very strong individual, not just verbally, but physically too. He could probably pull a stump out of the ground if he was faced with the challenge. I had a death grip on the branch while he yanked and pulled with all his might. My legs felt as if they were being pulled out of their sockets.

Suddenly there was a loud sucking pop as first one boot broke the terrible suction, then another, as the second leg broke free. Fortunately neither boot came completely off or I might not have been able to retrieve it from the quicksand, but both were, of course, full of water and gooey muck.

With Paul's help, partially dragging, lifting and cajoling me to bear with it and get my ass to the outer and somewhat drier edge of the morass, I eventually was able to sit on a log while my buddy yanked the soggy boots off my legs and drenched pants, then drained them to the best of his ability. Exhausted and sore, I decided to rest right where I was, nurse my badly bent ego and let Paul go ahead to work the Pefferlaw-Itsy Bitsy junction pool without me.

It took several months before the pain and discomfort from the badly stretched ligaments in my upper legs subsided sufficiently to allow my return to my second love—after Sheila, my wife—stream fishing for trout. Not the most pleasant recollection, but absolutely one deserving of its inclusion in my memories!

Chapter 6

The "Pigeons" of the Kawarthas

The Kawartha Lakes area in Southern Ontario is a tourist and vacationing Eden for bass, pickerel (walleye) and muskie fishermen. Its wide variety of lakes, resorts and cottage developments host thousands of guests every summer from all parts of Canada, the United States and even Europe. Although I now restrict my angling activities to trout fishing, before I *graduated* into that echelon—and I risk the ire of thousands of aficionados of the game fish mentioned heretofore with that comment—I did spend many an enjoyable day chasing down a feed of pickerel, working weed lines for muskies, or tossing around cork and deer hair bugs and flies for both largemouth and smallmouth bass.

I was married (the first time) in 1950. With our parents and friends all trying to dissuade us, Joan and I decided to elope and booked a cottage on Pigeon Lake for our honeymoon. Good buddy Art Walker, and his wife Sylvia, agreed to stand in for us and accepted the invitation to come up to the lake for our second weekend to join us for a little muskie fishing. Although I would hesitate to deem Pigeon a magical body of water, it certainly holds a wonderful memory for me as I am sure it does for thousands of other anglers as well.

It was the opening of the bass and muskie season, so after we were settled in the cottage Joan gave me permission to try a little top-water fishing for bass in the bay outside our cottage. I worked around the lily pads with my favourite lure of the day, a black Jitterbug popping plug.[1] I could never figure out why top water lures can be purchased in a wide assortment of colours, when all the fish sees from below them in the water is the plug's underside, a mere silhouette against the sky above. Therefore, if it is the silhouette that attracts the fish, then solid black should present the strongest and most consistent silhouette from any angle.

The sun had set and although reluctant to quit, I was with nary a strike to show for two hours of casting; whatever bass that might have been in the area seemed to have acquired a bad case of lockjaw. I made a perfunctory over the shoulder cast towards the deeper water beyond the lily pads, intending to head back to the dock while towing the noisy Jitterbug behind the rowboat. There was little that could be seen in the dark moonless night, but my hearing was not similarly impaired.

A loud, single "plop" followed by a furious thrashing around on the surface as my rod threatened to depart the boat, renewed my enthusiasm for the task at hand. The fish, a four-pound pickerel, was subsequently netted with little fuss. Prior to that evening I had never heard of, or experienced top-water fishing for pickerel, fish that although mainly nocturnal foragers, are seldom found feeding on the surface in shallow water. A half dozen three to five-pounders followed, four of which I kept, before I suddenly remembered that it was my wedding night.

Shortly thereafter, I could see the light at the dock blinking on and off repeatedly and it gradually sunk in that Joan was sending me a message the only way she could. I paddled the rest of the way in, tied the boat up then strode proudly up to the cottage where she stood, holding the screen door open for me. She was not upset and smiled broadly as I asked her to get me some newspaper so that I could clean the four fat pickerel I held up for her inspection.

That night on Pigeon Lake was never repeated for me, but remains one of my most potent memories—for a variety of reasons! It was a great week and a wonderful honeymoon, but seemed to wind down as soon as it began. Art phoned towards the end to say that he and Sylvia were packed and on their way and asked if there was anything we wanted them to bring with them for the cottage. I had to bear the brunt of Art's "humorous" remarks after I related the "facts" of our wonderful wedding night, the fishing facts that is.

The four of us trolled for pickerel the next day and caught enough fish for a shore lunch on big Boyd Island in the centre of the lake, but although we discussed working the weed lines in the hopes of catching a muskie with four of us in the boat it seemed rather impractical. Art, a transplanted Maritimer, however, had never hooked or seen a muskie and persisted in his request that we give it a try. We trolled around to the shallow and weedy inside of the island and the four of us cast around the weed-bed edges for a couple of hours, but all to no avail.

We cranked up the motor as we decided to wind up the day trolling the deeper waters, hoping to catch enough pickerel to take home for a feed or two. We actually trolled three lines, while Joan perched on the front of the boat, casting her plug slightly ahead and sideways so as not to hang up on the trolled lines. Muskies seldom wander far from their weed-bed lairs in the shallower waters, but there was one out in the deeper water off the island that hadn't read the same book as myself.

The second Pigeon Lake magical moment woke us up from our hot, July First weekend lethargy when Joan was nearly yanked off the front of the boat by a savage strike from a muskie that immediately began a series of tail-walking, leaping and cartwheeling hi-jinks. Sitting next to her, because I was in the stern manning the motor, Art grabbed her as she was about to go overboard, still clutching the rod with its reel screaming, and helped her off the prow and onto the seat beside him.

Both women were yelling as Art and I were shouting instructions, but Joan didn't want any part of it. She threatened to throw the rod in the lake when the giant muskie surfaced momentarily near the boat before cartwheeling and charging off once again for deep water. Art took it from her as she pleaded for help, but she asked him to pass it to me to play the fish. Normally a quiet and reserved woman, Joan screamed, "Don't you bring that thing in the boat! If you do, I'm out of here. I'd rather be in the lake than have that monster thrashing around and snapping at my legs or whatever!"

Fortunately the muskie stayed out of the dense weed beds as my ultra-light spinning outfit certainly was not designed to tackle brutes the size of that giant fish. It struck out for deeper waters where patience and constant pressure eventually brought it to heel alongside the boat. Both women were now hanging precariously on the opposite side while Art and I dutifully photographed then released the muskie to do battle another day.

I can still close my eyes, fifty-four years later, and visualize the entire muskie adventure. By the way, although we did not have scales with us, Art and I estimated its weight to be approximately thirty pounds.

As a commercial traveller for a wholesale hunting and fishing tackle firm in the fifties and sixties, I was privy to many tips and rumours that arose in the vicinity of my outdoor-store clients. There was a small tackle and bait shop in the tiny village of Omemee and the proprietor asked me if I had ever fished the small, stump-filled lake that bordered the village. The "lake" was merely a large pond that had formed on the Pigeon River when it was originally dammed, forcing the waters to spread out over the bush and trees that had surrounded the river.

"You know," he said, when I replied that I had not fished it, "there's a muskie in there that has already tested a half a dozen guys this summer. The fish came away the winner every time. They say he's at least thirty-five pounds and the local folks have named him, "Old Rufe." I see you've got your car-top strapped on the Chevy again. If you have an hour or so why don't you give it a go?"

I could hardly wait to finish writing up a fill-in fishing tackle order from him so I could test my own luck with "Old Rufe," ignoring the fact that I only had fly-fishing tackle with me in the car.

It was mid-afternoon when I slid my boat into the weedy waters of this man-made pond on the Pigeon River, but by the time I packed up, with the sun settling over the horizon, I had hooked and caught at least two dozen muskies, none of which was more than thirty-odd inches long. Most were in the five to eight-pound class and provided continuous, fantastic action with exciting top-water acrobatics. There seemed to be one of these beside or beneath every stump in the pond and they tore up several of my best Mickey Finn streamer flies with their enthusiastic cartwheels and slashing strikes.

However, "Old Rufe" didn't seem to be on my agenda that day, although there was an enormous eruption on the surface at one point when I was attempting to extract my fly from the roots of a huge old stump. I did not actually see the fish, but no little five to eight-pounder could possibly have created a tidal wave of the proportions that that fish did. Obviously Pigeon Lake and Pigeon River have both provided me with lasting memories that deserve to be chronicled.

Chapter 7
A Mystery At Tedious Lake

Tedious, for some reason or another, has recently been renamed Long Lake. Do we really need another Long Lake? There must be several hundred already tagged with that rather boring handle. Now take the name, Tedious—that was an interesting and, I'm certain, quite an exclusive and memorable label.

The magical waters of Tedious Lake certainly provided me with a memory that will never fade. After more than sixty-five years of fishing, when it comes to "fish stories," I have an infinite supply. Although this tale was part of my first fishing book, *Fishing Hats,*[1] written twenty-five years ago, it deserves to be retold as my number one true fish story.

Tedious Lake, about two miles long and a half-a-mile at its widest, parallels Highway #119 in Haliburton area. It lies a few miles north of the village of West Guilford, before one reaches Kennesis, the much larger and better known lake, a further ten minute drive north. Tedious provided my young buddy, Jurgen Brech, and me with the most momentous ice-fishing thrill of our lives. Although winter fishing can be tedious at times, it is difficult to understand how this beautiful lake, nestled between craggy hills on both sides, was ever tagged with such a derogatory name.

Our little AAA (Ardent Anglers Anonymous) group of fishermen rented a small cabin for the winter season near Redstone Lake in the Haliburton area. From there we could either drive, skidoo, or snowshoe into some of the finest trout waters in the province. It was a wonderful season of ice fishing, the best we had ever experienced. Along with the great fishing, working from our rented cottage, actually a deer-hunting cabin, we were also fortunate to have discovered many new and productive trout lakes.

Ontario's Ministry of Natural Resources maintains an excellent trout restocking program in Haliburton, complementing the somewhat limited natural reproduction in the lakes, although some streams with better running water and gravel bars do provide the means for the trout to propagate naturally.

Although we fished nine different lakes over fifteen consecutive ice-fishing weekends that year, our efforts were concentrated on two that were quite remote. Just a stone's throw from the cabin, however, lay Tedious, one of the best stocked speckled trout lakes in our area. It had received scant attention from us, or anybody else for that matter. It was probably another case of the "far fields looking greener."

After an opening (January 1) that was the coldest in memory for any of us (52 degrees below zero was reported and recorded on several official thermometers in central Haliburton that night), we opted for a more leisurely weekend. Pete Pokulok, Jurgen Brech, Ernie Percy and I had skidooed into A/B Lake on the Saturday and managed to bog the machines down in slush only a couple of times. Pete cut eight holes with the old power auger, while Ernie tinkered with his tackle and Jurgen and I gathered firewood. The buzzers that indicate a trout taking the bait kept us hopping and, by the time our shish-kebobs were broiling over the glowing coals of the fire, five specks were in the bag.

Even with four of us there, we were beaten to the beeping buzzers every time by Jamie, my ever-present Brittany Spaniel. He was a dog with amazing energy and endurance (my buddies said simply that Brittanies are stupid and hyperactive). Although not having missed a trip in nine years, Jamie had yet to match the feat accomplished by his predecessor, Trigger. That old fellow, my second Brit', hooked and landed a seventeen-inch-long rainbow trout all by himself, ice-fishing! A "fish story" you're thinking—yes—but a true one, with three witnesses.

The incident occurred ten years earlier on Mosque Lake in the Land O' Lakes district, when a mid-winter thaw had melted the snow on the ice. It subsequently froze into a giant skating rink, making the slippery surface negotiable only with the aid of ice creepers (studs) strapped to the bottoms of our boots. Looking like Bambi in that memorable scene in Walt Disney's movie, Trigger would occasionally find himself hopelessly spread-eagled on the ice if he forgot to dig in his claws.

The dogs have always reacted to the sound of the fishing buzzers—they seem to get as much pleasure as we do when a trout is lifted from the water through a hole in the ice. If we are not keeping an eye open, they will steal the flopping fish then bury it in a snowbank. Several times we have had to return trout that had been stolen by my dog from other fishermen on the frozen lake.

With the temperature hovering around freezing and no snow to anchor the base of the buzzers, it became necessary to secure them with pieces of our sawed and split firewood. One rig, set up in a shallow area over a rocky shoal where the rainbows search for crawfish, had already produced two fat trout. The dog was becoming quite excited with the action. Then the unimaginable happened—had we been able to capture the next few moments on film or video it could easily have been sold to a movie studio for possible inclusion in a nature film.

"Beep—Beep—Beep!" Same buzzer! This time, even wearing ice-creepers, we were no match for the already agitated Trigger. The problem was that he found he was unable to stop and skidded right into the buzzer rig, with his momentum dragging the entire set-up five feet beyond the hole. Simultaneously, the startled trout was yanked through the hole and onto the ice. A hell of a fish story—but absolutely true!

However, back to the A/B Lake trip. After we had eaten, the action slowed down, but with seven fat specks to divvy up there were smiles all around as we packed up our gear. Later on in the warm cabin we watched *Hockey Night in Canada*, then debated the next day's destination. With the barometer falling noticeably, the safest course of action seemed to be a day on Tedious, only five minutes from the cabin.

Sunday dawned far too early for our lethargic crew and the heavily overcast sky did not augur too well for the day's angling potential. Occasionally though, a barometer dropping out of sight will push fish into a feeding frenzy, so with that thought in mind our spirits were buoyed somewhat as we pointed the snowmobiles north. Thirty minutes later, the lines were in place, while Ernie and Jurgen still struggled to get a fire underway against the shore, using the damp wood they had dragged from the bush.

It began to drizzle. Rain, the bane of all winter sports, makes snowmobiling well-nigh impossible and is more discouraging than even sub-zero temperatures to ice fishermen. Three hours later with it still raining heavily and only a couple of released yearling trout to show for our persistence, Pete broke the crew up completely, moaning, "And my wife thinks I'm having a good time!"

It soon became worse and, as we fought to keep the fire flickering for a little warmth while we huddled around it, Ernie and Pete suddenly decided to call it a day. No sooner had they packed their gear, when the rain changed to snow—enormously heavy, wet snow. Jurg and I were only able to watch their departing progress for a few yards as the Skidoos disappeared through the curtain of white snow. A little while later, Jurgen, barely able to hear the snow-bound buzzers, took a brace of fourteen-inchers. The fire was soon abandoned to the elements so that we could concentrate on keeping the rigs free of snow and ready for action.

At precisely 3:30 in the afternoon the "mystery" began. (I had just checked the time after clearing the snow from the hole, before hunching down on the folding stool.) The buzzer was anchored in deep snow above twenty inches of ice and only eighteen inches of water. Suddenly water gushed upward, overflowing the hole and turning the surrounding snow into slush. It was as if a massive weight had just been dropped on the ice surface. Before I could regain my composure, the buzzer was wrenched from the snow, almost disappearing down the hole before I could grab it.

The buzzers are rigged so that the line releases, but flows free if a large trout hits. At least that is what is supposed to happen. Whatever attacked this minnow did it with such ferocity that everything jammed and the line broke. My screams of anguish brought Jurgen on the run. He listened incredulously to my attempted explanation of what had just transpired, while I re-rigged the set-up with a new hook and minnow.

The snowfall was becoming ridiculous, piling up so rapidly that the Skidoos, although parked only a few feet away, were almost indistinguishable from the snowdrifts. Before Jurgen could get back to his own set-up, the water boiled out of the hole again. Then a pause—and once more! What could it be? An enormous fish, intrigued by the little light filtering through the hole in the ice then rushing at it helter-skelter? To have caused the voluminous eruptions I was witnessing required much more power than any fifteen-inch trout possessed. As Jurgen, his own rig now forgotten, dragged his stool over to my hole to join in the excitement, I wondered if we had some sort of primeval monster beneath us—indeed, a proverbial Haliburton "Loch Ness" type critter.

This was truly a remarkable situation—our stools along with the buzzer and us were located in a slushy pocket around the hole, surrounded by rapidly deepening snow. There appeared to be no let-up at all and, as we sat on our stools, the white stuff was soon shoulder high. We learned later that a record low-pressure front had descended on the area that memorable day.

It did not deter the "thing" beneath the ice, however, as once more the water heaved when the minnow was grabbed. Fortunately, I had replaced the customary slip-knot with a loop to guarantee the line's release after a hard strike. It was vicious—without pause. The line streamed down the hole—10—20—30 feet. I grabbed it then struck to set the hook. Forget it— game over—the six-pound line parted like a 7X fly-fishing leader tippet.[2]

With shaking fingers I replaced the hook and minnow. We did not have long to wait. Bang!—the line was yanked off the trigger wire once again—then slack—minnow stolen. To make matters even more complicated, it was rapidly becoming dark as the snowfall continued. The "thing," already with two of my hooks buried in its maw and three minnows to its credit, then went into a temporary respite, probably to plan its next attack.

It was now pitch black. The setting made an eerie picture as Jurgen's flash camera recorded the scene for our future reminiscence. Incredibly, the action soon began again. After one or two swooshing passes beneath the hole, the "fish" began acting "cute." Instead of the previous gung-ho attacks, it now simply ripped the minnows off without disturbing the hook, while barely activating the buzzer. We changed the position of the hook in the minnow—to no avail. It stole *eleven* more without once being hooked! We were beginning to feel that it was all a strange dream—or nightmare. No "fish" could be that intelligent—or voracious. Nevertheless, there were two minnows remaining, seven-inch golden shiners, so we rigged up once more. It was corny, but seemingly appropriate, so I asked Jurgen, "How does that old Fisherman's Prayer go again, Jurg'?"

He repeated it aloud:

> *God give me grace to catch a fish*
> *So big that even I,*
> *When speaking of it afterward*
> *May never need to lie.*[3]

Unfortunately it did not seem to help, as another half-hour (it was almost seven o'clock) went by without a look-see. We wondered if we should call it quits, but with one minnow left we were considering trying again. Our thought was punctuated by a single "Beep" as the line bounced off the buzzer for the umpteenth time.

"He's hooked, finally—I think!" I cried, as the line played through my fingers. This time, I played it with extreme caution. It seemed very heavy, but somehow, a little sluggish, (fifteen minnows and three hooks—no wonder) as it was eventually led into the tunnel-like hole. Jurgen had his camera in one hand and flashlight in the other. Just as a dark snout momentarily appeared near the surface, he dropped the light so he could take a picture. The line broke for the third time as our "critter" escaped once again. We still had been unable to make a positive I.D.

I glanced at my watch—7:15—almost four hours since it had all begun. Then taking the last minnow from the insulated pail. I broke its air bladder so it would sink before pitching it down the hole.

"Help yourself—it's a free one!" I shouted at the hole as we began packing up.

With the visions of the afternoon's events recurring constantly, it was a very quiet drive home. Tedious Lake! Not bloody likely! A truly magical water and fantastic memory!

Chapter 8
Blue Lake of Temiscamingue

I have had the good fortune to fish Blue Lake on a number of occasions, but one particular trip stands out in my memory. The lake, deep in the heart of Quebec's Temiscamingue country, was where an old buddy of mine, Jack Wilkings, owned a beautiful cottage. It was situated on a promontory at one end of the lake with a full frontal picture window and a spacious deck. From there you could see almost the entire seven-mile length of this relatively undisturbed fabulous trout fishing water.

The trip that created the memory for Blue Lake's inclusion in this book, had a cast of Jack, Don Petican, Donnie Allen and myself. Whenever Blue Lake is mentioned in casual conversation since then, a number of situations occurring on that particular weekend are easily recalled. Perhaps the most memorable of these, though, is the remarkable and fabulous fishing all four of us experienced in Blue's waters on that occasion.

It takes the better of half a day to reach Jack's cottage from Toronto. He and his buddies usually tack a couple of extra days onto a weekend trip to Blue Lake, often taking advantage of the extra day in a long holiday weekend. Blue is such a large lake with so many prime bays, islands, shoals and river mouths in which to wet a line, that to properly fish the hot spots requires at least a couple of days on the water.

On this specific weekend, by the time we had arrived at the cottage on Friday afternoon and unloaded our food and gear, there was little time left to fish. Jack, a rather formidable cook, had brought along a sumptuous lamb leg roast. Making full use of the extensive herb garden growing in pots on the deck, he proceeded to marinate and prepare it for the barbecue, while both Dons, tired after the long drive, decided to replenish their batteries and take a catnap.

When Jack estimated that it would take almost three hours before his culinary efforts would be ready for the salivating crew—and having been given a new Cortland fly line by the manufacturer for testing,[1] I decided to go down to the dock and without using one of the boats chained up there, test the waters in front of his cottage.

The fly line that I was supposed to test was a Hi Density sinking line that I felt would allow me to cast a fly out far enough from the dock to see if there were any of Blue's storied brookies cruising around looking for a wee snack. I took a few minutes to stretch the line to remove any memory that may have remained in it after being on the reel's spool for a few days since it came in the mail. Hi D lines are notorious for this nuisance factor. Obviously, a line with much curling and/or twisting will not perform as well as one that is more supple without spooling memory.

A pleasant surprise, the first of many that weekend, awaited me. The line shot out from the tip of the rod like a rocket, carrying the leader and its lethal weapon, my trusty Despair fly[2] well over eighty feet out from the dock. The water in that part of the bay in front of Jack's cottage is quite deep, averaging about twenty feet. My intention, using a sinking line, was to fish the fly, a nymph pattern, near the bottom simulating the various larvae that would be rising from the depths to hatch on the surface as evening approached.

However, the Despair hardly touched the water when there was a tremendous boil on the surface, indicating the underwater swoosh of a big brookie as it engulfed the fly. Unaware that I now had an audience—fifteen minutes later I hoisted a twenty-four-inch long, five-pound brook trout for examination and unexpected applause from the overhanging cottage deck. Both Dons had been too restless to stay asleep for long; that and the smell of the roast wafting throughout the cottage got them up to see what was cooking when Jack told them that I was down on the dock fishing.

As most anglers are aware, for some strange reason the largest fish taken on a trip is often the first one hooked and that brookie, the initial trout caught on this memorable weekend was no exception as it turned out to be the largest of the trip. But as beautiful as it was, it was the next two days of fishing that I will never forget.

After we devoured Jack's excellent lamb roast along with his favourite parsley-buttered red potatoes, green beans, a bowl of mint jelly and half a bottle of mint sauce, we decided to take it easy, play a little poker. The drive and pigging out on Jack's cooking had taken a toll on our vitality. Our batteries needed recharging so we would be able to do battle on an even footing with Blue Lake's brookies and lake trout the next day. And what a battle it became!

Only moments from the dock, two to a boat, we struck out in the direction of an island fronting the mouth of a stream coming from another lake about a mile away, Sand Lake. Don Petican had chosen to stick with his spinning outfit while I had decided to go with my fly rod with the new Cortland line. In the other boat, Jack was also using a fly outfit, while Donnie Allen stayed with his spinning tackle.

As is our custom, when using Hi D lines, which are most often necessary when fly fishing on lakes, Jack and I had both fed them out while we motored across the lake in order that the drag of the water would remove any memory. I had momentarily forgotten that my new line didn't necessarily require the treatment but left the line stretched out behind the rapidly moving boat anyhow.

From thirty or forty feet away I heard Jack yell, over the whine of both outboards, "Fish on!"

We could hear his reel screaming before he was able to cut the motor on his speeding boat. As I cut my own motor, I could hear him yelling again, "It's a wonder I didn't tear his...head off or break the leader—but the crazy fish is still on."

Reeling my own line in as we watched Jack play his trout, a fine four-pound laker, I too was greeted with a smashing strike on the Despair fly as it twitched its way through the depths back to our boat. We had agreed that other than any brookies over twenty-one inches, normally three to four-pounders, we wouldn't keep any trout to take home until Sunday, taking the chance that the fishing would still be productive the next day. The usual ratio of brookies to lakers in Jack's lake was one in ten, with the lakers averaging about a pound or two more than the brookies. Both fish were released and before either motor was cranked up, all four of us were into lake trout again. Lines were criss-crossing the water in every direction as the trout all had minds of their own as to which direction would provide their best chance to escape.

I am not going to document the individual results of all the trout that were caught that weekend because this book is not really big enough and for some it would become boringly repetitious. Suffice to say that there were brook and lake trout hooked, caught, released—and lost, in the hundreds, on both spinning and fly-fishing tackle. After the first half-dozen trout engulfed my Despair, I decided to keep track of the actual number of fish hooked and boated before being released on my fly line alone. I don't believe the other lads, simply enjoying the sensational fishing for the excitement and thrills it was providing, did likewise.

However, my tally of actual fish caught on Sunday afternoon when we decided to head back to the cottage for an early dinner of trout fillets and a good night's sleep before the long Monday trip home, was an unbeliev-able one hundred and eighty-four trout. Mostly lakers that we discovered hovering around the top of the thermocline[3] about twelve to fifteen feet beneath the surface, my total did include a dozen or so fat brook trout in the two to four-pound class. All the fish were taken on the Despair flies, even when they became so tattered after five or six fish that most of their dressing had disappeared. My fly box was pretty well decimated by the time we decided to pack it in.

Everybody reported similar results, with a six-pound lake trout that Jack chased around the lake for at least a half an hour before it was boated being the largest fish of the weekend. Everybody agreed that the magical waters of Blue Lake had supplied each of us with a cache of memories that would never be forgotten.

Chapter 9

Sullivan—A "Pot-of-Gold" Lake?

This speckled trout lake is easily one of the most difficult to reach that I have ever fished. Part of its magic is just that—its remoteness. Our first attempt to find and fish it was about forty years ago after spotting it on an old topographical map then making inquiries about the lake's fish content at the Lands and Forests office in Tweed in Eastern Ontario. Their records showed that it did indeed hold brook (speckled) trout, and fish had been reported taken there in the five to six-pound class by gentlemen who had accessed the lake by small float plane. The other thing that intrigued me on the old topographical map was the nearby McCready Mountain, apparently the highest mountain in Eastern Ontario. There were no roads anywhere near the lake, only an indication on the map of several trapper trails in the vicinity. However, this is a story about "Fred" as much as it is about Sullivan Lake.

As mentioned earlier, in those days (the fifties and sixties), when we did the majority of our fishing in Eastern Ontario, most of the waters that we fished were worked by heading out from our customary base, a cottage on Buckshot Lake in the heart of the Land O' Lakes district. Sullivan Lake was at the extreme northern edge of the area and, according to the topographical map, there were a number of lakes, swamps, hills and cliffs to surmount if we were ever going to wet our lines in its pristine and, *imagined* magical waters.

The adventure was discussed a few times by my buddies and me but forestalled until our imaginations were so satiated with the potential of the attempt that it could not be put off any longer. We pored over the topographical maps until our eyesight blurred trying to determine the best route to follow for our eventual exploration of the supposed "pot of gold," Sullivan Lake.

If it had been winter, with the lakes frozen and the bush trails covered with deep snow, we could have taken a less circuitous path. However, with several lakes to negotiate by boat, it was decided that we would have to drive south to the village of Plevna then continue on a sideroad wending its way between a number of lakes until ending at Mackie Lake, at least another half-hour drive from the village.

We learned from Bev Woolnough, the proprietor of Birch Lodge where our cabin was located, that a gentleman by the name of Judd Tooley owned a lodge on the north end of the lake and kept a few boats moored at the road's end for his guests. Apparently we could use them to travel down the lake to Tooley's, pay him a couple of bucks, then portage about a mile further north to the next lake, Long Schooner, where he also stashed a couple of boats. We would then travel all the way up Long Schooner to a narrow opening between an enormous cliff and a rocky point, and work our way through to the next body of water, Round Schooner Lake. Both the Schooner lakes were understandably devoid of cottage life back then and probably are no different today.

The next leg of the trip would see us boating up Round Schooner to the base of a big hill, then strike out over the hill to what appeared to be a large swamp on the map. After circumventing the swamp to another smallish body of water,

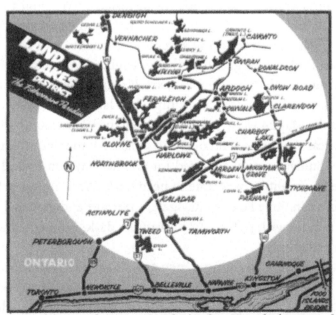

Map of the area known as Land O' Lakes. Note the location of Round Schooner Lake and Schooner Lake, top centre. Map taken from The Outdoorsman, *1963. Courtesy of Barry Penhale.*

Rock Lake, and walking around it to what looked like a trapper's trail on the map there still were a few hurdles to overcome, including almost impenetrable bush and several cliffs. Then, eureka, there would be Sullivan Lake.

As you can see, our plan to fish Sullivan, which we had also shown to Bev Woolnough, was going to require a considerable amount of patience, travel and hard work. Trout fishermen are known to follow a different agenda than most other fishermen, getting up in the middle of the night to begin their sorties, travelling miles off the beaten track on a hunch and so on, but this trip appeared to be beyond ridiculous.

Nevertheless, four o'clock on the chosen morning found us eager and quivering with excitement as we loaded our gear and struck out from the cabin. We were armed with our written itinerary, the all-important topographical maps, compasses and a substantial supply of insect repellent. The initial phases went according to plan. However, with the sun already beating down on us, it was a dishevelled and tired lot arriving at the shore of Long Schooner Lake. At that moment, Sullivan Lake seemed almost unattainable, but we decided to persevere and make do with whatever fate had in store for us.

Long Schooner is just that—long—so we trolled a couple of lines almost the entire length, while a couple of the fellows cast towards the most likely-looking points around the mouths of deep bays. We caught nothing in Long Schooner, but worked the channel through the narrows into Round Schooner, catching and releasing several nice smallmouth bass. But when we came around the bend into the lake itself, it was an awesome sight. Definitely round with only a couple of small rocky islands as we came out of the narrows, it was quite large and simply had lake trout written all over it.

As it was the May 24 weekend, traditionally the lakers should still be comparatively near the surface and near the shoals. Although it was nearing the noon hour, Sullivan was abandoned for another day and Round Schooner was worked over until it was time to head back. With the sun setting early that time of year, three lakes to navigate, a portage and the trip back to the cabin, we did not wish to test our luck in the dark. Fishing Sullivan would have to be postponed.

The hiatus was not too long. Once again, our imaginations went into overdrive and two of us, Don Petican and I, decided that we would have another go at this "pot o' gold" at the end of the rainbow a couple of weeks later. This time we swore we would not be distracted by other fishy-looking waters and would stay on course all the way to Sullivan Lake. The plan worked. Well, it almost worked. We stuck to our guns until we climbed the big hill on Round Schooner, near McCready Mountain, hiked around the swamp to a lake and rested for a few moments at the mouth of the small creek, ebbing out from the swamp into the small body of water shown on the map as Rock Lake. The sun had risen, but it was not yet too hot and the mosquitoes were ravenous. As we re-applied our repellents there was a splash, followed by several substantial, nearby dimples on the surface out in the lake just a stone's throw from where we were sitting. The fish continued feeding, actually boiling on the surface several more times.

Of course, it was "damn the torpedoes," "gung ho" and all that. Rods were quickly set up and put to work. Don caught the trout, a brightly coloured brookie that was probably the same fish that had been tantalizing us since we broke through the bush and arrived at the shoreline. We continued to fish Rock Lake with neither of us paying attention to the time. It was an ideal body of water to fish without a canoe, or craft of any kind, as it was small, less than three-quarters of a mile long and only a few hundred yards at its widest, with the shoreline quite rocky and numerous vantage points to work both our fly and spinning outfits.

As so often happens, that first fish caught and released by Don was the largest of the day, but we did catch another half-dozen or so before we realized what time it was, almost mid-afternoon. Working our way around the shoreline to fish all the likely-looking spots had taken much more time than anticipated, and much of our stamina along with it. However, sandwiches and thermoses were broken out and quickly dispatched. We decided to gamble and try to locate the trapper trail to Sullivan Lake and see if we could actually get there in time to give it a *little* fish before we would have to strike out for home.

It was not to be. The magical waters of Sullivan Lake would remain unsullied by our feathered creations and hunks of metal with hooks, probably until the lakes froze over and we could make the trip by snowmobile instead of all the fuss of in and out of boats, portages and so on.

Meanwhile, my buddy, Don Petican, purchased a small cottage from Russ Wells on Mosque Lake, so the cabin at Buckshot was abandoned in favour of fishing the abundantly rewarding waters of that lake and surrounding waters. Nevertheless, the "far fields look greener" philosophy grew even stronger and we could hardly wait for the January 1 legal season ice-fishing opener.

However, because the larger lakes had not yet proven safe to skidoo on, we were restricted to merely fishing off the dock beside Don's cottage for a week or so, before being able to move further away and fish further down the lake. One could look out the cottage window while seated at the table and actually see our Fish O' Buzzer set-ups[1] down by the dock. The buzzers could also be heard clearly in the cottage when activated by a trout's taking the minnow.

This is where the story of Fred comes into play. As game wardens in Ontario are often shuffled around from one district to another, Fred Day had recently been transferred to the Tweed office and the Land O' Lakes area in Eastern Ontario, an hour and a half from Mosque Lake. One morning while we were finishing breakfast and contemplating as to whether we should change the minnow on the four rigs near the dock, there was a loud knocking on the cottage's front door. It should be noted that the front door faced the trail in and the other side of the small peninsula where the cottage was located.

Although we had met him briefly at Buckshot Lake, Fred re-introduced himself, flashed his I.D., then inquired if the fishing lines in the water were ours. Speaking for both of us, I replied, "They certainly are, they're mine. I own them, but we're both using them. We're allowed two each aren't we?"

He then asked to see our licences and jotted some of the information down on his notepad before waving a couple of summons at us then saying, "I'll give you a choice, Mr. Deval. I can give you a summons for fishing with more than the legal limit of lines and another for leaving your lines unattended—or give you both summons for the unattended lines. Which will it be, sir?"

Being completely aware that the "unattended" law to which he was referring, simply stated that ice-fishing anglers must be within two hundred feet (now I believe the legal distance is 75 metres) of their lines, I took the initiative by speaking up. I clearly indicated that we were both definitely within the prescribed allotted distance from our rigs and we were indeed attending them. Before he could respond, I had Don go down to the lines and jiggle one of the trigger wires on the buzzers. A few moments later when Don tweaked the line I said, "I guess you can hear that quite clearly, Mr. Day, can't you? Wouldn't you agree then that our lines are, indeed, being attended?"

To our amazement, he declared that he could, but stipulated that that was not what the regulation intended. He gave us a single summons for fishing with unattended lines and warned us that we should be thankful that he was giving us a break, suggesting that he could seize all four lines as evidence if he wished. Right on the spot I determined to go to court to fight the charge.

After Fred's departure, we were curious as to why hadn't we heard his snowmobile approaching the cottage. We were soon to find out when we went out to move our set-ups and fish further down the shoreline. As we drove around the peninsula to check out new spots, we discovered that he had left his machine across from Don's cottage in the small bay where the ice was solid, then snowshoed across, stacking his snowshoes by the trail outside the cottage before knocking on the door. He must have spotted our rigs earlier from the other side of the lake and, seeing no one fishing beside them, assumed that they were not being attended. Unable to cross the still unfrozen larger body of water, he drove around the shoreline to the point where he could snowshoe across the small bay.

I next met Fred Day in the small courtroom in the village of Sharbot Lake, a good four-hour drive from Toronto, where, of course, I was prepared with the Fish O' Buzzers. A simple demonstration of their efficiency proved to the judge that they, indeed, could be heard, therefore—attended "for at least two hundred feet." I was unable to resist flashing a smile in Fred's direction as I departed the courtroom—an exonerated fishy felon.

I suppose that smile and the lack of a conviction grew under Fred's skin because he would show up several more times at various places we were fishing to check the tackle to see if we had more than two set-ups each and the two allowed hooks per line. If there were others fishing with us, to check to see if they had licences and, although knowing that we were licensed, would insist on seeing ours as well. One day he asked if we fished any of the nearby lakes, such as Grindstone, Lucky and Quinn. We replied that we did indeed and one morning discovered that he had followed our skidoo tracks from Don's cottage all the way up the nearby hydro line to where we were fishing on Quinn Lake. The man was persistent, to say the least. It seemed now that he must have felt he had been slighted somehow and was doing everything he could to wreak vengeance on us for our cheekiness.

Several weeks had gone by, the weather had turned much colder, so with all the lakes tightening up and a fine snow cover for skidooing, it was time to attempt the hike to the "unsullied" Sullivan Lake once more—unsullied by us, anyhow!

Backpacks were loaded with our lunch, maps, compasses, buzzers and a hand augur to bore holes in the ice. This time mosquito repellent was unnecessary! The trip was absolutely gorgeous, a newly fallen blanket of snow covered everything and driving the machines through the bush was like driving through a tunnel with the heavily laden branches forming a roof over our heads. The sunshine sparkled on the snow-covered lakes like a million diamonds, with the blanketed rocky outcroppings looking like giant marshmallow mounds. The conditions were as close to perfect as one could wish for snowmobiling, lots of snow but with a rather firm crusty top caused by the sun's rays. We had little trouble making excellent time across the lakes, through the bush and up the hills then, lo and behold, we broke through the bush. Finally we had our first look at what, until then, had seemed to be the almost unattainable magical waters of Sullivan Lake—albeit, the frozen waters of Sullivan Lake.

It took less than an hour to get there from Don's cottage on Mosque Lake and by eight o'clock we had *five* buzzers set up and ready for action. Four were on the inshore side of the lake's only island, with the fifth placed above a hole dug on the other side, a couple of hundred yards away from the other set-ups. It was there as a special treat for Fred if he followed our tracks and showed up later.

We did not have long to wait for action and by noon hour had caught four or five brook trout in the three-and-a-half to four-pound class, releasing all but one each kept for the pan. Then, while we were enjoying lunch and the pristine solitude of our surroundings, a figure suddenly emerged from behind the island and barked at us, "That your buzzer behind the island, Deval?" "This time you've gone too far, I'm afraid," he continued as he approached us resting on our Skidoos and eating lunch. "I'm going to have to seize your tackle," he added. "Two lines per person is all you're allowed," he gleefully reported. "You know, technically, we could seize your Skidoos, too, but obviously that can't be done here. I'll tag them and note the licences and we'll see about that back in the office at Tweed."

Still working on my sandwiches, I suggested, through a mouthful of food that maybe he would like to check the one on the other side of the island first. Taking the final bite of my sandwich, I offered to go with him. Attempting to keep straight faces, Don and I followed him to the fifth buzzer set-up. I stopped him as he was about to yank the Fish O' Buzzer out of the snow anchoring it in place, and suggested that he check the line first. He pulled in the eighteen inches of line and stared incredulously at the silver and red magnet tied on its end with no hooks fastened anywhere.

He growled, "Okay, Deval, what the hell is this?"

"I think you must know what it is, Fred," I replied, "A magnet! You see someone told us that the lake had some big steelhead trout in it, so we thought we would see if we could get one with a magnet."

He swore and furiously kicked the buzzer over, then refastened his snowshoes that had previously been stuck in the snow near the buzzer before coming around the island to confront us, and took off without a further word. As he slunk across the lake we could hear him continuing to snarl, but I doubt that he was able to hear the gales of howling laughter emanating from behind the island. We have since made three or four other attempts to get to the lake, summer and winter, but they, too, proved to be of no avail. The recollection of this and the many efforts made by us to reach and fish Sullivan Lake certainly must qualify for its inclusion here.

Chapter 10

Poaching Pierce's Pond

In my earlier years of exploring the streams and various waters that reportedly held brook trout, the names of various ponds in the Toronto vicinity would often arise in casual conversation. In addition, being the Canadian champion fly caster, I was occasionally invited to give demonstrations and conduct seminars at several of the more exclusive private ponds, such as the Caledon and Glen Major clubs.[1] The size of some of the trout in these ponds, often in the three-to five-pound category, along with their seemingly eager response to a well-presented fly or spinner always intrigued me.

I could never have afforded to join one of these exclusive clubs but that did not deter me from occasionally wetting a line in them. I fished with a chap back then whose real name shall remain anonymous in this book. I will simply refer to him as Ken. We fished together in many of the streams in our area and also in several of the ponds, private, or otherwise. I believe it's usually referred to as poaching. To Ken, though, poaching was simply one method of cooking eggs.

The challenge of fishing these ponds, uninvited and without being caught, however, seemed to outweigh the potential of the blemish to our reputations if we were ever apprehended. Although Ken was far more experienced than I in this unlawful practice, I did tag along with him on several occasions and I will admit that the adrenaline rush experienced with the illegal aspect was probably greater than that felt during the actual catching of the trout. Ken had told me about the one or two occasions where he had been caught and kicked off the private property with stern warnings that the authorities would be called if he was found on the property again, but luckily in the three or four outings when I joined him in these illicit acts we had yet to be discovered. Then there was Pierce's pond! Ken had heard that Mr. Pierce, an older gentleman in his eighties and a retired doctor, had purchased a small piece of property with a spring-fed pond and had had it stocked with two to three-pound speckled trout. I never did learn how Ken obtained this sort of information. Perhaps he had contacts in the various private trout hatcheries that produced trout for the owners of these private ponds.

Ken had already fished Pierce's and caught several specks, releasing all but one, a fat three-pounder. The pond, almost a mile off the main road near Goodwood, Ontario, could be reached in an easy hike down a railway line that passed on the perimeter of the property. He fished it by crawling close to the edge of the water then, while lying flat amongst the bulrushes, from one side of the pond he could cast a spinning lure while keeping an eye on the house opposite him on the other side. Unable to resist the temptation, I decided to join him on the next planned assault on Pierce's pond—a big mistake!

Ken was right about the logistics of the railway track, a walk-in with easy access to the non-fenced pond and its beautiful and plentiful brook trout. We had already caught and released several fine fish, but had kept a couple between us for the pan that had looked a little too much the worse for the wear and tear to be put back in the swim. Unexpectedly, a quivering but loud voice came from behind us, "Okay, what the hell makes you guys think that you could get away with sneaking in here and stealing my fish!"

As we surreptitiously, but fruitlessly attempted to cover our fish with the shore-line weeds, a gentleman, apparently Mr. Pierce, stood a few feet behind us with an old double-barrelled 12-gauge shotgun in his quivering hands, nervously levelled directly at us. It was difficult to tell who was the more tense, he, or Ken and I, as we could clearly see that his finger was not outside the trigger guard, but inside and on the trigger. We cautiously regained our feet, turning around slowly so as not to further upset him and simultaneously, we both began apologizing profusely. I know the fear must have been obvious on my face as I pleaded with him, "Sir, would you mind pointing your gun somewhere else, please. We're truly sorry. I promise you that we will never, ever come back here and fish your pond again."

He lowered the gun and took his finger off the trigger. Ken and I breathed a sigh of relief as he ordered us off his property, declaring that he had our car licence number and promising to call the OPP and have us arrested should we break our promise.

"Oh and leave those bloody fish right where they are, too!" he added.

We scurried off into the bush and back down the railway tracks to where the car was parked, feeling somewhat remorseful but at the same time relieved. We drove home with barely a word spoken between us until I dropped Ken off at his place near Stouffville. His home was only about a twenty-minute drive from Mr. Pierce's pond and half an hour from my home in Scarborough.

As he strode down the lane towards his house, I yelled out the car window that I was finished with such antics. It would be trout streams from now on for me. It certainly was an adrenaline rush, fraught with its highs and lows, but fishing Pierce's pond was absolutely the last time I poached anybody's private pond. The experience, although different, has become over time a decidedly potent memory for me.

Chapter 11
The Phenomenal Echo Creek

During my almost fifteen years on the road selling hunting and fishing equipment in Eastern Ontario as a commercial traveller for a wholesale firm, Canada Fishing Tackle and Sports,[1] I took advantage of the opportunities to fish almost every creek, stream and river in my territory. From Lake Huron in the west, my region stretched eastward to Quebec and Lake Ontario in the south to Algonquin Park in the north.

The fishing was not the only perk I had going for me in this job. Although I was seldom wearing appropriate fishing garments, I would often stop at whatever waters, however minuscule, outside the many cities and towns where I had clientele and make a few casts to see if there were trout close to the highway bridges over the streams. These stops were usually more productive than not, and many times I would march into the local sporting goods stores and offer the proprietors a couple of pan-size brookies for their own tables.

Needless to say, the merchants would predictably always ask either or both, "Where did you catch 'em? What did you catch 'em on?"

Answering their queries would usually bring on remarks such as, "I'll be damned. Always thought there was nothing in there but the suckers and chubs the kids catch. You'd better put a couple of dozen of that lure you were using on the order, along with my regular repeats. Okay?"

Up in the Ottawa Valley area there are many small streams that I would visit before driving into town. I fished one small brook named Sharps Creek several times on the way to Arnprior and Renfrew, a couple of smaller centres north of Ottawa. Each time, although I managed to catch a few brook trout, they were quite small, too small actually to offer to any of the dealers.

When I mentioned this to one of my clients, Ray Clemow, in Haleys Station, a village north of Renfrew, he asked if I had ever fished Echo Creek, a little stream that runs into the Madawaska River below Combermere. As I had not, he offered to take me there and even fish with me the next time

I came his way. But he made me promise not to tell anyone about his "real trout stream"—with real fish.

Working my territory more quickly than usual after that, I discovered that I was going to be at Haleys Station a week sooner than I had said to Ray. As promised, I phoned him from Renfrew the night before and arrived at his shop just before noon, not exactly the best time to go fishing. After noting that he had, indeed, placed his "Gone Fishin" sign on the front door of the shop, I mentioned my poor timing to him. He simply shrugged and indicated we would "catch 'em" anyway.

Pointing to my already assembled spinning rod, he said, "Glad you remembered your hip boots, but you won't need that thing." Seemingly he had a couple of outfits already for us, with a can of fat dew worms, along with the requisite can of mosquito repellent. However, I informed him that fishing with worms was not my customary cup of tea. I told him that I preferred to use a fly or an artificial lure. Since I had been told that Echo Creek was a very small stream, I hadn't brought a fly rod, but instead a little spinning outfit, my favourite approach to fishing smaller brooks and streams.

Before he could take umbrage, I said, "That's not to say that fishing properly with live bait doesn't take skill to be successful, but using a spinning rod correctly in difficult conditions, also takes considerable skill, if you're going to stay out of the trees and catch the odd fish."

He seemed agreeable and we headed out. Following his circuitous directions (deliberately, I imagine to make returning on my own another time difficult) we neared the end of a muddy trail that petered out into *nothing* an hour later. According to Ray the creek was just in front of us, beside a clump of bushes. To me, those bushes looked more like a Costa Rican rain forest.

I pulled on my hip boots as Ray set up his fishing rod which turned out to be one of those old, steel, telescopic fishing rods, some of which when fully extended were almost fifteen feet long. He threaded the fishing line through the guides, and not bothering with a leader, tied on a large hook. He next fastened a fat dew worm to its point, leaving the bulk of the worm to wriggle freely to attract a trout's attention.

Seeing me just standing there watching him incredulously, he said, "You sure you don't want one of these rigs, Gordon? I don't know how you'll be able to cast a lure here with the heavy bush. It hangs over the creek almost everywhere. By using this thing I only have to pick a spot and pull out the rod until the tip's over the water, then lower the bait down through the brush and branches."

Despite his offer, I decided to take my chances and see what I could do with my spinning tackle. We worked our way closer to the creek, which I still had not been able to see, but which Ray identified by its sound. There's nothing more beautiful for a trout fisherman than to hear the sound of a babbling brook gurgling its way through the bush or over obstructions in open meadow streams. I could certainly hear it but still could not see even a hint of water. I held my ground and watched as Ray pushed section after section out on his rod until the juicy dew worm was dangling over what he guessed to be the middle of the stream. A couple of heavy split shots (tiny lead sinkers that fasten to the line through a split in their makeup) a foot or so above the hook, along with the weight of the worm, allowed him to easily feed the line through the guides and lower the bait towards the water.

Immediately, there was a furious splashing somewhere in front of us. Without hesitating he sharply raised the rod and in the same motion flipped a fourteen-inch, gorgeously coloured brook trout over his shoulders, dropped the rod and pounced on the startled and flopping fish. I shook my head in disbelief, never having seen such an incredible sight, "I ain't never seen nothin' like that before, man! Wow!"

Ray broke the first trout's neck and tossed it into his ancient wicker creel. He then repeated the entire procedure except this time the trout, which he had a little difficulty lifting with the long rod, seemed to come through the overhanging bushes rather reluctantly before it crashed right at my feet. An even more beautiful brookie than his first, it tipped the scales at a little over three pounds. This was rapidly becoming a truly magical fishing experience that would rival almost any other.

"Okay," he said, smiling, "that's enough for me and my missus. Let's see now if you can fish Echo Creek with that spinning rod of yours, eh!"

The challenge was definitely on. Chomping at the bit to have a go at Echo's lovely brook trout, I moved a short distance upstream from Ray's pool, parting and holding the brush to one side with my left arm as he had demonstrated and poked the tiny rod, that is tiny in comparison to Ray's fifteen footer, through the opening. Using only the tip of the ultra-light rod to execute an Arrenberg cast, a type of flip cast used in one of the World Casting Competition disciplines, I propelled the spinner upstream. With this cast the lure remains below the caster's waist throughout its trajectory, allowing for accuracy, and in fishing the avoidance of overhanging brush and branches. The little spinner plopped into the fast-moving stream ten or twelve feet up the current, forcing an immediate retrieve with the water seemingly rather shallow. Should the lure be allowed to sink as it would be caught on bottom.

This magical little stream provided me with an instantaneous thrill when a brookie smashed the lure, even before the initial revolution of the silver spinner blade. It put up a fine struggle before I was able to lead it towards my position in the brush on the bank. I have caught brook trout in smaller waters but never in conditions similar to those of Echo Creek. Such scenarios always place a premium on the necessity of handling one's tackle skilfully, including the telescopic outfit with worms for bait that was being used by my friend and client, Ray Clemow. I carefully placed the trout back in the swim after working it gently back and forth in the water to force water through its gills, a necessity to replace the vigour back in the exhausted fish if it is to survive.

Ray was obviously impressed with the fact that I did not require worms to fish his creek. Between the two of us, fishing for only a couple of hours that afternoon we probably caught and released a dozen more fat brookies ranging from about fourteen inches to another big fellow that Ray latched into that was over nineteen inches long. An incredible size for such small water, it would have tipped the scales at three-and-a-half pounds. They were all carefully released.

I suppose the secrets of the phenomenal production of the Echo Creek waters are: firstly, its remoteness; secondly, its inaccessibility to most fishing methods and, thirdly, and most importantly, apart from an odd one for the pan, the catch-and-release policy practised by Ray and his buddies on this precious little stream.

I worked for Canada Fishing Tackle and Sports for a number of years after first meeting Ray Clemow. Never again after his taking me to his wonderful stream did I deem it necessary to drop him off a couple of trout as I had done with so many other dealers in my territory. He remained a fine friend and fishing buddy, and we fished numerous other waters together, including Golden Lake for pickerel and the Ottawa River for sturgeon. Ray even took me grouse hunting one fall and demonstrated an unusual and highly successful method for bagging a brace of these delicious birds—but that story will have to wait for another time.

Chapter 12

Pleasurable Pursuits on Grenadier Pond

As we get older, much older that is, we tend to often look back at our youth with fondness, occasionally even drifting into wishful thoughts that we could have done this thing—or that thing—differently. Some of these reminiscences occasionally result in daydreams that take us back to the incident so realistically that we actually feel we are once again participating in the event. One of these memories, often recurring to me in my few idle moments, took place in the heart of the City of Toronto, at Grenadier Pond, nestled in its huge High Park. The "pond" is actually larger than many of the trout lakes that we have fished over the years.

Being eighteen years old is a wonderful time of life when many doors are beginning to open for the future—advanced education, possible careers, and a different way of looking at the opposite sex—with all the wonderment that goes along with one's sexual experimentation. When I was eighteen I had a girlfriend, Mona, who accompanied me on a number of fishing trips. One was to Uxbridge where we bicycled all the way from Toronto to fish in the brooks below the village. The results of that particular day in the bush were recounted earlier. Another trip taken together was when we were invited to my uncle's rented cottage on Pigeon Lake, near Bobcaygeon, Ontario, where our eighteen-year-old libido overruled our caution and the boat cushions scattered around in the big boathouse were put to use for another purpose several times, until my Uncle Bob stumbled upon us one afternoon. Chuckling, he looked away but suggested we go up to the cottage where "it's a lot more comfortable," as he and my Auntie Joan were going shopping in the village.

Perhaps the most vivid recollection, the only one to really justify Grenadier Pond's ever being deemed a magical water, at least by us, was the day I asked Mona if she would like to do a little fishing in downtown Toronto. I qualified

Fishermen in Grenadier Pond, High Park, 1939, from the James Salmon collection. Courtesy of the City of Toronto Archives, Fonds 1231, Item 629.

that somewhat by explaining that while Grenadier Pond actually was only close to downtown Toronto, it did have a lot of fish in it, not trout but pike, bass and panfish. On Sundays we could rent a rowboat. She agreed to make a lunch for us.

The old jalopy that I had bought from my uncle, a used-car dealer, was in for repair so we took advantage of the streetcar ride that went the entire length of the city and culminated in a circle around the lunchroom in the middle of the park. My girlfriend was wearing the fashions of the day, a white, frilly peasant blouse with puffy sleeves and a huge, full length and colourful billowing gypsy skirt. These details are only easily recalled because I took a lot of pictures of her that day, some of which I occasionally run across in one of my old photo albums.

We rented a big, old, flat-bottom boat, rowed out a couple of hundred yards and I proceeded to set up our tackle. According to legend, Grenadier Pond was tagged with its colourful name as a sort of memorial many years before I was born. The oft-told tale that has withstood considerable analysis is that in the eighteen hundreds an entire legion of soldiers (Grenadiers) disappeared into its murky depths during a forced winter march on the ice—a colourful legend but one without substance.[1] A codicil often added to the myth suggests that the pond is *bottomless.* I suppose that fallacy persists because of the extremely deep and soft muddy bottom the lake possesses. Actually, although it definitely has a muddy bottom that would be impossible to stand in, even in the shallows, the warm-water pond is not at all deep, but is completely gorged with weeds making fishing rather difficult when using anything other that a float, sinker and live bait.

Already into tournament casting, I owned an excellent bait casting outfit, a hexagonally shaped, rapier steel rod (the best available in those days) and one of the most expensive reels of its time the famous Pflueger Supreme.[2] In my attempts to induce Mona into the sport of casting, I had purchased exactly the same outfit for her and this was to be her initial exposure to casting. Any fishing she had done with me earlier had consisted simply of still fishing with live bait.

Casting in extremely weedy waters such as those in Grenadier Pond necessitates searching for surface pockets in the weed beds, aiming for these targets and not allowing the lure to sink too deeply. I demonstrated the proper technique for her and after several casts encouraged her to give it a try. That was a big mistake! We should have stuck to a concrete children's wading pool until she gained familiarity with her new outfit. Her hand, slippery from wiping her brow, was unable to retain its grip on the rod's cork handle. The entire outfit, rather than just the lure, flew out into the weed beds and promptly slid out of sight. Tears began to flow and she apologized over and over again as I contemplated the prospect of stripping to my underwear and diving into the weeds to search for her outfit. Scared when she realized what I was about to do, she pleaded with me not to attempt such a dangerous act. She continued as I pulled my pants back up from my ankles, and promised to buy another rod and reel for her. But it dawned on me that perhaps if I fished around with my own tackle where it had gone in, I might be able to hook and retrieve it.

However, the fates were against us. It was not to be. The weeds were so dense that I could not get the heavy pickerel jig that I had tied on for the purpose close enough to the bottom and I quickly realized that the attempt was absolutely futile. Accepting the inevitable and forcing a smile, I rowed out to the middle where it was likely a little deeper and thus easier to fish. We both relaxed and settled down near the middle of the pond before taking turns with my rod. Now when she was casting it was quite obvious that she was keeping a virtual death grip on the rod handle. Trying to make a cast without hanging up on the weeds every time soon became rather tedious so the tackle was laid to rest. With noon hour approaching we tucked into our picnic lunch while drifting aimlessly around the pond.

About that time we noticed that there were boats everywhere. Everybody seemed to be coming out for the afternoon, some fishing, but most simply paddling and rowing around and enjoying the afternoon sunshine. Mona still appeared a little upset and apprehensive so I suggested that she move up beside me so we could snuggle. Smiling broadly, she stood up then carefully re-arranging her enormous skirt, slid down beside me. Looking daredevilish, she tossed almost half the voluminous skirt over my lap. I will leave the ensuing action to the reader's imagination. Suffice to say that even as other boats passed closely to us on the calm pond we were not deterred in our pleasurable pursuit—and I definitely do not mean fishing! Too bad those billowing peasant skirts went out of style long ago, but I guess they are at least, partially responsible for Grenadier Pond's being listed among my magical memories.

The 1974 North American Casting Championships, held in High Park provided my entrance back into the competitive casting world after a sixteen-year hiatus to spend more time with my young family. It was the first time the event had ever been staged in Canada, and it was hosted by the old Toronto Anglers and Hunters Association (TAHA). However, within the membership there were no competitors capable of casting all twelve disciplines.[3] The Toronto casters had always been excellent accuracy casters and practised regularly at the pond, but for some reason or another when "old buddies" Art Walker and Ron Duncan and I retired in the fifties, none of the other TAHA casters took up the challenge of the more difficult distance disciplines. I was proselytized out of retirement to dust off my equipment, get back in the game and compete on their behalf. I had not competed in any tournaments since 1958, but after a few days of practice a week or two before the event, the fire returned. I discovered that I was still competitive enough to not embarrass the country or myself and won a number of medals accordingly.

The accuracy events were held on the shore of Grenadier Pond, with the distance events in the upper portion of the park. Several records were set in the tournament, and the fishing and casting world was introduced to the remarkable talents of Steve Rajeff. Only seventeen years old at the time, he was already establishing himself as a rising star in the game and the power to be in the future of the sport. Steve cast an unheard of at the time distance of 208 feet in the popular Trout Fly Distance game, a distance I was never able to achieve until the World Championships in Olso, Norway, in the late eighties. Several of the disciplines had changed their rules and makeup during my absence from the sport, but for an angler who fishes as much as I do, they were comparatively easy to adapt to. After I resumed competition at Grenadier Pond and High Park in 1974, I began teaching several other accuracy casters the intricacies of casting for distance with flies and plugs, so they could compete in world and international competitions. As a result several of the TAHA members did begin working on all the games. The tournament in High Park, along with the surprising results of my resurgence, was the catalyst leading to several members of their club eventually becoming world-class all round casters.

One of the casters representing the Toronto club in that first tourney in High Park was Charlie Phillips, whose father, the late Joe Phillips, was one of their finest accuracy plug casters. Charlie was a budding young accuracy caster destined to become one of the best all round tournament casters to ever represent the club. I have a distinct memory, magical if you wish, of young Charlie, not yet a teenager, sitting on one of the casting docks firing deadly accurate casts at the targets with his bait casting outfit, all the while casually working over a mouthful of chewing gum. Charlie eventually became, and still is, the president of the Canadian Casting Federation, which eventually replaced the Canadian Casting Association begun by a few others and myself in the fifties. It had become defunct after the first World Championships in Kiel, Germany, when several of us retired the following year.

Another interesting development discovered during the tournament was that media interviews were being conducted at Grenadier Pond by the daughter of one of my best fishing buddies, Tony Whittingham. Many people today would recognize the name Valerie Pringle, but then she was known to us as Val Whittingham. In one of her first ever assignments in her job for radio station CFRB, she was interviewing Steve Rajeff, the young and rising star in the casting tournament world, as well as interviewing Allyn Ehrhardt, myself and other competitors.

Twenty-one years later, now a seasoned television hostess in a number of different shows, Valerie was once again interviewing me for television news when our Scarborough club was hosting the 1995 North American Championships, the first time it had been staged in Canada. During the lengthy interview, she not only had me demonstrating casting for her photographers, but I talked her into having herself filmed while giving it a try. Not surprisingly, she handled the equipment with great aplomb, much as her father, my buddy Tony, would have done.

Chapter 13
The Magic of Sludge Lake

Like Tedious Lake, now just another Long Lake, this is one more case of a lake having its name changed because one or two cottagers disliked the connotations suggested in the original name. It is now officially called Cedar Lake. Both Tedious and Sludge had enough originality and exclusivity in their names that I find it difficult to believe that the powers to be acquiesced to the name-change requests. However, we continue to refer to the lake by its original name and will continue to address it as such here.

Sludge is a most unusual Haliburton lake. It is situated right alongside Highway 35, actually close enough to the shoulder that it is possible for one to cast out a car window into the water. Over the year, the lake had been reduced to simply a small body of water teeming with suckers and panfish, probably because of the thoughtless actions of a few fishermen dumping the remnants of their live bait from minnow buckets and traps into the water at the end of their fishing day. Not only is that an illegal procedure, but it is a sure way to ruin a trout lake within a couple of years. The results of their carelessness was even more dramatic on Sludge as it is such a small lake with only a single comparatively tiny area deep enough to remain cold in warmer weather. Although it is a spring-fed body of water, being so shallow for approximately eighty per cent of its volume, the warmer water panfish species quickly overran the lake eliminating the trout population.

However, thanks to the progressive actions of the biologists in our Ministry of Natural Resources, along with encouragement from scores of trout fishermen, Sludge Lake has regained its former status as a magical water and one that has provided us with several very special memories. As a first step, the lake was poisoned with rotenone[1] and, after several successive treatments, all the undesirable species were completely eradicated. The lake was then allowed to rest for a couple of years before being restocked with rainbow trout. The biologists also decided to try an unprecedented procedure. Although realizing that most true trout anglers prefer to fish in the boondocks, deep in the bush on rather inaccessible lakes, they felt that many other fisher-men did not necessarily adopt the same principles. It was decided to carry on a massive restocking program. Normal trout stocking procedures for tiny lakes such as Sludge are to plant anywhere from eight hundred to fifteen hundred fish annually. Nevertheless, twenty-four thousand rainbow trout fingerlings and yearlings were planted in the lake over a four-year period with follow-up plantings annually from eight to fifteen hundred more.

It was about that time that I met the biologist, Wayne Williams working for the MNR out of the Minden offices. He had heard the story about Fred Day and knew that my buddies and I, ever since the incident with Fred and the magnet, called all game wardens "Fred." I told him not to worry, we would address him as "Chief Fred." Actually we got along quite well, and he introduced me to a number of the local "Freds," one of whom, whose last name escapes me, was Bob, a chap we were destined to run into on a few occasions. That particular fellow was a rather large burly chap with a great moustache.

Wayne had heard a little about our club's fishing activities in his bailiwick and when I first called him to introduced myself and ask if he had the current stocking sheets for his area, he was most agreeable. He commented on our reputation for extensive fishing experience in the area and, since he was new, wondered if he could call us sometime for some background information.

It was in that conversation that I learned about the Ministry's unusual program for the revival of Sludge Lake. When I expressed my surprise that they would pour that many trout into a lake alongside the busy highway, he explained that the approach was experimental. Depending on the outcome, consideration was being given to repeating the procedure in other lakes that had been contaminated by undesirable species.

He even wondered if we would check out the lake a few times and let the wardens know how the trout were doing. With this being the second year of restocking, the net surveys conducted over the past Fall had been promis-ing. I assured him that we would, but as it was still winter and the lakes frozen that we would probably leave it until ice-out, when we would have a much better idea of how the 'bows were faring. It seemed that a couple of fishing sorties to Sludge Lake during May would be a good idea. The combination of proximity to Toronto and the enticement of heavy stocking should make it easy to generate enough interest to put a trip together with a bunch of the guys.

With almost a month remaining in the hard-water season, a few of my buddies, Jack Wilkings, Donnie Allen, Pete Pokulok and I, decided to squeeze in another ice-fishing trip to A/B Lake before ice-out time and the tentatively planned "assault" on Sludge Lake. We had fished A Lake three or four times since the January 1 opening, but had not cut a single hole in the nearby B Lake. We opted to forego what was probably the best ice-fishing time of the year on the one lake in favour of fishing the other, smaller of the two. We also decided to film the day's activities to add to the fishing movie we had been shooting since the initial January trip. The skidoo trip in to the lake was uneventful and the trout co-operated in fine style with several smaller brookies having already been released while a couple of five-pounders had already been packed in some of the remaining snow, still on shore.

The camera, set up on a tripod, had filmed much of the action when another snow machine could be heard approaching the lake through the bush. With a couple of lines allowed per person when ice fishing, we had eight rigs set up over a comparatively shallow area where the water drains over the beaver dam into B Lake. We chose the spot to fish with the idea that the lake's specs might be attracted to the flow and the various vittles being washed in their direction.

When the big, high-powered snowmobile broke through the bush, we could see its driver was dressed in the garb worn by the conservation officers (game wardens) in Ontario. Another "Fred," only this time it was Bob, the moustached gentleman that Wayne Williams had introduced me to in Minden a few weeks earlier. Although Jack wondered aloud if Wayne had suggested his checking us out after our initial chat, it seemed improbable to me. When the biologist had called me back, as he said he would, to ask about the five or six lakes we fished in his area, the call at the Ministry's expense had lasted almost two hours. He had apologized for, "Taking so much of your time, Gord," and thanked me profusely.

After checking out our licences and counting the rigs, Bob asked about our Fish O' Buzzers and how they worked. Jack, standing closest to him, suggested that the officer watch one of his. Just before Bob had arrived on the scene, Jack had missed a couple of strikes and forfeited his minnows to what he estimated to be at least a "ten-pounder." I suppose he believed the same fish would return for a third helping—and he was absolutely right.

"Beep! Beep! Beeeeep!" Jack's buzzer sounded before the line slid off the trigger wire and began running down through the hole. He leaped over to grab it and this time successfully set the hook, while Bob looked on dumbfounded.

The noise caught him by surprise. While Donnie operated the camera to film the entire panorama, another buzzer started up—this time one of mine. Bob was looking over Jack's four-pound brookie as it was held up for inspection and being recorded on film. He congratulated him then, shaking his head as the Fish O' Buzzer operation was demonstrated for him by Pete, asked where he could get one of "these things?"

When I told him that after I had designed and assembled the first one, I had them made for me, he wondered if I would sell him one. As I was not carrying any extra ones with me, I directed him to Bill's Bait and Tackle shop back in Minden. He had bought and sold quite a few from me over the last couple of years. Bob promptly thanked us, started up his snowmobile and left.

Donnie had kept the movie camera running the entire time he was there and had snapped a couple of 35 mm shots as well. It made a terrific bit of film for the movie we had been working on. That film has since been shown to hundreds of fishermen in several countries.

The best part of that particular memory, however, occurred a week later, when Jack and I decided that it had been cold enough that the ice would still be safe to make a last trip to A/B and fish B Lake once more before ice-out. As our Skidoos broke through the bush onto the lake, we both stood up on them in surprise at the sight that lay in front of us, exactly where we had been fishing the week before. Unaware of our arrival, sitting on a stool and hunched over a single hole in the ice, was Bob, the same "Fred" who had checked us out a week earlier. He appeared mesmerized by the Fish O' Buzzer he had set up beside it.

A couple of weeks later, with the ice out of the Haliburton Lakes, eight of our club members, in two cars with canoes and my fold-boat strapped onto the roofs, headed up north to accept the challenge and invitation to explore the fishing—and catching—potential of Wayne Williams' Sludge Lake rejuvenation project. We had agreed ahead of time that none of us would drop anchor so that we could move around more on the tiny lake. In this way we would not only be simply investigating the fishing, but the various depths in the lake as well.

The result was fabulous! More than a dozen silver-slabbed two to three-pound 'bows were caught, with only a couple having to be kept that would probably not have survived if released. The males were adorned with a slash of vermilion on their cheeks and down their sides, displaying their spawning colour glories. Inexplicably, a four-pound smallmouth bass was also caught, probably thoughtlessly put in the swim by one of the cottagers.

Wayne Williams was pleased to learn from our report that the fish were all in excellent shape with most of them spending as much time performing aerial acrobatics in their attempts to get off our lines, as they did charging around beneath the surface. On several occasions, all four boats contained anglers simultaneously fighting rainbow trout. In addition to those that were actually caught and released, probably another dozen took care of the release factor on their own, breaking lines or becoming unhooked. With the water still retaining its ice-out temperatures, the fish were scattered all around the lake in water as shallow as three feet to approximately eighteen feet or so in the single deeper location near a small island. It appeared that only about twenty-five per cent of the water in Sludge would be deep enough to stay sufficiently cold throughout the warm summer months to support the trout.

The lake was fished once or twice more that summer and produced action on both occasions then rested until the hard-water season when we simply parked beside it and walked out to set lines up on the far shore. Fish were on the lines both times, but only one was caught and already it was showing phenomenal growth, reaching a shade under four-pounds. Sludge was beginning to display signs of truly being a magical water.

Following an ice-out trip to A/B the next spring, a few of us tried our hands on Sludge once more, again with similar results, excellent action with 'bows running to as much as five pounds. A few weeks later, with the temperatures still cold enough to encourage Jack and me to make the hour-and-a-half drive to test the lake's potential once again, it was decided to check out whether the trout were still in the shallow water and receptive to our offerings. As we had contemplated, the water had stayed cold enough to keep the trout from moving into the lake's depths.

We caught several quite close to shore, with the main memory highlight for me being a gorgeous seven-pound female 'bow who towed our little boat all over the lake before surrendering to the constant pressure exerted by the long fly rod. Although I have caught much larger 'bows in some of our steelhead (trout that migrate from the lakes) rivers, that Sludge Lake beauty remains the largest one I have taken from an inland lake.

It had to be kept as the gills had been damaged by the fly and later when it was cleaned and gutted at home, as is done with most of the trout we keep, the stomach contents were analysed. There, looking like a small cigar, was the largest caddis larvae I have ever seen, or even heard being described. It was removed, still in its case, constructed of what appeared to be fragments of oak leaves off the lake bottom. I rinsed, then froze it in a big pill tube of water as a memento to show to my buddies. The case was more than five inches from tip to stern, whereas the majority of caddis, the number one food staple for many brook, brown and rainbow trout, rarely exceed an inch in length.

We have not fished Sludge Lake since, preferring to be, as Wayne Williams indicated, "a little bit nuts," and fish the lakes such as A/B, deeper in the Haliburton Highlands. However, nowadays when we head up Highway 35 on our way up north to Haliburton, the car appears to slow a little as we drive alongside Sludge and pensively recollect the magical moments it provided for me and my fishing buddies.

Chapter 14

From Novice to Accomplished Angler

I have hundreds of memories and they all do not necessarily have to do with fish, or even with magical waters. Many of them have more to do with people. A number that often recur and are related to other fishing and casting buddies, concern another fine friend and fisherman, Peter Pokulok. I first met Pete after Donnie Allen and I were planning an early ice-out go at Brule's fine lake trout. Donnie called and asked if another friend of his could come along with us. "He hasn't done a hell of a lot of fishing, but feels he would like to find out what it's all about. We'll be fishing from a boat so I don't think he'll slow us down or anything. It's not like we were going to go fly-fishing on the Ganny or something."

During the drive up to Brule in the Land O' Lakes, I learned that Pete had tried his hand in a number of sports previously. He had been a linebacker for the Montreal Allouettes football team, competed in trapshooting championships in Vandalia, Ohio, and worked as an assistant pro at a golf club.

Quite a bit younger than I, he had been told by our mutual friend that there was a lot more to fishing than just tossing out a hook baited with a worm. Apparently when he heard that I had had considerable success in the competitive tournament side of the sport, fishing became his next sporting pursuit. Don explained to him, however, that before we would take him under our wing in the tournament side of the game, he would have to tag along with us on several fishing trips, to make sure that he really wanted to get seriously involved. Although fire was not involved, "trial by fire" is an oft-used expression that is perfectly appropriate when describing Peter's initial exposure to our sort of fishing.

Brule Lake is a fairly large body of water, four or five miles long with a narrow opening at the north end leading into a smaller body of water connecting to the main lake. Russell Brown, a gentleman who operated a small camp at the access to the smaller portion of the lake, had an old fleet of wooden skiffs that would not have been placed in the water yet as his camp would normally not be open as early as we were planning to fish the lake.

Ice-out time, whether fishing for brookies or lakers, is our favourite time of the year to get out on the water. The blackflies and mosquitoes have yet to become active and hyper; we seldom have company on the lakes and on occasion the results can be extremely rewarding. This excursion was planned for mid-April. Donnie and I were keeping our fingers crossed that the ice on Brule would be at least partially off in the area where we planned to fish, a little beyond the opening into the main lake. We planned on taking our own aluminum car-top boat, believing that Russell's old wooden boats would not be available. With a solid keel and prow on the old car-top, it could be used as an ice-breaker if necessary.

The final few miles on the trail leading to the lake presented a bit of a challenge for us as the frost had not completely gone out of the ground, which meant that wherever the sun could weave through the treetops to the trail there would be a soft, muddy morass to negotiate. Being stuck in muck at ice-out time was nothing new for Donnie and me, and along with Pete's muscle, we managed to dig and wrestle the Chev out of a couple of nasty mudholes. When we came over the last hill before heading down to Russell Brown's camp, we were a little disappointed to see that the lake was still substantially covered with ice.

Pointing across the bay, Donnie commented to our neophyte that experience had taught us how to make our own open water across this bay and where we should find the ice off at the end of the main lake, way over where the water drains out of this area. Pete, looking puzzled, helped me carry our car-top boat down to the dock, while Donnie looked after the motor and gas. We pushed it off the dock and, using a couple of paddles, broke up and pushed the honeycombed ice far enough away that the hundred-and-ten-pound car-top settled nicely into the water without effort. I grabbed a handful of the elongated ice crystals to show Pete how rotten the ice was at this time of year, making it fairly easy to break through it with the boat or paddles in most places.

Donnie demonstrated how the ice crystals could be kept at bay using the paddle as both a spear and a shovel as I cranked up the motor and pushed the boat into the ice field in front of us. The ex-football player, Pete, looking petrified, was yelling over the roar of the outboard engine, proclaiming his lack of faith in our methods, especially with the absence of life preservers.

Pete Pokulok holding his prize catch, a seven-pound brook trout.

Ignoring his concerns, we suggested he use his weight to our advantage by rocking the boat from side to side. The resultant wave action would also help break up the ice. With luck, we reckoned we would be across the bay and fishing in about twenty minutes.

An hour later we rounded the point where the channel leads to the main body of water and were pleased to discover that, as we had surmised, the majority of the big lake was basically ice-free. There was enough breeze that we were able to maintain a nice drift along the shoreline so that Pete could troll with the fly rod while Donnie and I made angled casts slightly ahead of the drift to allow our flies time to sink before repeating the procedure. It proved to be quite an effective process with both the cast flies and Pete's trolled bucktail streamers doing the job of inducing Brule's lakers into attacking our offerings. By the time we decided to call it a day there had been enough action with a brace of four-pound trout each to keep for the table, that Pete, like the fish he had caught, became hooked on trout fishing.

Before the summer was over, Pete had fished with us on a number of streams and lakes and had become quite proficient with both fly-fishing and spinning equipment. In the gym, working with our club throughout the winter months, he also quickly became adept with his accuracy skills on the targets. By the time spring rolled around, his naturally competitive instincts were apparent as he could hardly wait for the tournament season to commence.

Casting at the Toronto Sportsman Show and then in a couple of local competitions, Pete began collecting awards by the handful so that by the time the major tournaments, such as the Canadian, Great Lakes and North American Championships were coming up, he was more than a little eager to try his hand competing against the big guns in the casting world. In the Great Lakes event, he opened eyes with his proficiency and skills, winning medals in all twelve accuracy and distance events in the "B" Class category, beating many other competitors who had been casting much longer than he.

The following year his interest in fishing grew to the point where he, along with a couple of partners, opened Barklay's, a fishing tackle and outdoor sporting goods shop[1] in Oshawa. Shortly thereafter, he then became a bass fishing pro and went on the bass pro-fishing circuit, making a name for himself in that facet of the angling world as well.

My wife, Sheila, is the hardest working fisherman that I know. Regardless of the weather conditions and the co-operation of the fish, it is a rare day when she wants to pack it in before the rest of us. She simply loves fishing and possesses a burning desire to do well even on those days when the trout seem to think otherwise.

Her determination and persistence is even more amazing when one realizes that because of her physical limitations, Sheila is not capable of reeling in her line—or playing her catch—as you or I would do. A disastrous Berry Aneurysm[2] that she suffered twenty years ago left her with partial paralysis on her left side and the complete loss of the use of her left arm and hand, as well as left-side neglect with her vision. She is unable to "see" left of centre without moving her head.

However, after tagging along with me as a spectator to various casting competitions, she firmly said one day as she admired the medal I had just won, "You know, I could do that—casting I mean. I want to win one of these things for myself!" And she asked me to show her how.

Pleased with her request, I told her so, realizing that she was getting bored and frustrated just watching everybody at these events. However, it hadn't occurred to me that she wanted to try casting herself as she would not be able to reel in her line. This was going to require some hard thinking on that angle, but I would see what I could devise.

The result was a brace that would be held in place on her left wrist and hand with Velcro straps. Rummaging around in my tournament casting equipment, I located a large butt guide, (the large bottom line guide on a fishing rod) then securely fastened it on the front of the brace. Using a spin-cast reel she would be able to make her casts then reel the line in by placing the reel handle into the guide and cranking her entire rod. Although certain that the system and rig would work sufficiently for her to participate and even use for fishing, I had doubts that she would have sufficient strength in her good arm to allow her to perform with the outfit for more than a couple of casts.

I should never have underestimated her resolve and persistence. Within a year or two, Sheila was winning medals in tournaments all over the place, including the North American Championships, where she set a record in the Ladies' Spinning Distance discipline of almost two hundred feet. In addition she was not only accompanying me on fishing trips but outfishing me more often than not. The most amazing thing about Sheila's casting though is the determination she displays with the hours spent on the practice targets. She is usually the first to begin and it is almost impossible to convince her that a little rest is every bit as important as the actual practice. She can bang away

Sheila Deval proudly displays the medals she won at the Long Beach, California, National Championships in 1998.

at the targets by the hour. That same tenacity is also apparent when we are fishing and quitting before dark is inexcusable in her mind.

Although some of Sheila's successes on the tournament trail have provided me with wonderful memories, the truly magical ones have more to do with her fishing accomplishments. Mentioned earlier was the time when she skunked her old man, me, and caught the largest speckled trout of the weekend, five-and six-pounders, as well as seven of the total of twenty-nine caught by eight of us on a club trip to A/B Lake one weekend.

Her first sortie into the difficult world of steelhead trout fishing, the powerful migratory rainbows that run the rivers flowing into the Great Lakes, provided her and myself, of course, with a permanent memory. I would hesitate to deem the Beaver River, at least that portion of the river that enters Georgian Bay below the town of Thornbury, a magical water, but for a couple of months in the spring and then again in the fall, it probably does deserve the title.

When the big rainbows leave the depths of Georgian Bay at that time to run the rivers flowing into it, the Beaver comes alive with the excitement of hundreds of fishermen hoping to catch one of these silver warriors. Often the banks of the half mile or so of water that is fishable from the dam to the lake are so lined with fishermen that they must take turns to present their lures or roe bags.[3] As drifting roe bags or worms seems to be the standard lure for the majority of folks fishing for steelheads, anglers wishing to fish with artificial lures must place their casts accurately or suffer the wrath of the drift fishermen, those fellows floating their baits through the current, rather than casting and retrieving them and whose lines seem to cover the river like a net at times.

My wife is an expert caster though, and once it was pointed out to her that she would have to time her casts and place them between the drifters' lines, she had no trouble. Because there is so much debris and heavy snagged line fouling the riverbed, it is necessary to avoid fishing the bottom or it quickly becomes an expensive proposition with your lures donated to the layer of garbage. We had both managed to get in a few casts without attracting the ire of the drift fishers when suddenly the quiet setting came alive with a fresh-run silver steelhead rainbow leaping all over the place in the pool we were fishing. Demonstrating their good sportsmanship, most of the drifters promptly reeled in to allow the lucky angler freedom to play the fish unheeded by all the lines. Fascinated by the aerial acrobatics of the rainbow that had to be at least ten pounds, I had not noticed that the "lucky angler" was my wife, Sheila.

Her yells for help finally woke me up, when I realized that the powerful trout might be more than she could handle on her own. However I was reluctant to take the rod and play the fish for her and simply offered her verbal encouragement, "Just hang on and try to pump it in when you can. Don't try to reel it in—you'll just twist the line. Remember, you can only reel line in when you pump the rod and gain a little slack."

My advice was a waste of time because the trout had other ideas. Shouts came from across the narrow river, the other fishermen cursing me for not helping her.

"It's her fish—let her have the fun of playing it!" I yelled back.

Sheila seemed on the verge of tears as her trout decided that it had indeed had enough of the pool and took off like a jet downstream for Georgian Bay. The fish was so strong that the clutch on her spinning reel gave out and the wrist brace that her reel handle was firmly planted in while playing the fish, was yanked right off her wrist. The big steelhead cartwheeled out of the water one more time before exiting the pool completely. The lure came out of its jaw. Examining it later, I saw that one of the tines on the treble hook was broken off, another was bent completely out of shape and the third that had been bravely holding the fish was almost straightened out completely.

Sheila now was crying and her frustrations boiled over when she accused me of not helping her when she needed it. It was a beautiful fish and she had really wanted it. Not only had I been reprimanded by the other fishermen on the river, but now by my wife, Sheila, as well. To the best of my ability I explained that I was hoping that the fish would have tired eventually if her brace had not been ripped off, and then she would have been able to bring it in on her own. That way she could truly say that she had caught it all by herself. Wiping away the remaining tears, she somewhat reluctantly agreed and nodded affirmatively. As she often recalls the experience, it's obvious that the memory of that majestic cart-wheeling rainbow trout has not dimmed for Sheila. However, it has been overshadowed several times with other Georgian Bay rainbows that she has hooked, played to a standstill without help and kept to be deliciously prepared in our smoker.

One of these, a muscular eight-pounder, was hooked while trolling near the mouth of the Big Head River and, by the time it was boated almost an hour later, our little car-top boat had been towed and blown several miles out into the open water of Georgian Bay. The fascinating memory for me of that occasion had nothing to do with Sheila's fishing prowess, but the small flotilla of boats that followed our progress out into the vast blue bay while she played her catch. These men seemed enthralled with the idea that a woman with only the use of her right arm could fight a big fish for such a long time. Because she was playing the trout cautiously, not wanting to lose it as she had when the Beaver River steelhead tore the brace off her arm, she was not rushing it but trying to force the fish into surrendering. That created the impression for the other fishermen in the boats tracking us and monitoring her progress that the trout had to be a great deal larger than what we yelled to them. Since then, her indomitable spirit has soared several times when she conquered other large Georgian Bay rainbows—without my help!

Georgian Bay and several of the tributary streams flowing into it has provided other innumerable thrills and recollections for me, with the earliest being when I was fourteen or fifteen years old when Uncle Bob took me out on the big water in a charter fishing boat to troll for lake trout. It is a large body of water that could easily be considered as one of the Great Lakes, but actually is a smaller section of giant Lake Huron. Ask anyone who has fished or boated on Georgian Bay and their response invariably includes comments about the clarity and beautiful blue tint to its waters.

When my uncle took me on that memorable outing I had no idea of the style of fishing that we would be doing. Having already achieved a modicum of competence with my spinning and fly-casting equipment, I was taken aback when the captain of the charter boat that my uncle had hired indicated that my "stuff" would not be needed as I would be fishing with the gear he had on board. That gear, I soon discovered, was a strange-looking apparatus consisting of a huge pulley-type arrangement, loaded with miles of heavy braided copper wire. An enormous wabler was fastened on the business end and once the lure and wire was hand-fed out far enough to reach the depth that the captain deemed correct for lake trout, a bell was somehow fastened to the wire line near the terminal end.

"When you hear the bell clanging, son," he said, "just grab the handle on the big 'reel' and wind it in. When you get your fish alongside the boat, I'll net it for you."

The net referred to looked big enough to envelop my uncle's car in its mesh. To me, the style of fishing seemed inappropriate and unsporting and whether we were to catch fish or not, rather unpleasant when compared to fishing with the light equipment I was accustomed to using. Our "lines" were set as instructed and we simply sat and waited for the bells to clang. We did not have long to wait and soon we had several fat ten-pound lake trout in the ice-cooler on board. My memory of that "fishing" experience would hardly fit the general intent of this book had it not been for what transpired the fourth or fifth time the bell rang on the line on my side of the big boat.

With several other previous efforts to wind fish in with the giant pulley-reel having failed when, with no rod to absorb its attempts to get free, the fish had simply broken free from the big wabler, the excitement waned to the point where I became rather casual to the winding-in procedure. That changed dramatically when a big, silver slab of trout began performing cartwheels almost a hundred yards behind the boat. The copper fishing line glistened in the sunshine during the aerial acrobatics.

The captain, who previously had barely slowed his boat to allow us to reel in the lake trout, took the craft almost to a halt and yelled, "That's a rainbow trout, son. You don't want to lose that one. There's not too many of them around and they're damn fine fish to eat, too. Wind it in slow." "*You mean, slowly,*" I almost said.

With the boat now drifting sideways in the wind, the other "lines" were cranked in to prevent tangling and, using my hands rather than the big winding mechanism to cushion the trout's lunging histrionics, the gorgeous rainbow was soon carefully drawn alongside. Then, wrapped in the giant net, it was hoisted aboard. That fish was the first rainbow trout that I had ever seen.

That was back in the mid-forties and the 'bows had just begun appearing this far away from where they had initially been stocked in the Sault St. Marie area from brood stock imported from British Columbia.[4] Since then, of course, with the rainbows multiplying dramatically throughout the entire Great Lakes system, my buddies and I have had the pleasure of doing battle with more appropriate tackle with thousands of these wonderful combatants, both on the big waters of Georgian Bay and many of its feeder rivers.

One of those occasions involves Little Ollie. Oliver Johnson first appeared, although perhaps "appeared" is the wrong word as he could barely be seen through the pile of fly-tying equipment and my fishing books, in front of the booth that our club was operating at the Toronto Sportsman Show almost twenty years ago. Busy throwing Despair flies together for the up-coming fishing season, I didn't notice him standing in front of the table, the top of his head hardly visible. But when I discerned a little voice above the general din of the show politely asking, "Are you Mister Deval, sir?"

I stood and looked around. When I replied affirmatively that I was, he asked if it would be possible for him to cast with our club on the platform over at the pool. Seemingly someone had told him that he could, but only if he belonged to a casting club. And almost immediately he politely asked the cost of membership in our club.

Now I am not a big man, not quite five-and-a-half feet tall, but here was this little wisp of a boy who could not have weighed more than sixty pounds inquiring about casting and joining our club. Needless to say, I was speechless, but only for a moment as his mother who had been standing nearby and listening intently, moved behind her son and supported her son's request. She indicated that he had some of his own equipment that his father had purchased for him, and reinforced the expectation that whatever dues were required, she would pay if he were allowed to join our club.

Still somewhat stunned by the little fellow's diminutive appearance and the manner in which he conducted himself, I nevertheless responded immediately. I did not wish to miss this opportunity to witness what appeared to be shaping up as an exciting situation. Reaching across the table to shake his hand, I welcomed him to our club and asked his name and his age.

"It's Oliver, sir…Oliver Johnson. My friends call me Ollie and I'm ten, but I'll be eleven in a couple of months. Is that old enough, Mr. Deval?"

I replied without hesitation that his age was not a problem and that we would love to have him join our club. I told him and his mother that the club had had several lads even younger than he in past years. When I offered him the use of one of the spinning outfits we had in the booth, he continued to astound me, saying he preferred to use his own, and proceeded to show me his fly rod, passing a rod case to me to look at. It was a full size five-weight fly rod and I facetiously inquired if he had a line and reel to match. Attempting to mask the incredulous tone in my voice, I asked if he could cast.

"Of course! I prefer fly casting to using spinning tackle." he replied, proudly.

His mother gave me the information we required and the money for Ollie's dues to join our club. I then trotted him over to the platform to see what he could do with his fly-casting equipment. As we walked towards the casting pool, I thought of the competition coming up in about an hour. There was a Junior Division for kids under sixteen in the plug accuracy, but unfortunately there was no Junior Division in the fly accuracy event. He would have to compete against the men and women in either the "A" or "B" Class Division if he wanted to participate in the fly game. When I made this suggestion he continued to astound me by suggesting he would like to try them both, but thought he should cast the fly accuracy in the "B" Class. He had watched some of the men practising at hitting the targets and thought he could do it. With my brain still reeling, I simply suggested we should see what he could do first.

I helped the little fellow, all four-feet tall, onto the casting platform and along with everyone else watching in the area was fascinated by the aplomb and competence he displayed with his fly rod. Before the afternoon was complete, Ollie had collected the first place trophy in the "B" Class Dry Fly Accuracy event and a second or third place award in the quarter-ounce Spinning Accuracy contest. All the competitors he faced in both events had previously had considerable competitive experience.

Within a few months I had taken Ollie with us to a number of competitions in Canada and in the United States and he won medals and trophies in all of them. He also fished with some of the other folks in our club, tied flies and accompanied my grandson, Jason and me on several camping and fishing trips, even assisting me with my maple syrup operation. Little Ollie was truly a quite precocious lad. I learned from his mother that although he had just reached his eleventh birthday, he was conducting nature art classes for older youngsters at the Royal Ontario Museum. During one of our spring fishing and sap-collecting trips, he came back to the cabin to report that he had been observing a "yellow-bellied sapsucker," a bird that because of its unusual name I had always assumed to just be fodder for a comedian's jokes. Ollie insisted, however, that he had seen one on the tree above the maple syrup pots and knew precisely what it was. He pleaded with me to come and see it for myself.

Of course, I went out and saw my first ever, positively identified by an expert, yellow-bellied sapsucker! Little Ollie then inquired what my favourite bird was—other than ducks and geese. I replied that it would be a toss-up between loons and cardinals. A couple of weeks later his mother drove him up to our house and he presented me with two incredibly lovely oil paintings done on birch bark, one each of a loon and a cardinal. Unfortunately, I never did find out why he had said, "Other than ducks and geese."

Obviously there are a great many other memories involving Little Ollie, but the one that initially moved me to write about this truly exceptional

Ollie Johnson engaging in serious conversation with Gord at a little cabin in Haliburton in 1992.

young man occurred on a club-fishing trip to the Big Head River that flows into Georgian Bay in the Town of Meaford. Ollie's mom had called me the evening before we were to leave and reported that she wouldn't be bringing her son up the next morning to go fishing with us. Ollie had told her that the only boots he had, a pair of kid's customary black rubber boots, were not suitable for wading with in the river that he would be fishing in with us. I told them that I had an extra pair of chest waders that he could use and that I would somehow tie and fasten them on the young man so that he would be able to fish the river. Using one of our wading staffs, he would then be able to safely negotiate the stiff current. I assured his mom that we would all be keeping an eye on Ollie, as well, at all times. She need not have worried. Her son once again displayed his competence in all things to do with fishing.

Looking like some sort of apparition from outer space, almost completely ensconced in the vastly over-sized chest waders, with several extra pairs of socks to fill the feet of the boots so he could walk, he declined the suggestion that he fish from shore rather than attempt to cope with the steep current any more than absolutely necessary. Then, within an hour or so after he and I began fishing, he hooked and landed two rainbow trout in the four to six-pound class. One was released, the other fastened to the stringer on my belt for him to take home to his mother.

A little later when the other fellows who had left us to move way upriver came grumpily back to report "there are no fish in the river," he put on a show that I will never forget. As I hoisted the stringer to display Little Ollie's catch, he emitted a man-sized yelp, and in his excitement momentarily forgot his good manners and addressed me by my first name. "Wow! I've got a big one on this time, Gord! Oops," he added, "I'm sorry about that, Mr. Deval—but this is a really big fish!"

It was obvious to all of us that he was into a big chinook salmon as we hustled out into the current, not to help him play his fish, but only to grab and keep a firm hold onto the back of his waders to make sure the salmon didn't pull him off his feet. The chinook, charging all over the river, looked larger and heavier than Little Ollie's sixty or seventy pounds, but he played the big fish with all the patience and skill of an older and much more experienced angler, using the spinning rod and the reel's slipping clutch to his advantage to control the fish perfectly.

The chinook, not Ollie, tired in fifteen minutes or so and was led into the shallows by the young man. There with the assistance of his fellow club members, it was hoisted for several photographs before being carefully placed back into the swim as per Ollie's request. Although his salmon, estimated to weigh about twenty-two pounds, certainly weighed less, it seemed almost as big as the young fisherman. The pictures of him and his great catch continue to hold a prominent place in one of our club fishing albums.

Ollie with his "really big fish."

Sadly for us and apparently also for Ollie, we subsequently heard that he had to move to Connecticut with his father who had gained permanent custody when his parents broke up. We did correspond with each other for a year or so, but then unfortunately lost track of him, but the very special memories of our experiences with Little Ollie are etched enduringly in my brain—and in my heart.

Chapter 15

The Trout of Loughborough Lake

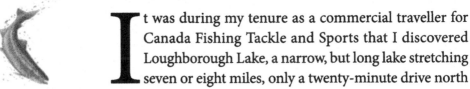

It was during my tenure as a commercial traveller for Canada Fishing Tackle and Sports that I discovered Loughborough Lake, a narrow, but long lake stretching seven or eight miles, only a twenty-minute drive north of Kingston, Ontario. It is actually two large bodies of water connected by a three-mile narrow stretch which could almost be deemed a river. It served up a number of memorable moments for me, several of which are deserving of inclusion here.

The first to come to mind occurred during a spring sales trip when I made an unscheduled stop at a highway bridge that crosses the lake at its narrowest point, midway in the river. I had taken a shortcut from my previous visit to a couple of shops in the village of Sharbot Lake and, as was always the case in those early days of my being on the road, could not continue on without making a couple of perfunctory casts from the corner of the bridge. My spinning outfit, always at the ready, was equipped with a fairly heavy bucktail jig, the perfect lure for making exploratory casts in what appeared to be fairly deep water with a substantial current. The jig was allowed to sink to the bottom, but before I could begin its customary, bouncing and erratic retrieve, it was picked up by a lunker lake trout.

I clambered down the end of the bridge and eventually worked it into the shallows, then dragged it up the shore. By the time I hoisted it with both hands to show it off to the handful of others who had stopped and parked their cars to see what all the fuss was about, the crowd had grown ten-fold. It included a Provincial Police car with a couple of cops who were valiantly attempting to break up the crowd on the bridge and get the traffic rolling once again.

It became obvious why that fish had left the depths of the lake to swim up the comparatively shallow "river," when it began disgorging smelts, some of which were still alive, the moment it was lifted from the water. It had moved upriver to feast on the spring bounty of the annual smelt run. Before I could escape to my car with my "prize," someone stopped me and pointed out a reporter from the local newspaper rushing towards me to do a story on my "catch." "He'll probably want pictures, too," he added.

All this fuss over a twenty-pound fish, about half the size of the huge lakers we had caught previously in Muskoka! I was rather startled at all the attention, but realized later on after the reporter left and I continued into town, the discovery of a trout caught just a healthy stone's throw up Division Street, one of Kingston's main thoroughfares would be unusual. The next day a picture and story was on the front page of the *Kingston Whig-Standard*, the city's principal newspaper.

What the folks who stopped to watch the excitement and the reporter who covered the event seemed to find fascinating was that I had not been dressed in a typical fisherman's gear, but in my working business clothes— tie, jacket, street shoes and all. Of course it was not unusual for me in those days on the road to stop and test my luck at pretty well every promisingly attractive stream and body of water that I happened upon.

As I still had several days to go before completing my customary, two-week sales trip into Eastern Ontario, the big trout was spirited into the hotel room after I checked in. Using two or three newspapers, I managed to eviscerate and clean it up without too much mess. The big trout's stomach contents included twenty-eight smelts. Before I could be caught with the "evidence" of the unusual hotel-room project, the leftovers and papers were surreptitiously carried out in a trash bag and deposited in a garbage bin at the rear of the building. The next day, the big lake trout was given to one of my clients on the first call made that morning.

As soon as I got home a couple days later, I rounded up a few of my buddies and the next day we headed back to Kingston hoping to locate other laker trout that might be making the upriver trip to gorge on the smelt run. Of course we were all armed with an assortment of lures resembling smelts, but to hedge our bets, we also had an abundant supply of smelts with us, purchased from a Loblaws grocery store before we left home.

That turned out to be a hectic weekend! One that we will all remember. Although the cottage season was not yet underway, we managed to locate a camp owner who was willing to rent us a cottage big enough for our eight-man crew, While most of us were unloading the car, unpacking gear and readying the sleeping quarters, two of the fellows meandered down to the dock dragging a couple of the car-tops down the slope behind them. Whether it would be necessary to have the boats with us to fish from for the weekend was about to become a moot point.

After they slid the boats into the water and tied them to the dock, they returned to the cars and rummaged around the pile of gear yet to be taken in to the cottage until they located their fishing tackle. A little further investigation and they soon discovered which of the three big Coleman coolers held the food—and more importantly, the packages of smelts. Lines were rigged and the big baits were unceremoniously tossed out on weighted lines to allow them to sit on the river bottom without being washed inshore by the heavy current.

They then rejoined the rest of us to continue readying the cottage for our visit, but a yell from one of the other fellows put them both in full flight and racing back down the hill to the dock. One of the rods fastened to the side of the dock had come loose and it looked as though a trout or something was about to take off with it. It was then that the fun and games really began. They did manage to get there before the rod slid completely off the dock and a few minutes later proudly held up a fine eight-pounder for those of us looking out the kitchen window to see. In short order, there were three or four other rods rigged in the same manner, each with a whole smelt and fastened to the dock in a variety of ways. By evening after a giant pot of chilli had been consumed, three more trout had been caught, with one, a twelve-pounder kept and cleaned to take home for the smoker. Of course, it provided even further evidence that these lake trout, well away from the depths of the main lake and out of their normal element, were quite content to be pigging out in a completely different environment, the shallow waters of the Loughborough narrows.

During the evening poker game we came to the conclusion that, although it was fun and there was always the chance of tying in to a really big fish like the one I had caught off the bridge a few days earlier, it was deemed that it would be even more pleasurable if we could catch these big trout on artificial lures rather than packaged smelt. Up and at 'em early the next day, two of the fellows had tackle set up on the dock before breakfast while the others readied the boats, motors and tackle to do battle at the mouth of the river where it enters the main body of the lake. The prevailing feeling assumed that the trout probably staged there before moving up the river in pursuit of the smelts.

We all caught trout. It was one of the most memorable fishing trips that I have ever participated in with perhaps twenty-five or thirty lakers in all providing heart-stopping action. The fish averaged eight to ten pounds with the largest, kept for the chap's wall, registering twenty-four pounds on the scales. Although a number of the trout were caught on the smelts, many were also seduced into striking a wide variety of lures such as Rapalas, Crocodiles and others resembling the smelts that the trout found so alluring.

Loughborough Lake is now a pet project for the Ontario Ministry of Natural Resources.[1] The legal date to fish for its lake trout was pushed back a couple of months to allow the trout more time to finish their spring fest on the smelt run. They could then retreat safely into the depths of the big lake were they would not be as susceptible to an angler's offerings as they were in the cold, shallower waters of the narrows in spring-time. Loughborough's lakers are also stripped of their eggs and milk in the fall during their spawning run for the rearing ponds operated by the Ministry.

That stop that I made, way back then on the bridge over Loughborough's magical narrow waterways to toss a jig in on an investigative cast, will always remain a prominent memory.

Chapter 16

Lake Simcoe: A Most Fishable Body of Water

I have written about my first catch of brook trout near Uxbridge, my first browns caught in the Ganaraska and recognized the Georgian Bay water as producing the first rainbow for me. This section, representing a very early memory, recalls the first lake trout I ever caught.

Once again my Uncle Bob, who, as you have probably already deduced, figured in much of my early fishing career, is once again involved. It was 1946 and he had just sold a car to a fellow who owned a cottage along Oro Beach on the shore of Lake Simcoe. I was sixteen and already well established as one of my uncle's fishing buddies. One day in early May he called and asked if I would like to go fishing for lake trout with him to Lake Simcoe. Never declining an offer like this, I, of course, accepted but expressed concern regarding proper equipment. I only had my fly-fishing and casting equipment.

He dismissed my concern as he had in his possession a couple of deep water trolling outfits and I would be welcome to use one. But more importantly, he thought the coldness of their water in early Spring could mean that the trout might not be too deep. If we were lucky, we might find them poking around some of the shallower shoals looking for a feed of perch or something. He suggested that I bring my casting rod and stuff.

The fellow who had bought the car from my uncle had given him directions to his cottage and told him that he was welcome to use one of the boats he had tied up to his dock, but that he should bring along his own outboard motor. However, once we were out on the lake and had the copper wire outfits set up with huge Canoe spoons (actually shiny seven-inch metal wablers) attached, Uncle Bob discovered that he was unable to get his old motor to slow sufficiently for proper trolling with the heavy tackle. After a frustrating half an hour of fiddling with the thing and running out of his repertoire of cuss words, he gave up. We were simply going to have to use it the way it was. But he had an idea. We would troll just one of the big rigs and hang on to it in case some foolish trout was fast enough to catch up to the damn thing and hit the spoon. I, however was to cast a plug on an angle out ahead of the boat so that it would manage to sink a little before I began working it in.

"You did tell me that you could cast more than a hundred feet now, didn't you?" he asked. "Well let's see what you can do today. Okay, kiddo?"

I had an old plug in my tackle box called a Deep Diving Heddon River Runt[1] that I though might get down deep enough to entice a trout even with the boat moving much more quickly than was desirable. Proceeding to cast, according to my uncle's suggestion, we trolled around for several hours and got nothing for our efforts but sunburn and sore arms until Uncle Bob's rod was almost jerked out of his hand. He cut the motor immediately and swore that we were caught on a shoal.

The wind was blowing us back in the direction the fouled copper wire was indicating while he cranked the big reel. I took advantage of the situation to cast and allow the River Runt plug to sink towards bottom so that it could be worked in on the retrieve much more erratically than was possible when we were trolling at high speed. I had learned years earlier that a lure

Bob Wilcox, "Uncle Bob," fishing on Lake Simcoe in 1946.

worked in variable fashion is considerably more attractive to a fish than one that is simply tossed out and reeled in.

Even before my uncle could position the boat to free his lure from the rocky shoal, a lake trout smashed into my plug and surged in powerful fashion towards the depths in the middle of the big lake. The ensuing tug-of-war and give and take with that lake trout that turned out to tip the scales at sixteen pounds was not only my first ever with the species, but by far the largest fish of any kind I had caught up to that time, surpassing a twelve-pound muskie I had caught two years earlier when I was fourteen years old.

A couple of lovely five-pound bass, a smallmouth and a largemouth, already graced the walls in our recreation room. Now thanks to my uncle's kind offer, my first ever lake trout, although eventually dwarfed by the two monster lake trout caught in Muskoka Lake, is still on the wall beside them. Lake Simcoe produced many other powerful lakers for my sons and me over the years.

But before I tell you about another trip there, I must pass on a little more information about this wonderful body of water. Lake Simcoe, less than an hour's drive from potentially five million people, a very large per cent-age of them anglers, must be considered one of the premier large bodies of fishable water in Canada. Simcoe is home to more than a hundred species of fish in all, from sturgeon to sticklebacks including most of the game species to be found elsewhere in Ontario. Regularly producing smallmouth bass up to and over six pounds, pike to twenty, whitefish to seven and lake trout to twenty-five, the lake is popular because of its easy accessibility and superb fishing with the millions of American anglers just across the border from where we live in Toronto. It also supports a fabulous winter ice-fishing season for the hard-water anglers, producing buckets of perch, crappie, smelts, to go along with many limit catches of fat whitefish, lake trout and pickerel. In winter the lake is dotted with as many as five thousand ice-fishing huts, many of which are private as well as those available for rent from commercial operators ringing the shoreline from east to west and south to north.

Simcoe is a big lake with a surface area of well over five hundred square miles and depths exceeding a hundred and twenty feet in places. It does have several islands, Snake, Fox, Georgina, Thorah and Strawberry, and numerous shoals that we fish for lake trout before the water temperature rises and the perch and smelts move elsewhere. One of the most repeated memories of fishing this magical water, is the story of what happened to me on that second outing when we were making our lake trout fishing movie.

Twelve-year-old Ron Deval with a twelve-pound laker and a twelve-pound pickerel caught in Lake Simcoe.

Usually Randy, my younger son, or along with his brother Ron, would accompany me on the majority of my fishing jaunts that spring, but for one reason or another, probably hockey practice, neither could go on the day when I wanted to add footage to the movie I was making. I was planning on spending the morning up at the lake fishing near a familiar shoal. I felt there should be a good chance of getting into some of Simcoe's big lakers that were probably also heading there, intending to reduce the lake's enormous smelt population. They move up from the depths in the spring to feed on the perch and smelts on the shallow water shoals before retreating as the water warms.

It was really a wild idea to begin with, but when conceived, it seemed that if it worked some interesting film could be the result. The plan was to mount the movie camera on a tripod, set it up in the front of the car-top boat and aim it at me in the rear, the intention being to capture on film what fishing for the lake's big lake trout by oneself is all about. I would simply have to reach forward to trip the camera's switch when ready to record. All was working splendidly as I shot a variety of footage including close-ups of fastening and adjusting the lure to maximize its action in the water, the utter relaxation while stretched out and trolling, as well as a little of the action experienced when playing the lakers. All this was topped up with shots of vanquished trout being raised aloft for the *coup de gras* after each battle. Although awkward, it proved to be a workable scheme and a fair amount of film was shot. Of course there would have to be considerable editing before being completed later on.

A new film canister had been inserted in the camera and a couple of fifteen-pound fish had already been landed when my "relaxation" was rudely disturbed by a particularly savage strike. Large fish like these lakers do not normally smash a lure like a rainbow trout or muskie would, but simply latch on to it and move off casually with their "prey" until the lucky angler strikes hard to set the hook firmly in their jaw. The unexpected ferocity of the strike so disturbed the tranquility of the scene that I momentarily lost my cool and leapt forward from an almost prone position to activate the camera, completely ignoring the tripod's somewhat tenuous perch on the aluminum floor in the front of the boat. Because of the shallow waters that were being fished I had been trolling with a much shorter line than one normally would, the lure bouncing along near bottom only forty or fifty feet behind the boat. Splash!!!

"Oh no! Damn," I yelled out to the sky above, "there goes my bloody camera—and the film along with it!"

While I was furiously trying to regain slack line that had occurred when the trout had struck and rushed towards the boat, out of the corner of my eye I saw the feet of the tripod as the camera descended, head first to the bottom. Fortunately, while continuing to play the trout, I had enough presence of mind to look about me in all directions to triangulate my bearings, just in case that I was somehow going to be able to retrieve the camera with its precious film. However, the chances of either being able to survive the dunking seemed minuscule at that moment. The trout, a muscular eighteen-pounder was subsequently whipped then released with a cuss word or two in its direction for the part it had played in the camera's deep-sixing.

Later, on the half-hour drive home, it occurred to me that I had a client, Gerry Leuden, who owned a sporting goods store in Scarborough and was a scuba diving enthusiast—in fact he was the president of the Scarborough Scuba Divers Association. In previous conversations with him I learned that these folks were always on the lookout for a different reason to stage one their club's underwater forays, whether it be to retrieve an outboard motor that had not been fastened correctly then flipped off a boat fifty feet from the dock, to unclog an underwater line to a cottage, or to search for an assumed drowned person.

I wondered if Gerry and his buddies would be interested in attempting to retrieve my errant movie camera from the bottom of big Lake Simcoe. I need not have given it a second thought. Once I had explained to him the next day what had happened, then answered a few questions to his satisfaction, he assured me that they would jump at the opportunity. His main concern was whether I would be able to place the divers anywhere close to the camera's location. When I stated that I would also take my own boat out and anchor right were I believed it went in and would guarantee that it would be within a fifty-foot circle of where I was anchored, he asked incredulously how I could make a promise like that, with Simcoe's being such a big lake. I assured him that after fishing this location, a shoal half a mile off the shore of Snake Island for at least twenty-five years I was able to triangulate the boat's position, using Snake and Fox Island, along with a buoy positioned at one end of the shoal.

I also informed him that I knew the lake bottom there, too, almost as well as I knew the basement floor in my house. Searching wasn't going to take place in weeds or muck, as the shoal consists mostly of assorted rocks and boulders interspersed with the odd sand bed. All in all, it should be easy to find.

He then asked me why I even bothered when obviously the camera would be beyond repair and the film it contained, useless. I had already heard the same story from a chap in a camera shop located in the same mall as Gerry's store, Argosy Sports. But for me, even if it seemed foolish to others, the possibility of retrieving even a part of the film would be worth it to me. As for the camera, it was insured. There was just that possibility that the water hadn't totally filled the case or the film canister. Besides, this was an excuse for them to go diving. He agreed with that and made a few phone calls while I was still in his shop then suggested that we meet the next day at Willow Beach.

At eight the next morning, I sat fidgeting with my tackle in the car-top at the dock while anxiously looking back up the road leading to the public dock. With a half an hour still to go, several cars pulled up behind mine on the road and at least a half a dozen men and women, all carrying wet suits and diving paraphernalia descended the stairs to the dock and introduced themselves to me. Someone said that Gerry and the others would be along momentarily, having realized that it would be too difficult to launch the diving barge at this stop with those steps. Hence they had gone up to the marina to put it in there.

I had no idea what they were talking about, but a few minutes later I heard the drone of a powerful motor then saw the "barge" coming around

Members of the Scarborough Scuba Diving Association searching for Gord's movie camera in the waters of Lake Simcoe.

the corner of the shoreline towards the dock. The divers all began pulling on their wet suits and checking the regulators on their tanks. Gerry explained that they used the barge for most of their diving excursions because it had all the equipment aboard that they might need, such as compressors, extra tanks and so on.

I headed out towards the island with the big barge following. Although there was more scepticism than optimism among the folks when we were waiting at the dock, understandably so when looking out at the huge lake, there was considerable camaraderie apparent amongst the club members that augured well for the success of the mission. After I dropped anchor then indicated to the folks on the barge parked nearby that the camera and tripod would most certainly be somewhere within a hundred foot circle of my car-top, they began slipping, one by one, into the still cold water. This was early May and with the ice being off the lake only a couple of weeks, the water temperature was approximately a heart-stopping forty-four degrees Fahrenheit. The divers would not have been able to perform the search if they had not been wearing scuba diving wet suits.

Deciding it was prudent to not do any casting with people cruising around, near and beneath my boat, I busied myself instead by taking 35 mm pictures of the entire exercise. No more than five minutes transpired, when fortunately I happened to be focused on a trail of bubbles popping to the surface. They indicated the progress of the diver whom I felt was most likely to be in the immediate proximity of my missing movie camera. I snapped the photo of what followed; one that highlighted this entire magical memory experience.

The bubbles gave way to a bulge in the surface water as the "lost" movie camera emerged, breaking the surface and still attached, of course, to the tripod, triumphantly clutched in the hand of one of the female divers in the "search and rescue" crew. Only thirty feet or so from me, she yelled in my direction, "Heh, Gord, is this the thing we're looking for?"

Okay! However this memory does not finish here. It has an even more remarkable finale! I thanked Gerry and his club members, who were somewhat disappointed with the exercise ending so abruptly after it began, then made a special show of appreciation to the young lady who actually located and retrieved the errant movie camera. It was then taken to a dealer to determine whether it was feasible to have it repaired and to also remove the film canister that I planned to take directly to the Kodak plant in Weston. The camera was deemed worthless as it would cost more to repair than it would to replace it with a new one. Once armed with the dealer's name and other information, I completed and submitted an insurance claim. At the Kodak plant I was told much the same story. After I explained what had happened at the lake and that I wondered if there could still be useable footage, the clerk at the counter exclaimed, "You've got to be kidding, man!"

Amazingly, the camera, still attached to the
tripod, was retrieved.

Tossing the canister back and forth between his hands, he said it would have been totally ruined by the water, but wondered how long it had been in the lake. I told him that it was there less than twenty-four hours, then asked if I could have a word with the manager of the technical department where film was processed. The fellow complied but assured me that I would receive the same answer.

Fortunately for me the technician who appeared shortly thereafter while I paced back and forth like an expectant father outside a hospital delivery room, was a fisherman. I had previously given our club business card to the clerk when I had first arrived at the service desk and holding it in his hand the gentleman dressed in a white lab gown inquired, "I see you're a fisherman, too, Mr. Deval. What can I do for you, sir?"

I told him the story, although it seemed like the hundredth time it had been related since the camera went for the "deep six." He confirmed what the clerk had said, that there was not much chance of my film having survived the dunking.

He also explained that all of their films are strung together and processed one after the other in an uninterrupted flow. If something were to happen to disturb the process, such as my film jamming the equipment (as it could if it got stuck together when it was wet or whatever) then a number of other films could also be ruined. They simply could not afford to let that happen.

Refusing to admit defeat, I continued to plead, wondering if it would be possible to put my film on the end of the line so that if it does jam the equipment, there would be no others to follow. Or, perhaps the film could be processed on its own after all the day's other films had been done. Even if there were only a few feet of film saved that could be used in the trout-fishing film I'd been working on, for me, it would be a fabulous ending to a great story and movie.

He laughed, and said that if I was willing to divulge where I was catching all these trout He personally would stay past closing time. When everyone in the lab had left, he would see what he could do with the film. I was to call him the next day. "Maybe we will be lucky," he added.

The film was processed and when I picked it up at the service counter the next day the clerk just shrugged and said, "No charge......I told you so. We don't charge for films that we can't process."

When I got home I opened up the specially wrapped film and discovered a brief note, obviously from the friendly technician who had worked overtime to process the still water-logged movie canister:

Dear Mr. Deval:

Well your idea did work, sort of. I was able to save almost half the exposed film and some of it's damned interesting as you'll discover. Now tell me, sir, when are we going fishing?

There was footage of several of the trout that had been caught previously, then an astounding piece of film taken by the camera as it tumbled from the boat towards the bottom of the lake and continued to run until it had been completely exposed. I have since shown this film to many friends and fishing clubs and when I explain what it is they are seeing, they are all amazed.

The bottom of the boat and the lines of rivets that seal the hull are easily spotted, undulating in appearance as the camera sank, while the really exciting scenes are a couple of brief shots of the trout that caused all the fuss as it cavorted beneath the boat in and out of the camera lens' field of view while it descended to the rocks below. Every time I see this film on the magical waters of Lake Simcoe, my memory is rekindled.

Chapter 17

I Always Wanted to Fish in a Stream Called Piss Creek

The first time I wet a line in this little brook, a feeder stream to the much larger Cavan Stream, west of Peterborough, I caught four or five small, but fat, brookies, keeping a couple to take home for the pan. They were caught on both sides of the highway bridge that crosses the stream without my having to leave the dry comfort of the bridge proper. Wishing I had my R & R (rough and ready) fishing clothes and boots with me, my mind was quickly made up to return as soon as possible to try my hand on the creek with the fly rod.

I am not sure how we tagged the stream with that obscene handle, but it might have been suggested by another old buddy of mine, Ron Duncan, when I asked him if he would like to try a little fly-fishing on a small creek that I found that looked like it was open enough to toss a fly around without having to worry too much about back casts hanging up in the bushes. He asked what it was called and when I replied, "Damned if I know, Ron. I saw it on my way back from a sales trip to Peterborough when I decided to take a different route. I looked it up on my maps at home and found it runs into Cavan Creek, or whatever. Do you want to call it that, or what?"

"Let's call it Piss Creek," he replied, "I always wanted to fish in a stream that was called that for some reason or another." Ronnie Duncan always was a little weird, but the name stuck and has been called that by my friends and me for almost fifty years now.

Although the name we tagged the stream with might be considered disparaging, the little creek's fishing potential never was—until the last few years, that is, with some houses being built on its pristine riverbanks, resulting in overexposure to live bait fishermen drowning worms. The Cavan Stream always contained substantial numbers of the much larger brown trout, with a few occasionally wandering into some of its tributaries like Piss Creek.

Most of these folks fishing the smaller waters were hoping to locate one of the big, out of their real element, browns, and fished with quite a bit heavier tackle than was necessary for the small stream. The result was that many of its more gullible brook trout fell victim to the proffered dew worms, big hooks and fishing outfits gradually annihilating the natural native brook trout stock.

An earlier chapter involving Blue Lake described a memory of a remarkable weekend of fishing its waters when we discovered that the lake's fish seemed to be on a suicidal binge. We were unable to keep them off our flies and lures. One after another beautiful speckled and lake trout tore into our offerings that weekend like there was no tomorrow and, although the fish were nowhere near the size of those in Blue Lake, Piss Creek was about to offer a similarly exciting action bonanza. Although much smaller, what these fish lacked in size when compared with Blue Lake's trout was easily offset with their enthusiasm.

Ronnie Duncan and I decided that we would test the waters of Piss Creek the following Sunday, with wet flies being his choice while I opted to fish dries.[1] At least we would begin in that fashion with the idea being it would be interesting to make a real effort to find which would be more rewarding on a small stream like this one. We had a couple of dollars riding on the outcome to make it more interesting and agreed that we would work the stream's pools alternatively, with one watching, while the other fished.

The specks, mostly six to nine inches with hardly any over ten, were ravenous and struck whatever was tossed in their direction, wet or dry, with Ron's eventual total of trout caught and released exceeding mine by about a dozen, ninety-two to my eighty. All were caught on flies with their barbs flattened to facilitate the live releases. It was easy to remember those numbers because, other than that fabulous Blue Lake trip, I had never, either before or since, experienced that kind of continuous angling action. Every pool and riffle that we fished produced at least one or two brookies, with some containing a half a dozen or more, all of which seemed to be on either a suicide bent, or so hungry that they were eager to snatch at any bit of fur and feather tossed in their direction. Whether it was my dry fly offerings floating on the surface, or Ron's underwater wets cast and fished, it did not seem to matter. Both were producing equally well until they became shredded by their constant abuse. By the time we had decided that "enough was enough," like eating too much fudge all at once, our respective fly boxes were decimated.

My buddies and I fished Piss Creek many times over the years since that magical memorable outing with much more normal results. Most days we were skunked or simply raised and caught enough brookies to make the outing interesting, but never again did the creek produce similar results to that memory of that first day of fishing the stream with Ronnie Duncan.

Obviously, the browns moving in from Cavan Stream and the over-exposure it experienced from the new folks moving into the new developments in the area slowly put Piss Creek on the back burner of our favourite trout streams. I last fished it a couple of years ago on opening day with Paul Kennedy. He had heard the story of that incredible first day of fly fishing on the creek several times and suggested we choose it for our opening day trout fishing endeavour. Paul and I had fished opening days for a number of years together and, of course, I agreed.

We fished several accessible spots on the tiny creek with nary a single speckled trout for our efforts. The outing was not without several thrills, however, including a nice brown trout that Paul kept for the pan and a frenetic rainbow that must have escaped from one of the private ponds newly built in the area. It danced around for almost ten minutes before it was calmed down and beached. A four-pounder that seemed considerably out of place in such a small stream, was nevertheless placed back in the swim to possibly generate *another* thrill on *another* day for *another* angler.

I will fish Piss Creek again, even if simply only in deference to the recollection of that initial exposure to that day's wondrous fishing!

Chapter 18

A Wonderful Lake With No Name

Wonderful, wonderful A/B Lake! So many memories exist of the many days, delightful and otherwise, spent on this magical water that it was difficult to choose which to recount. I decided to select those that, in my mind, were the best of the lot.

There are a couple of spring-fed lakes in Haliburton connected to each other by a narrow strip of land with about a hundred yards of water flowing from the upper lake, through a beaver dam on one side then into the slightly lower lake on the other side. Wishing to keep those lakes relatively anonymous we refer to them, not by their real names, but as one—A/B Lake. Although we have caught larger speckled trout and more of them elsewhere, there is a magical quality about A/B that differentiates it from all the other lakes that my sons, my buddies and I have worked over all these many years.

Interestingly enough, we have probably been skunked on A/B more often than we have actually caught fish. A couple of my fishing buddies, both expert anglers, Jim Lloyd and Paul Kennedy, spinning and fly fishing in the spring and summer months, ice fishing in the winter, fished the lake several times over a few years before they experienced any action at all for their efforts. Another fishing buddy, Ashok Kalle, who has also joined us on numerous fishing trips to A/B, has yet to produce so much as a hit from a brookie on his tackle. My largest on this water was a six-pounder caught on a fly in B Lake.

With so many other excellent places to wet a line within the same approximate distance (150 miles) from Toronto, we occasionally wonder why we head up north to work these waters so often—and we certainly visit them often. The answer lies somewhere within the following stories. This lake is an absolutely gorgeous body of water—occasionally the brookies go into a feeding frenzy and what appears to be a fishless lake one day, comes alive with action the next. With no cottages or whatever on the lake, and stocked regularly by our Ministry of Natural Resources, the trout seem to grow larger and more rapidly here than in most similar-sized lakes, producing specs for us in the six- and seven-pound category.

Prior to the seventies most of our lake fishing for brookies occurred in the Land O' Lakes area, but as the region began to become littered with cottages in even some of the more remote waters, my buddies and I did a little research on the Haliburton area. We quickly discovered that there were indeed as many trout lakes there as in our former favourite, Plevna to Ompah, stomping grounds. In addition, our inquiries turned up the information that brook trout in the six- and seven-pound class had been caught in several Haliburton lakes in recent years.

A couple of these trout showed up in the long defunct *Toronto Star* fishing contest.[1] Further investigative work then led us to what we now call A/B Lake. Initially, Pete Pokulok and I skidooed miles checking out several lakes in the northern reaches of Haliburton with the same real names as A/B—unfortunately, and as most fishermen are aware, there are only so many names for lakes to go around. For example, there are hundreds of Long Lakes, Clear Lakes and so on.

The lakes that Pete and I fruitlessly checked out were mostly barren, but my son, Randy and I decided to continue from where the earlier explorations left off. After running our Skidoos across several large lakes eventually

In the late 1900s A/B Lake was accessed by Skidoo. Note the helmets hanging in the trees.

we discovered our elusive lake. At first there were no signs that we were on the right track. Even though we were already several weeks into the ice-fishing season, there was not a single sign that the lakes had been fished since the season began on the first of January. No skidoo tracks, shore-dinner fire remnants or gads stuck in the snow existed to indicate that fishermen had been there and drilled holes in the ice!

Nevertheless, verification did not take long in arriving. Something seemed to suggest that this was the lake we had been searching for, so the hand augur was put to work and Randy carved the first hole in A/B Lake of the many thousands that we have cut there since that January day some thirty years ago. While I began drilling the next hole, Randy's buzzer was barely set in place when a trout nailed the bait, a golden shiner.

A three-pound speckled trout that, because of its being our first A/B Lake catch and one never knows perhaps the only one, was kept, photographed and cleaned on the spot to check its stomach contents,[2] then packed in snow to prevent its freezing solid. Fresh-caught fish will retain more moisture if treated in this manner, therefore maintaining their delectability for longer periods. Providing they are kept cold, on ice or refrigerated, trout treated this way are still delicious up to a week after they are caught. An example of this is the fact that most fish taken commercially in fresh or salt water are immediately packed in ice to retain their freshness, rather than simply freezing them. Once a fish is frozen it should be retained in that state until being readied for the pan and not refrozen unless absolutely necessary.

Before I had time to set my own buzzer in place, Randy had already enjoyed a second battle with another fat brookie which only being lip-hooked was given its freedom and put back in the swim to provide thrills for us, or another angler, on another day. On that introductory day of fishing A/B there were not a lot of trout caught, but every one of them was at least nineteen inches long and three pounds or larger.

A few days later, Randy, his wife Judy and I, trekked into the lake for a second go at its brookies, with similar results. A/B Lake was quickly assuring itself of a permanent place in my memory bank as magical water. A couple of weeks passed before we were able to test our luck again on A Lake. Even with five of us carving holes all over the small lake and even in its smaller adjacent cousin, B Lake, nary a single minnow was forfeited to the trout, all of which seemed to have totally disappeared. I had to endure a battery of derogatory comments aimed in my direction. We were experiencing the lake's obstinacy for the first time and soon learned that A/B Lake was a most unpredictable body of water to fish. One with moody trout displaying symptoms of lockjaw one day, then a few days later ready to strike at anything lowered into its depths. We did learn that on some of those days when they turned their noses up at our live bait offerings, they could occasionally be induced into striking a well-worked jigging lure.

Towards the end of that first ice-fishing season after some superb days filled with action, interspersed with days where the lake appeared devoid of trout, one of the most indelible moments in my memory occurred. Three buddies, Jack Wilkings, Donnie Allen, Pete Pokulok and I decided to make a final trip to the lake before the ice became too dangerous on the larger lakes that we had to traverse to reach its pristine waters. Several brookies that had tipped the pocket scales between five and six pounds were the biggest caught by our crew until that exceptional weekend.

We always fish for brook trout close to shore, believing that that is where they locate the bulk of their food—larvae, minnows and crawfish. Often the thickness of the ice being fished through is greater than the depth of the water beneath it. Towards the end of winter though we fish even closer. With the sun melting much of the snow along its banks there is an abundant supply of food for the trout in the shallow inshore waters, much of it being washed into the lake beneath the melting shore ice. That, along with the lake's smaller fish, minnows and sculpins attracted to the shoreline to forage there, provides an abundant feast for A/B's brookies.

With our lines being placed even more closely to shore than was our custom, some of them were situated in as little as eighteen inches of water beneath two feet of ice. Unlike many days on this magical lake where all the action seemed to be confined to one or two of our crew's efforts, it had been a productive day with everybody sharing the day's accomplishments and being rewarded accordingly. Most of the trout were released, with only a few that had taken the minnow too deeply or were bleeding, having being hooked in the gills being kept for the table.

At that time of year with the daylight hours gradually growing longer, we are able to leave our lines in and fish until well after five in the afternoon. A longer day, with more hours spent fishing, means a more tiring day and later arrival home. Pete had earlier moved one of his Fish O' Buzzer rigs further down the shoreline and adjacent to a rocky ledge that appeared to continue to the bottom underwater. "If there's a 'biggie' around here, today," he suggested as he pulled his rig, "it's probably a little further away from all the traffic we've been creating, walking up and down the ice over this shallow area." Fish cannot hear voices or sounds from the air above the ice or water but are notoriously spooky in their reactions to vibrations created in the water or ice surface that are foreign to them.

About a mile long and half a mile at its widest, A Lake is set between cliff-like shores on three sides with the fourth being where it empties into B Lake at the end of a shallow, rocky bay. Thus the sunlight, travelling from the shallow end of the lake to the tall cliff end at the other, soon disappears from sight. The sun had already passed behind the trees above the cliff. Darkness and colder temperatures would not be far behind. Only occasionally moving away from our campfire now to kick out the ice forming rather quickly over our respective fishing holes, the four of us were reluctant to venture far from the flickering flames and dying coals as the cold began to permeate our bone marrow. Pete, however, let out a whoop that woke us all from our lethargy, "Heh, did you hear that? It's my line, the far one!"

He hustled down the shoreline to play his "catch," most likely the last one of the ice-fishing season. The rest of us were reluctant to leave the weakening warmth of the fire until Pete yelled back to us to come and bring a flashlight. He added, "Something fucking big's on my line!"

We grabbed a couple of flashlights as daylight was now ebbing rapidly and took off to assist him and assess the situation. A problem had arisen. It seemed that Pete's big trout had swum under a log or something. It took at least thirty feet of line off the rig and now Peter couldn't move it at all, although he could still feel it on the end of the line.

Standing around, feeling helpless and at a loss for practical suggestions or even consoling words of advice, we were not much help. I did ask, however, "Have you tried that old trick of keeping the line taut, while tweaking it like a violin string with your fingers? That'll sometimes trigger a response from the fish and if you're lucky enough it'll free itself, swim back beneath the log the way it went under the first time, then you'll be able to play the damn thing."

Meanwhile our team joker, Jack, grinning from ear to ear, had wandered out in the direction and distance where Pete estimated the trout was. Looking as though he had gone crazy, he began violently jumping up and down a half a dozen times on the ice. "This ought to do the trick," he shouted back at Pete.

Meanwhile, Pete was not having success with tweaking the line and asked me to try. I was somewhat reluctant to even touch the line for fear it would break the moment I did, but Pete continued to plead with me as I stood over his position, hunched by the hole and rapidly losing any hope of resolving the predicament.

*Jack Wilkins of Toronto, now deceased, was part of the early
1990s ice-fishing foray to A/B Lake. Here Bob, the warden,
puts "the pinch" on Jack.*

A good half an hour had passed since the trout had triggered the buzzer
then ripped the line off Pete's rig, but when I held the still taut line between
my fingers it was obvious that the foolish fish was content to simply out-
wait Pete when actually it could easily have broken off with a firm wave of
its tail. As Pete had already indicated, you could feel vibrations coming from
the fish's undulating motions even though the line was obviously being held
tightly against the log.

I then tried my own version of the pitsicatto plucking on the tightly held
monofilament fishing line. First tweak it—then let it go slack—then tweak
it again. After a few moments of the alternative treatment the irritated trout
boldly freed itself and began to take out more line, still in the wrong direction, however. Triumphantly, I went to pass the now freed line to Pete, when
it suddenly went slack.

I swore, then realized it was simply swimming in our direction, beneath
and not above the cursed log that was Pete's earlier nemesis. I took up the
slack and passed the line to Pete so that he could renew battle with his big
trout. It temporarily became hung up once or twice more on other obstructions with Pete's moans being the loudest of our crew each time, but he
prevailed until finally working the brute close to the hole.

Now the trouble really began. The hole was eight inches in diameter, more than twenty inches deep with only a foot and a half of water beneath it. Pete's trout was deemed to be far too long to get into the tunnel-like hole and to the surface. It would have to be literally either bent at right angles, or somehow persuaded to swim into the hole trapping itself where it could be snared and raised to the top.

It was now pitch-black dark, but somehow or another, Pete's luck held. The line, badly frayed from its being chafed on the various underwater logs and obstructions, also managed to hold together with the hook securely planted in his trout's maw. A final series of give and takes and the big brookie's snout could be seen in the beams of the flashlights as it was eased upwards through the hole. When its head broke the surface we all yelled simultaneously, "Grab it! It's huge!" With the fish's buoyancy removed as it was being hoisted from the hole and water, the line that had performed so heroically until that moment, parted under the weight of the giant brookie.

A former linebacker for the Montreal Allouettes football team, and all of six feet four inches tall, Peter Pokulok crashed to the ice, plunged his arm down the hole and grabbed his catch in the gills before it could slide completely back down into the shallow water beneath the ice. Sopping wet, but with an enormous grin on his face, he held the beautiful fish aloft for our admiring inspection in the flashlight beams and light from the flashbulbs going off as photos were taken. It was measured for posterity, twenty-seven and-a-half inches long and a fraction over seven pounds.

Pete's trout now lies resplendent in a glass case on the wall in his recreation room, a permanent reminder for him of that wondrous day. However the occasion also represents one of the most magical memories not only for me, but for all of us in all our fishing pursuits over the years. To this day, Pete's brookie remains the largest any of us have produced from the A/B Lake.

Then there was Jim Lloyd's fish, his biggest ever brook trout. I had been fishing with Jim for several years since he first joined our club and quickly learned everything he could about trout fishing from us. We fished most of the streams and rivers within an hour or two of where we live in Toronto, along with a few of the lakes in the Land O' Lakes area.

Soon proving himself to be a fitting candidate to be invited on one of our trips to Quebec's mighty Broadback River, Jim had the misfortune to go on perhaps the poorest of all the twenty-two of our Broadback River excursions. We always plan that particular trip for the end of August and first week of September, the last week of the Quebec fishing season. Once the colder temperatures arrive, the big brookies move from the depths into the shallower rapids to spawn. The water temperatures are normally in the fifty-six to sixty-four degree range at that time of year in northern Quebec, ideal for the river's trout seeking a little bedroom action. The air temperatures are in the same approximate range.

We refer to brook trout over twenty-one inches as "mounties," that is suitable candidates for taxidermy. Unfortunately, Jim did not catch a mountie—none of us did on that particular Broadback excursion. The water was so warm, over seventy degrees Fahrenheit, that for the first time we were actually able to swim in the river and retrieve several of our lures hung up on logs around the camp. It was left to A/B Lake to come to the rescue if Jim was ever to catch a wall-hanger brookie for himself.

Although previously he had unsuccessfully fished A/B once or twice, Jim continued to accompany us on most of our outings to this magical but frustrating body of water. Jim demonstrated extreme patience and outlasted the lake's propensity for making life miserable for anglers, going fishless for a couple of years before finally breaking the apparent jinx with a couple of three-pounders. One of our most intriguing memories of fishing A/B Lake was about to occur during that season when he figuratively "broke the ice." Paul Kennedy, another of my expert angling buddies with whom I had fished

Gord with his Brittany spaniel, Tigger, on A/B Lake.

all our favourite streams and lakes from the first time we met (but who had also been skunked on several excursions to A/B Lake over a couple of years), joined Jim and me on another mid-winter ice-fishing trip to A/B. Unlike Jim, however, Paul had already been to the Broadback with us on a superb trip that produced mounties for him as well as the entire crew.

Both Paul and Jim were understandingly negative about the prospects of their being successful on another trip to A/B, but the challenge and allure presented by the waters of this lake alleviated their negativity somewhat. Both realized it was going to be a fine day of fishing, if not catching. The outing proceeded as usual, with Jim and Paul doing an excellent job of building and tending the campfire and cooking their lunches while not having to put up with the distractions of their buzzers being activated by A/B's brookies. Luckily, for me at least, I was able to set my buzzer over my favourite spot on the lake, a great shoal only a few feet out from our camp-fire set-up on the rocky shoreline. I had often said it would be a nice trick if I were able to take the hole home with me at the end of an ice-fishing day, put it in the freezer and bring it back for the next cold water outing. It soon became obvious that it was cut in the correct spot after a couple of A/B's lovely brookies fell to my "deft approach" before lunch was ready.

While Jim was attacking the last of his spareribs, nicely grilled over the hot coals, he and Paul were also eating their heart out at my "luck" and the lack of theirs. Jim almost gagged on a mouthful of charred pork when his buzzer finally signalled action on his line, the first after several years of fishing A/B.

Rushing to his set-up, Jim yelled at Paul to bring the Handigaff[3] which places a secure grip on the slippery fish when it is brought to the surface. However the A/B Lake fates seemed to be still aligned against him. By the time Paul and I had strolled over to partake in the action, Jim was clearly upset. The fish, and he thought it would be well in excess of seven pounds, had already stripped fifty feet of line off his spool. He hadn't been able to stop it or even slow it down, and now it was not budging, perhaps caught under something. A sudden movement was short lived, but Jim was certain it was still on the line.

Paul speculated that the line was likely running against the bottom of at least two logs. If a hole could be drilled and if we could hoist the log to the surface we might be able to pass the line over the end of the log and free the fish. With the water being about ten or twelve feet out there it was a pretty far-out idea, but one worth trying. I told Paul to run to shore, grab the axe and get a branch at least ten feet long with another branch on one end. He was to cut it so that there would be enough left of the second branch to hook the log, but not too long to be able to get it through the hole. In the meantime I would drill and cut a hole over the spot where Jim believed the first log was situated.

Unbelievably, the big brookie was co-operating and remained on the end of the line as Pete's mountie had done while we executed the other unorthodox scheme. The first branch, carefully trimmed by Paul, was lowered down the new hole and fortunately Jim's assessment of its location was right on the button. He worked it with a circular motion until Jim could feel some slack on the line, suggesting that Paul had located the log.

Miraculously, the branch hooked near the end of the log. Jim and I heaved sighs of relief as the log was raised out of the hole while the taut monofilament line was passed over its end. Flushed with our early success and grinning from ear to ear, I asked, "Is it still on, Jim? Can you still feel it?" He could.

Immediately I began to drill the second hole where Jim estimated his trout and the log it had swum under were located. As that did not work, Paul took the drill and moved back twenty feet or so to drill another hole, then fished around attempting to hook Jim's line. No luck—so he drilled another, tried again, then on the third attempt was able to fish the line to the surface where it was secured until Jim could move up and hang on to it. The procedure was repeated several times, with Jim eventually hanging on to the line, more than a hundred feet and a dozen more holes out from where his buzzer had been set up. It was a strange sight, the line of holes, fifteen to twenty feet apart, extending well out into the lake. Checking to make sure the fish was still on the line, Paul drilled his last hole where it was now indicated by the line's direction. This time he couldn't even feel the bottom—too deep. Only the "tweaking" procedure remained.

Jim tweaked the line several times and was caught off guard when his trout reacted to the aggravation and tore off once more towards the middle of the lake, but the badly frayed line that had been wrapped around his hand could not be released quickly enough. It broke. The sad look on his face told the story. It was all we needed to know that this particular game was now history. A/B Lake had prevailed once more and Jim would have to wait for another day to break the fates that seemed to always be directed in his direction. Nevertheless, fishing is why we pursue this sport, not catching.

However, Mr. Lloyd would not have long to wait. The vagaries of the gods that govern the fishing on these waters were soon to be put to the test again on

Jim's behalf. Several weeks after the adventure with his big runaway brookie which had been unavoidably "released," the three of us were at it again on A/B with Jim and Paul determined to wreak vengeance on the lake's predilection for hot and cold *fishing*, often with hot and cold *catching*, as well.

It began to appear that the lake's reputation would hang tough, as it was fairly late in the afternoon before the first buzzer sounded. It was mine, but the fish was not well hooked and escaped without so much as a tug or two on the line. Paul continued to go without a hit, but Jim's buzzer which he had placed in the identical spot where he had hooked the big one previously, sounded the alarm and got him off his stool beside the dwindling fire and into action with a grin on his face.

"Do you think it could be the same one?" he wishfully conjectured as he hustled out to check the line that was already running freely towards the centre of the lake as his "biggie" had done before. This time, however, the trout turned tail, and Jim had to work furiously to regain the slack as the trout swam back towards him. This fish did not have the smarts that his previous trout had displayed and was whipped by Jim in short order and successfully hauled through the hole and out onto the ice.

Jim Lloyd finally broke his jinx with a six-pound speckled trout.

Looking straight up at the sky, he pursed his lips, kissed his hand then blew it straight upwards to express his thanks to the lake's gods for that memorable moment. Jim not only had broken the jinx, but smashed it soundly with his first ever A/B Lake speckled trout—and a mountie, too—twenty-four inches, solidly tipping the scales at six pounds.

Paul and I congratulated him, but that was it for the day's fishing. It was a pleasant drive back to Toronto with Jim unable to conceal his pleasure at the day's results, while Paul, still fishless, snored all the way home in the back seat. He would have to wait for another day to lose his own A/B Lake virginal status.

That spring we had an ice-out club trip to the lake, with a couple of gals and three or four guys, all fine fishermen. Paul Kennedy, electing to challenge the lake's victory streak over his previous efforts, decided to join us for this outing, normally one of the most productive of the year. Ice-out fishing for brookies in spring-fed lakes can be very exciting with great action on either fly-fishing tackle or spinning equipment, providing the timing is correct.

The ideal, if one is to experience maximum action, is to arrive when the lake has shed most of its mantle of ice with the remainder, perhaps ten to twenty per cent, in the form of drifting floes or some still covering parts of the bays and shoreline pockets protected from the sun by the logistics of their locations. On an exploratory outing a few days earlier, we had discovered that the logging road into the lake was still far too muddy for our regular vehicles to negotiate, thus the outing was set back a week to allow it to dry up sufficiently. Getting a car buried in mud with a half a dozen folks impatient to get fishing, is not really our idea of a good time.

On that initial trip we had been able to catch enough glimpses of several other Haliburton lakes to determine that there was still a substantial amount of ice cover remaining—at least on the ones we saw. We kept our fingers crossed that everything would work out in our favour before the club trip. It really was a Catch-22, with our hoping there would be little rain and enough sun to dry up the road, yet not enough to melt all the ice on A/B Lake.

Driving in a week and a half later, with three vehicles, canoes and fold-boats, eight eager anglers armed with both spinning and fly tackle, we discovered that the road, although still quite muddy, was passable and we arrived at the lake without incident. Our jaws dropped, however, when it became obvious

Ice-out time on the lake in April.

that A/B had closed the door to us once again. At least it appeared that that would be the situation as the lake had indeed completely shed its mantle of ice in the interim since our earlier exploratory trip.

On the previous year's ice-out club trip, blessed with perfect conditions, one of the best club fishing trips we ever experienced occurred. A/B was conquered—royally! There were twenty-nine specs caught on flies and wablers, by eight folks, with my wife, Sheila, playing the starring role by catching two of the largest, five and five-and-a-half pounds respectively, and actually boating seven of the total caught by our crew. Unfortunately for him, Paul Kennedy had been unable to participate on that particular day, so I assumed the honour of being the sole angler to get skunked.

When Paul learned about the great trip that he had missed out on, he was not amused, nor was he about to miss out on another ice-out junket. Not as discouraged as we were by the complete absence of ice on the lake, he jokingly insisted as we hoisted the canoes off the cars' roofs, that his luck had only one way to go and that was upward.

My retort was to remind him of the possibility of falling out of the boat into forty-two degree water. (Prophetically, a few months after I had recalled and written this account, Paul and his partner Ray Cockburn flipped their canoe and did just that, fell in, along with all their gear—and a boat load of trout. *The water temperature was forty-two degrees Fahrenheit!)*

The lake was worked hard by everybody, but the trout apparently had already had their fill of goodies washed in by the melting snows. Only two trout were taken: one, a fat three-pounder by Sheila and sadly, the other,

Sheila Deval fishing on the lake, using the brace on her left wrist,
circa 2000.

not by Paul, but by one of our club's newest members on his first club-fishing trip, Leon Schwartz. Regardless, all, including Paul, agreed that it had been an excellent outing.

Perhaps the second most productive time to fish these lakes for brookies is the last weekend of the season, the end of September. The water has normally cooled, attracting the cautious brookies out of their summer hiding places as they forage to fatten up for the long, up-coming spawning and winter season. The majestic Fall scenery is worth the price of the trip alone, even if the trout are displaying symptoms of lockjaw.

With his patience still undeterred Paul and I decided to wind up the season together on A/B. Here, as I record that day of fishing with one of my all-time best buddies, the old saying about patience comes, to mind:

Patience is a virtue.
Seek it if you can,
Seldom found in women,
but often found in man.[4]

Paul Kennedy had certainly demonstrated many times that he was blessed with an abundant supply of patience, and on the last day of the season he was rewarded accordingly when A/B finally surrendered a trout to him, a fine twenty-one-incher. Being his initial A/B Lake catch—after a moment's introspection—his brookie was dispatched and kept. Paul then decidedly laid to rest the lake's jinx that had been his nemesis by proceeding to catch a couple more fine specks that were duly and carefully released. Each release was performed with great ceremony and dignity.

There is one more anecdote that I have recounted many times to folks who enquire whether we ever camp at our magical A/B Lake. It deserves inclusion.

Ella and David Collins were two of the more ardent members of our club in the early years of its existence, with David accompanying me on many trips to our favourite trout streams and excursions to A/B, as well as the Land O' Lakes area. Both became fine casters and enjoyed the tournaments but more for the social aspects in meeting others with the same hobbies, than for the competitive aspects. Ella and my wife, Sheila, both worked hard on their fishing skills and enjoyed the club fishing trips, including those where we rented a couple of cottages for the weekend. We had done that on a few occasions previously on Kennesis Lake, from which we would skidoo in to fish A/B if in winter, or drive in if in the spring or summer months.

During one of our ice-out spring trips to A/B, Dave inquired if we ever camped on the lake. When I replied that Sheila and I had enjoyed camping there quite a few times, even leaving our tent set up for as long as a month on a remote peninsula at the far end of the lake from where we customarily accessed it, Dave asked if we would mind their joining us for a camping trip on one of our long weekends.

Gord holding the deadliest mushroom in the world—the Destroying Angel, Amanita verosa, *found near A/B Lake.*

I encouraged the idea, as we were planning to go on the long Labour Day weekend when the extra day would allow more time to enjoy the swimming, fishing and camping. My reference to swimming carried a caution to not let one's legs dangle down too far while treading water. Just hitting the top of the thermocline, the cold layer of water lying a few feet below the surface, would be enough to create the impression of swimming in the Arctic. Actually, I mentioned that Sheila and I would be doing most of our fishing early in the morning before we even have breakfast, when the lake is generally covered with a five-foot-thick layer of misty fog. I explained that when it burns off, it's back to the tent and brecky with the rest of the day spent relaxing, swimming, reading and so on until late afternoon. We usually have an early dinner before heading out on the water for the evening to test our luck again until dark.

Four months later, with the tent set up and already into our second day of camping on the lake, an incident occurred that I can still close my eyes and easily recall in its entirety. It had been an unusually warm couple of days and the four of us spent more time in the water, than we did on top of it. David and I had just come out after a lengthy swim down the shoreline to our ice-fishing location, hoping to retrieve some of the jigging lures that had been donated to the bottom structure during the hard-water season.

We were drying ourselves off in the sunshine and enjoying a game of chess while Ella and Sheila, looking beautiful clad only in their bikini bottoms and perched on a big shoreline rock, were also enjoying the warmth of the sunshine after their own dip in the cold waters of the lake. Our camp is situated in the remotest area of the lake, the opposite end from the only automobile access and where we park our car. The women were totally comfortable with their toplessness.

Suddenly, a rather guttural, heavily accented voice appeared on this pastoral scene, disturbing the serenity and asking for help. It was a voice with a strong German accent and as our wives made futile attempts to cover their breasts with their hands, he continued his request by explaining that he was seeking the way to Redstone Lake.

Still somewhat in a state of shock, I challenged his presence, "Who in the hell are you? Where did you come from, anyhow?"

The fellow not only had a thick German accent but was dressed in typically Old World German clothing, Lederhosen (leather shorts), braces, long colourful stockings and shirt, and wearing ordinary hiking boots. The only thing missing was one of those little odd-shaped, green Tyrolean hats.

Surrounding the stranger was a cloud of mosquitoes that had obviously followed him through the bush to our campsite. Unlike us, he seemed able to ignore the pests as he refused the can of spray bug repellent I offered him.

The extremely polite fellow, finally noticing our wives' attempts to retain a modicum of modesty, apologized in slow and perfect English, and turned to renew his trek around the lake. Recognizing that his chances of reaching his destination before dark were most unlikely, I offered to give him a lift by canoe to the other side of the lake where he could pick up a trail. After much resistance, he responded to David's order to get in the "damn" canoe. As David and our "guest" disappeared in the distance, the gals finally relaxed, left their rocky perch and went into the tent to dress for dinner as I began chopping wood and organizing the fireplace for the evening. My only regret is that in my surprise at the fellow's sudden appearance from the bush behind us I neglected to take a picture of him. I seem to recall that we all caught trout on that weekend, but the incredible memory of that A/B Lake weekend was definitely the startling emergence from the bush of the peculiarly garbed stranger, peculiar, at least for a gentleman trekking through miles of mosquito-infested Haliburton forest.

Chapter 19

More Trout Fishing in Haliburton

These magical waters, Limit and Beanpole lakes, are included together, as often when we plan to specifically fish one lake, or another, our plans change and occasionally, both are fished on the same day. Beanpole is a shallower and slightly smaller lake than nearby Limit and contains rainbow trout whereas Limit has both rainbows, splake (a lake trout—speckled trout cross) and the odd true speckled trout. Both lakes are stocked more or less regularly by the Ministry of Natural Resources and occasionally produce fish weighing as much as six pounds or more. The lakes are a two-and-a-half hour drive north from Toronto, with the trip into Limit taking longer as the last couple of miles necessitates either an ATV or 4-wheel-drive vehicle such as our Jeep, to negotiate its almost inaccessible bush trail. To get to either, requires a slow and careful drive down a hydro road, originally constructed as a corduroy logging route. There are also stretches of trail, often underwater due to flooded beaver dams. Corduroy roads are muddy trails with rows of logs laid across at right angles to create a semblance of firmness and traction for vehicular traffic. Most deteriorate into a nightmare driving exercise for ordinary cars, quickly demonstrating their ability to pinpoint any loose connections in the unlucky cars driven on them. The trail to Limit and Beanpole is no exception!

I first learned about Beanpole Lake from Murray Austen, an old fishing buddy of mine, whom I met in the village of Haliburton when I was on the road as a travelling sporting goods salesman in the fifties. He walked into a small tackle shop and was introduced to me as the town's best fisherman. We seemed to hit it off immediately when we discovered that we both loved hunting and fishing—especially trout fishing. I learned that Murray actually was responsible for stocking many of the smaller waters such as small lakes and beaver ponds in his area with brook trout.

With special permission from what was then known as the Ontario Department of Lands and Forests, Murray would obtain a couple of hundred trout fingerlings. He would place them, along with ice-cold water, in an insulated galvanized milk transferring pail, the type that traditionally back in those days, farmers used to temporarily store the milk in before shipping it to market. The heavy pail, almost three feet long was next fastened to a back-pack harness, and Murray would slog through marsh and bush to reach these minuscule waters. There he would carefully empty his precious cargo along the deepest shoreline he could access in order to give the fingerlings a chance to acclimatize before being snatched by mergansers and loons in the shallows.

He wisely kept records of which body of water received the fruits of his labours, and religiously adhered to his credo to not fish the lake for at least two years in order to give the brookies a chance to mature to a decent size. Many of these ponds already contained large stocks of minnows and, along with the plentiful supply of grubs, larvae and crawfish therein, the trout thrived to become worthwhile adversaries for him, some growing as large as three and four pounds. I was fortunate enough to have been invited by Murray to fish in a number of these comparatively tiny waters along with him and discovered that some them had become truly magical waters in their own right.

Earlier in this book I wrote about sensational memories I have experienced on other magical Haliburton waters, specifically A/B, Sludge and Tedious lakes. Those lakes, especially A/B, have borne the brunt of most of our trout-seeking forays since the mid-seventies. However, about ten years ago we seemed to be experiencing a dearth of fishing success in our favourite lakes, although according to stocking sheets published by the Ministry of Natural Resources, the lakes were still being well stocked. Several fruitless trips in a row caused us to think about new areas to explore. As fishing buddy Jim Lloyd and I began the drive home after another day's frustrating efforts on A/B, I happened to blurt out as we approached the still tiny village of Haliburton, "I wonder what my old friend, Murray Austen, is up to these days."

Jim had heard all about my early relationship with Murray when I was a travelling salesman and what a fine and knowledgeable fisherman he was, especially when it had to do with trout and his home territory of Haliburton. He suggested we look him up, after all we had time and were in his territory. Although I had not spoken with Murray for five years or so, I felt that we knew each other well enough that he would not be upset by my dropping in on him unannounced with another fishing buddy.

I suggested we call him first from a payphone. Murray was delighted to hear from me again and did not hesitate to invite us to visit him, saying he had some trout pictures to show me. After we spent a few minutes reminiscing about our early fishing ventures together, Murray pulled out a photo album of a few of his recent hunting and fishing outings. While we poured over the great shots of fat and gorgeous brookies, huge lake trout and moose and deer strung up from tree supports, his wife Betty suggested we stay for supper. They were having moose steaks, but we had promised our wives that we would be home by eight that evening.

What I really was after was "picking" Murray's brains for new fishing spots. I told Murray that we hadn't been able to catch a thing at A/B Lake for at least four or five trips and wondered if he would suggest someplace new for us to try. He empathized with our lot, being skunked four times in a row on A/B was a tough one to swallow, and asked if we had ever fished Beanpole Lake. According to him, the lake had "bloody" nice rainbows in it and was hardly fished at all. Moreover, he told us that Natural Resources stocked that lake every couple of years with 'bows and that the guys who hunt there also put fish in it now and then. It sounded like a good bet.

A week later, after locating the lake on a topographical map (it was not far from Algonquin Park's borders), Jim and I were bouncing along the ancient corduroy trail that led to a smaller cut-off trail through the bush to Beanpole Lake. It is always a magical moment when first viewing a new stream or lake that you are about to fish for the first time. The lovely vista that lay in front of us as we slogged through the last hundred feet of muskeg was certainly not an exception. The cold morning air had combined with the warmer surface waters on Beanpole to create a beautiful but eerie, misty panorama that stopped us in our tracks. Neither Jim nor I said a word; we just ogled the scene until a trout broke the silence with a cartwheeling jump and noisy splash a few feet out from shore where we were about to launch the little Instaboat folding craft we used for situations like this.

Beanpole turned out to be a great new source of exciting angling action for us over the next few years. The results of our first exposure to its charms easily placed it well up on the list of our favourite magical waters in which to wet a line. We had to work hard to catch fish, but the rewards were definitely worth the effort as the rainbows we caught, all between four and six pounds, fought like the devil, with most also putting on a frenetic show of airborne acrobatics for our pleasure as well.

Roger Cannon (in the background), Sheila Deval
and Jim Lloyd (picking up the pack) prepare for
a day's fishing at Beanpole.

Although speckled trout will always be our favourite angling quarry, rainbow trout will often put on a spectacular display of power and speed in their panic to get unhooked and free. Brookies seldom do, although their other attributes easily compensate for their more mundane demeanour. We have had many wonderful days of fishing on the waters of Beanpole, but as in the case with all trout lakes, there have also been other days when its trout all exhibited symptoms of lockjaw. Several instances of working Beanpole's waters immediately come to mind, however, when discussing the lake's pros and cons or in fishing discussions when it is first mentioned to one of our newer club members contemplating an opportunity to test their own luck on the lake for the first time.

Front and foremost is the classic tale of our good friend, fishing buddy and internet provider, Ashok Kalle. Ashok joined our Scarborough Fly and Bait Casting Association about ten years ago after I had purchased my first computer and signed on for internet services with his Pathways Communications Company. When he saw our club business card, he said that he would like to join if we could teach him how to fish. He claimed that he wanted to learn everything about fishing.

I quickly assured him that nobody—anywhere—"knows everything there is to know about fishing," but that we were certainly prepared to teach him everything that we knew. Ashok quickly became comfortably skilled with his spinning and fly equipment and a better than average caster as well. He and I had a number of outings to a variety of streams and locations, but for some reason or another he seemed to be hexed, like that famous character in the old Lil' Abner comic strip who had a tiny rain cloud over his head that followed him wherever he went. It did not matter whether we were fishing one of our favourite trout streams, or on a club trip with a dozen of us going north to do battle with A/B Lake's fish for a weekend, Ashok could not seem to catch a trout, no matter how hard he tried. He bought the finest of equipment but to no avail. This unfortunate jinx seemingly fixed to his shoulders would not go away. Even dynamite probably would not have produced a "catch" for him in those early frustrating days of fishing with us.

But then came Beanpole Lake to his rescue! A few of us had been experiencing the pleasures of fishing Beanpole for a couple of years, but Ashok, as determined as ever in trips to the Ganny and A/B, for one reason or another had not participated in any Beanpole outings. Finally he decided to join me there for a fall fishing trip.

It was his first Jeep ride in deep bush and swamp and he admitted that if he came away skunked again, especially after undergoing a nerve-jarring and bone-rattling trip like that one, he would have to give serious consideration to exchanging his fishing tackle for golf equipment and fly casting lessons for golf lessons. The day began like many on trout lakes with lots of casting practice and experimenting with different lures and flies and nary a strike from a trout between us.

Then Ashok's face lit up like the sun coming out from behind the clouds as his rod was nearly torn out of his hand by a savage strike from a gorgeous rainbow trout. He played the fish to a standstill like an old pro, slid it into his waiting net and breathed a sigh of relief that I am sure was heard throughout all of Haliburton. I breathed my own sigh of relief while I snapped several photos to record the scene for posterity—Ashok Kalle's first trout.

What seemed to excite him even more than breaking the spell that had hung over him and catching his first trout—and a beauty, at that—was the fact that he had a fish in the boat, whereas Deval did not. The excitement of Ashok's finally losing his status as a trout fishing virgin had barely calmed down when he let out another whoop. That trout was also handled perfectly and also dutifully recorded. We had decided ahead of time as we normally do that the catch would be shared equally no matter who caught what, so with a grin on his face and comment, Ashok gleefully said, "Better keep this one in case you get skunked, eh!" then eventually laid it reverently alongside his first.

These fish, stocked by the Ministry of Natural Resources do not reproduce. It is basically a "put and take" fishery and the MNR encourages anglers to keep the larger trout (within the legal limits) for their tables and release the younger fish to grow larger and produce thrills for other fishermen on other days. But I was not even able to catch one of Beanpole's smaller trout on that day as Ashok continued to remove any remaining remnants of the jinx that had hung over him since he joined the club. In all he caught two more lovely rainbows for a total of four terrific trout, all around the four pound mark. I will never forget the triumphant smile he wore during that day, and for the three-and-a-half hour drive home.

Another unforgettable happening on Beanpole occurred a couple or so years ago on another late fall fishing trip with Ray Cockburn, one of our club's original members. The lake's trout once again seemed to have all been caught as Ray and I worked our way through our lure boxes, hoping to find a

Jason Nasato (left), Gord's grandson, and Ollie Johnson in the Haliburton area in the early 1990s.

magic cure there. When we went ashore for a lunch break, fishless, our hands did not require rinsing before tucking into our sandwiches. While on shore, the wind, which had been negligible, became stronger so we decided that we would troll to the western end of the lake, then cast the shoreline while drifting back to the other side. When trolling we customarily work slightly deeper water in order to minimize fouling the lures on weeds or rocks. I had just refastened my favourite lure for this type of fishing, a Crocodile,[1] although two hours of casting with it earlier had produced zilch.

Shortly thereafter, as we approached the shallower water at the end where we would begin the drift and cast procedure, perhaps the largest rainbow trout I have ever seen, other than the steelheads from the Great Lakes that migrate the rivers in the spring and fall, smashed my Crocodile spoon. It shot three feet out of the water, then sped off towards the far end of the lake. Both Ray and I had a good look at the powerful trout when it was airborne, then once more after it had peeled most of the line off my reel in its non-stop dash to freedom. The silver slab of pure power whizzed down the lake so quickly that we could see spray flying off the monofilament line as it sliced through the water. At a couple hundred yards away, with most of my line already peeled off the small spool, it leapt well clear of the water in another heart-stopping moment—and the lure came out of its jaw. With great difficulty, as I was shaking like a leaf, the line was slowly retrieved while Ray and I spoke nary a word. Upon examination, two of the barbs on the lure's treble hook, obviously those that had valiantly tried to hold on to the 'bow while I hopelessly attempted to arrest its mad flight, were almost completely straightened.

Prior to and since hooking into that particular trout, my friends and I have caught rainbows there as long as twenty-six inches that weighed in excess of six pounds. The memory, though, of that one fish as my line screamed off the reel easily surpasses any of the other thrills that the magical waters of Beanpole supplied us with since Murray Austen suggested we give the lake a "boo" about ten years ago.

After Jim Lloyd and I had discovered the delights of fishing Beanpole Lake and fished there in spring, summer, fall and winter for a couple of years, it was time to look into the potential of another of Haliburton's lakes. A small trail branching off the bush road to Beanpole seemed to indicate that it could be worth exploring. According to our interpretation of the symbols on the topographical maps of the area, the trail, actually just a trapper's trail, led to another body of water, larger than but not too far from Beanpole Lake.

As our initial attempt to access the lake was prior to my purchasing a Jeep some seven or eight years ago, we quickly discovered that the trail was definitely not negotiable with an ordinary automobile. Even though my Chevy was equipped with heavy-duty everything and over-sized wheels, we were only able to penetrate the bush a few hundred yards or so with it. The house-sized boulders and deep pools of gooey mud made even walking almost impossible. Nevertheless, carrying our folding Instaboat, tackle and paddles, about a half hour later we managed to break through the nearly impenetrable melange of rocks, muck and fallen trees to a just reward—the sight of a lovely-looking lake and one, we hoped, was full of hungry trout. The boat was quickly assembled, gear strung together and we pushed out from shore full of expectations. Most fishermen will agree that anticipation is the driving force behind one's angling excursions, certainly on those investigative sojourns into previously unexplored territory.

Several hours later, paddling back to shore, we had to admit defeat. The sum total of our first crack at Beanpole's sister lake was one small splake. As we broke down the tackle and folding boat, then shook our arms to work out the kinks from almost five hours of fruitless casting, Jim said what we were both thinking, "Guess we should have fished Beanpole. Doesn't look like there's much in this lake."

Thinking over his remarks, I reminded him that we just as easily could have been skunked at Beanpole. Maybe the barometer was falling,[2] it's never easy to attribute a cause to "no fish." However, it did occur to me that ice fishing might lead to a different story. We always ice fish A/B on opening day, January 1 (the season is closed all fall for brookies); we would return to our "new" lake on another day.

Opening day on A/B proved to be fruitful as the lake almost always is after being rested for three months with the season closed during the spawning period and the trout eager to put on the feed bag after their busy sexual escapades. Jim and I had to verbally twist each other's arms after the fine outing on A/B, to stick to our original plan to fish Beanpole's sister lake a week later.

Skidooing in to the lake a few days later was a great deal easier than trekking and slogging the five-mile trail by shank's mare. It was also simpler than it had been negotiating the mudholes and rocks with the car on our

Paul Kennedy ice-fishing at "Limit" Lake in
2005. Note the scoop used to ladle slush out
of the hole.

initial trip in and, of course, much quicker. As soon as we had our allotted two holes each drilled and the Fish O' Buzzers rigged up, Jim set about getting the fire started. I knocked down a few dead trees and sawed them into suitable lengths in order to have enough fuel to keep it stoked up for the entire day. Even before the water in the teapot indicated it was ready for the tea bags, one of Jim's buzzers began making a racket that pulled him off his seat by the fire to race over and see what had taken his minnow. Grabbing the line streaming off the spool to set the hook and slow down the flight of the fish, he was able to tell immediately that it was definitely not a small trout attempting to head for the middle of the lake; "Feels like a big rainbow, better bring that fish-grabber thingamajig gizmo of yours—your camera, too!"

Jim played that fish, retrieving and feeding out line as needed for almost fifteen minutes before bringing the trout to heel just beneath the hole. Because it was still early in the hard-water season, the ice was no more than six or seven inches thick so the trout could easily be seen through the clear ice as it was shaking its head trying to dislodge the hook lodged firmly in its jaw. A few minutes more of give and take with the big 'bow and he realized that the trout was too big to get through the six-inch diameter hole in the ice. I ran for the hatchet we use to chop firewood, hoping that we could enlarge the hole before the hook came loose and the trout lost. My hustle was all to no avail. One particularly violent shake of the rainbow's head and the hook was wrenched free quicker than Jim was able to react.

Shortly thereafter, nevertheless, another of our buzzers went off, this time, one of mine. Although it was smaller than the trout that Jim lost, I was luckier than he and soon had a fat four-pound splake flopping around on the ice. Then Jim's re-baited buzzer spurred him into action once again and another splake, larger than the first was also flopping on the ice. The day just continued like that, first Jim would catch one, then it would be my turn. We caught so many trout that our bucket of minnows was depleted by mid-afternoon when jigging rods with tiny Rapala jigs[3] were put into action. The excitement continued until it was time to pack up and skidoo out of the bush before dark. All in all I would estimate that we had fifteen or twenty strikes on the buzzers—caught most of them and kept our limit, six each. Most of the trout, predominately splake, with a few rainbows and at least one brook trout, were in the three to four-pound class, while a couple were over five. None, however, was as big as that first trout that had grabbed Jim's bait and caused all the excitement before it was lost. It was the most productive day of ice fishing that either of us had ever experienced and led to Jim's suggestion as we drove home quite content with our "discovery" of another superlative lake in which to do battle with trout, "You know, Gord, we don't even know if this place has a name or not. There are three or four lakes, all fairly close to Beanpole and who knows for sure which one is which. We both caught our limit today and they were all big and lovely trout. What do you say we call it Limit Lake."

Like all trout lakes, although Limit has given us some wonderful catching days and created great and magical memories, it has as often as not, given the impression that the lake was fished out. Our first visit to Limit Lake was a classic example of that. However, three years ago, that memorable day when Jim hooked into the rainbow that was too big to get through the hole in the ice, was topped by another incredibly productively "catching" day, lending further credence to our theory, that like us, the fish are entitled to a day off now and then.

Four of us had fished the lake a week previously with only a single two-pound rainbow to show for the sum total of all our efforts. Jim and I, understanding the whimsical nature of the lake, opted to work the Jeep

The stool capsized, much to the amazement of Jim Lloyd.

through the rocks and muck once again the following Saturday, rather than take the easier route and fish Beanpole instead. As it developed, we were glad we did. That outing became one of the most unusual and memorable days I have ever experienced in my long history of fishing for trout. We hooked, lost, caught and released trout right from the get-go, with the action continuing right through to noon hour when we rested our arms to work on our sandwiches instead. At that point we each had already kept all but one short of our limits so that we could continue fishing in the hopes of catching even larger trout. It may not be illegal to continue to fish with a limit catch already in the bag, but it is certainly not wise, as another hooked fish cannot always be successfully released. If badly hooked, or bleeding it probably would not survive the release. While I was finishing off the last of my trout-salad sandwiches (the filling, courtesy of a previous day's catch) I happened to say that I never thought catching that many trout all morning long would become boring. Jim commented that it's the challenge and suspense that are the most important factors in fishing. He was right, it was just too easy that morning. That led me to suggest that we finish our day over at Beanpole.

Jim looked at me like I had lost all my marbles and said, "It's a crazy idea! We would have to load, unload then load everything once more then unload everything again when we get home—but let's do it."

Shortly after 2:00 we pushed the little Instaboat out from the lily pads in the shallows of Beanpole Lake, wondering if its trout were going to be as receptive to our offerings as were the fish in Limit. The *suspense and challenge* had definitely returned and we were once more in the desired frame of mind that is an absolute requisite if maximum pleasure is to be reaped from one's angling pursuits.

However, the suspense factor dissipated rather quickly because Beanpole's rainbows gave us little time to contemplate the worth of all that extra effort in moving from the one lake to the other. Within an hour or so after making the first casts, we each had a beautiful five-pound rainbow trout in the bottom of the boat. With a second catch, we had rounded out our limit. It was time to stop. Limit Lake along with its sister lake, Beanpole, had justified the moniker we had applied to it after Jim had first suggested it on that other remarkable day of trout fishing. Haliburton undoubtedly contains many other terrific lakes in which to fish trout, however, it is difficult to imagine that any of them are superior to the magical waters of A/B, Limit and Beanpole lakes.

So you think you've heard it all before! Well, here's an incredible tale that illustrates the meaning of credulity and will make a most fitting conclusion to these Haliburton lake stories. It involves several members of our Scarborough Fly and Bait Casting Association and Patrick Walsh, the editor of the magazine, *Outdoor Canada*.

On Saturday, a couple of weeks ago, six of our club members, Paul Kennedy, Ray Cockurn, Rob Tanaka, Sharon McIntyre, my wife Sheila and I, "jeeped" our way into Limit Lake to do a little trout fishing. Weather-wise, it was a gorgeous day with nary a cloud in the sky all day long, but quite windy and very, very cold. The temperature hovered around the zero degree mark when we arrived and did not exceed three or four degrees all day long. The surface water of the lake was just short of five degrees Celcius.

By noon hour a dozen splake and rainbow trout had already been caught, with Paul and Ray, in Paul's new canoe, having caught about a dozen, with nine (one short of their limit) kept for the smoker and table. While Sheila and I were enjoying a brief respite and bite of lunch on shore on the south end of the lake, our little walkie-talkie radio barked at us with a message from Paul, reporting how the fishing was and specifically telling me that if I wanted a picture of all the trout lying on the bottom of their canoe I should come right away.

We quickly packed up and struck out down the lake in my tiny folding Instaboat towards the two "lucky" anglers, still enthusiastically working the waters. The wind was on our tail and had picked up even more velocity with whitecaps rolling in the middle of the small lake where they were waiting for us. I cut the electric motor about fifty yards from the canoe, intending to let the wind propel us the remaining distance. But the wind was pushing our boat faster than we would have liked and we closed on the canoe a little too quickly. Then, instead of using his paddle to ward us off and prevent our bumping them, Paul reached out to use his hand to hold us off. Big mistake! He reached too far, overbalanced his canoe and it rolled over, dumping him, his partner Ray, the trout and all their gear into the frigid water. A few scary moments followed as the two fellows were momentarily in shock and sucking air furiously.

Sheila and I watched helplessly as seven lovely trout wafted through the water on their way to the bottom looking for all the world like falling leaves, albeit, silver falling leaves. Two, their largest, were on a stringer tied to the canoe. Fortunately, the men finally regained their composure. Whatever was still floating was tossed into our boat at Sheila's feet. One paddle was whisked away on the surface by the wind before it could be retained. Ray's tackle bag lodged under a seat was retrieved, while Paul's bag was nowhere to be seen. There was no time to search for it as my soaked and half-frozen fishing buddies had to be towed to shore.

An amazingly lucky break was discovered when the sopping wet victims scrambled up on shore and found yards of monofilament tangled around their legs and torsos. Untangling, then gently retrieving the spinning lines, they were able to retrieve both their casting outfits, pulling them from the water along with half a ton of weeds. Paul and I went back to right their canoe and tow it to shore. We all immediately headed to the end of the lake where the Jeep and its heaters awaited. Paul, still soaking wet, and I pushed off once more, however, and searched the shoreline and retrieved his expensive paddle from a weed bed several hundred yards from the "dunk."

Among the six of us, and with Ray's foresight in bringing a partial change of clothes, there were enough for both shivering fellows to get into dry garments for the three-hour trip to Toronto. Back home, later that evening, I searched the internet looking for a Scarborough-based scuba diving club and fortunately, discovered the Toronto Super Turtles Dive Club. Hoping that we would be able to find someone who might be interested in our tale of woe and be able to assist us in finding and recovering Paul's fishing tackle bag with its estimated five or six hundred dollars of reels, lures and gadgets, I scribbled and fired off a few e-mails to the gentlemen listed on their Web site. Too impatient to wait for their response, the next morning I decided to phone the directors of the club and explain my request. The first chap I spoke with was Bill Crich, the secretary and training director of the dive club. I told him what had happened the day before then asked him if he knew anyone in their club who would be able to take the day off and using his scuba diving gear, help us locate Paul's pack and my two-way radio. My spirits soared when he indicated it could probably be arranged. I reminded him that with the deer hunt beginning in Haliburton on the next weekend, and those chaps not taking kindly to fellows wandering around up there in the bush when they're running their dogs and tracking deer, it would have to be someone who could take a day off work. I added that by the time the hunt finishes, the lakes up there could be frozen solid. He surprised me saying that he could go himself if Wednesday was all right.

Three days later, the two of us, with all his considerable scuba gear loaded in the big Jeep, drove back up to the lake after first having to limp into a town on the way when an alternator burned out on the vehicle, delaying us by several hours and costing almost four hundred bucks. It was two o'clock by the time I dropped anchor where the canoe had flipped four days earlier as I waited for Bill to don his gear on shore where I had deposited him. I had "guaranteed" him that I knew the exact position of the accident and probable location of the errant pack, so it was decided that swimming in

Bill Crich retrieves the "lost" trout.

increasing larger circles around the boat would be the best procedure to follow. "It won't be more than thirty or forty feet," I assured him, "in one direction or another from my boat."

A few moments later, he popped up, removed his air intake and announced that he had found the fish. We figured the pack had to be nearby, and I passed him a landing net to scoop the fish up off the bottom.

Almost an hour later, with the water temperature on the bottom reading only three degrees above zero and still not having located Paul's pack, Bill reported that he had had enough. Apparently his wet suit had previously been damaged by contact with zebra mussels on a dive in Lake Ontario and was unable to provide him with enough warmth to continue the exploration.

Back in the Jeep and dressed in his regular clothing, he expressed regret at not finding Paul's pack, but was pleased to have found all the trout. He shared what he thought was a peculiar observation—all those fish were facing the same direction when he found them. It looked almost as if they had simply been placed there by somebody! I thanked him profusely for the mighty effort he had given under rather trying conditions and offered him a couple of trout, but he refused with thanks, saying that they should go to Paul.

Back home later, I cleaned, checked and distributed the trout and received glowing reports after they had all been eaten. Even after four days, dead—but being in the water they suffered no ill effects and were delicious. The temperature in my fridge is about the same as it was on the bottom of the lake.

Flash forward two and a half weeks from the "great canoe dunk" Paul Quarrington, Paul Kennedy, Patrick Walsh and I are returning to the little lake to do battle once again with its lovely trout. When we arrived we drew straws to determine who would fish with whom, and the two Pauls were partnered while Pat and I drew the short twigs. It was much warmer than our last outing, with the thermometer hovering around the twelve-degree mark and not a breath of wind rippling the surface at all. Without the glare of sunshine on the surface and with the sky slightly overcast one could see almost eight feet down through the water. We fly fished and tossed spinners and spoons on ultra-light spinning rods for a couple of hours, with the trout proving to be just as cooperative as they had on our last trip to the lake—to fish, that is—not scuba-dive.

By noon hour Pat had caught a five-and-a-half-pound rainbow trout, the largest, he said, of his fishing career, along with several nice splake. Paul Quarrington reported that he had already experienced one of the best and most productive trout fishing days that he could ever remember. His catch

Patrick Walsh, editor of Outdoor Canada *magazine, with his rainbow trout caught in the little Haliburton lake.*

also included a big rainbow, a five-pounder. Paul Kennedy and I brought up the rear with a number of fat splake including a lovely three-pounder taken by Paul. I had already told Pat that at twelve o'clock I was planning on spending about a half an hour or so jigging in the area where P.K.'s pack had disappeared. I had rigged a special outfit just for the purpose and intended to work the bottom further away from the "dunk" where Bill Crich had so diligently searched. It had been Bill's suggestion later on that the pack, if closed, might have held air long enough to have drifted quite a bit further away from the circle that I had initially indicated and that he had so thoroughly combed.

Equipped with Polaroid glasses and using fourteen-pound line on a sturdy outfit, a four-ounce lead, salt-water jig with a large treble hook, I made short twenty-five-foot casts downwind from the "dunk." The direction was easily determined when the canoe paddle retrieval was recalled. After the bottom was dredged a number of times, we moved along the line and repeated the process. After the third or fourth move we discovered we were gradually leaving the former eight to ten-feet depths and entering slightly shallower water.

Suddenly, Patrick shouted that he saw something red on the bottom. I remarked that it was probably a coke can that some thoughtless ass had tossed overboard, but he persisted. We paddled back until it was spotted again, this time by both of us. I went to work with the jig outfit and after a dozen tries finally managed to bring it to the surface where Pat jubilantly hoisted it from the water. Grinning like a Cheshire cat, he held up my walkie-talkie. I was amazed! Presumably then, Paul's pack should be nearby. A couple minutes more of paddling then the eagle-eyed Walsh quietly announced that he could see a big lump of something or another down there. Then I saw it, too, and confirmed his conjecture. Much easier to snag than the tiny walkie-talkie, it was hoisted cautiously to the surface where Patrick slowly raised it just enough to drain what seemed to be about half the water in the lake from its contents before bringing it aboard.

When we motored down to the other end of the lake at the pre-arranged time, one o'clock, to present Paul with our "catch" and eat our lunch, he took one look, grinned, then asked, "What took you so long, Gord?"

After lunch we fished for another couple of hours, with Patrick getting his just reward for his remarkable, observational skills by latching onto an even bigger rainbow trout, a twenty-five-inch-long six-pounder. The total catch on that incredible day was thirteen trout in all, three rainbows and ten splake. The big ones were all kept for the table.

The two trips to Haliburton were reviewed as we drove back to the city. It was agreed that the circumstances were remarkable: great fishing; the canoe dunking in freezing weather; finding such a cooperative scuba diver so quickly, the trout recovered by him from the lake bottom four days later, mysteriously almost side by side—and in perfect condition; another superb day of fishing with record catches; the walkie-talkie recovery and finally, the errant pack located and raised. All were deserving of being recorded. As a final note, the recovered two-way radio was cleaned up, new batteries installed and surprisingly discovered to still be working.

Chapter 20

Saugeen Country Booty

It has been mentioned several times earlier that my fishing buddy, Paul Kennedy and I have made it a point to fish the May 1 trout opening together for the past ten years or so. As already described, some of our trips have resulted in near disasters, or at the very least, out of the ordinary adventures.

Although usually on those occasions we chose to fish on the smaller trout streams, often just for brook trout, last year Paul and I did not follow our customary format as there had been a great deal of rain leading up to opening day. Realizing that the water in the small streams that we normally enjoyed would be too murky to fish successfully with flies or spinners (neither he nor I care to fish for trout with live bait such as worms), we opted instead to try our luck on the much bigger waters of the Saugeen River.

For some reason or another that I find difficult to explain, I hesitate to apply my magical waters tag to the Saugeen. Perhaps it is that although there is certainly much headwater in its system yet to be explored by my fishing buddies and me, our trips to the Saugeen have been restricted to the five miles or so of river upstream from where it drains into Lake Huron. It is an area that, during the spring and fall rainbow trout (steelheads) and salmon runs, is teeming with hundreds of fishermen every weekend.

Perhaps, too, the fact that the river is so accessible that it attracts almost anyone who owns a fishing rod—any kind of fishing rod—is another reason for my reluctance to declare the Saugeen a magical water. Although the river does play host to many skilled anglers who certainly know the best methods to ply its waters, it unfortunately also draws some of the least desirable, "poor sport" fishermen out of the woodwork. These are folks hoping to illegally snag a fish to take home to show to their neighbours before stripping the spawn from its belly to use as bait then discarding the desecrated carcass. However, the lure of tangling with one of the massive rainbow trout and gargantuan salmon that run the river is also an attraction for "run of the mill" anglers

Gord fishing at Denny's Dam, just above Southampton,
Ontario, in the early 1970s.

like Paul and myself, despite the occasional unpleasantries, such as someone carelessly snagging and ripping a hole in your waders. Or someone with a half-empty mickey in his hip pocket who resents your catching more fish than he does—who lets you know in no uncertain and unsavoury terms.

Regardless of what was said in the previous few lines, we have had some tremendously exciting days of fishing on the Saugeen River, including several memorable battles with rainbows up to eighteen pounds and salmon over thirty. It was with those thoughts in mind that I drove for about a half an hour north of where I live to meet Paul in Newmarket on opening day a couple of years ago. Living in Uxbridge, he simply had to drive west for about fifteen minutes, park, then transfer his waders and fishing gear to the Jeep.

Our plan was to meet at 4:45 a.m., load up, then drive to Southampton and the Saugeen River on the shore of Lake Huron. We anticipated the very real possibility of catching several of the gorgeous steelheads up from the lake on their spring spawning run. About twenty minutes after Paul came aboard the Jeep with his boots and equipment and about ten miles west of where we had met in Newmarket, an ungodly clanging racket began to reverberate from beneath the Jeep's hood. I couldn't believe this was happening—and on opening day!

Slowing to a crawl, I decided to pull over and let the engine cool down. We rested it as long as our patience would allow. We opened the hood to see if by any chance the problem was something simple and obvious—no such luck. Much more knowledgeable in automobile matters than I and skinnier, Paul offered to slide beneath for a look-see. There was nothing obviously beneath the front end where the noise seemed to be coming from so Paul concluded that it had to be something to do with the transmission.

As I get free tows from my auto club, I had the Jeep towed to the Canadian Tire store in Newmarket while Paul contacted his brother and arranged to meet me there. It was after seven by the time he drove up. With the sign on the store window indicating a nine o'clock opening, however, we locked the Jeep and decided to kill time in a nearby coffee shop. While there we happened to meet the manager of the store's service department who informed us that because of a backlog of work orders they would not even be able to look at the Jeep until the next day. He suggested we have the Jeep towed to a Mr. Transmission shop up the road a few blocks, where the owner, he confided, "loves fishing."

We finished our coffees and hiked up the street, hoping that the transmission shop would be open and the store's owner would be in. It was—and he was there.

Gord, in the early 1990s, with a chinook salmon caught at Denny's Dam.

We told him our sad story. Offering words of encouragement, he indicated that although he couldn't look at it for an hour or two, we should have it towed to his shop as soon as possible. Fortunately I have an unlimited tow feature in my auto club membership so back I went to the same fellow who had towed the Jeep back to town. Once more the vehicle was moved, then parked in the new location while we headed back to the coffee shop. Eventually we were summoned and told that fixing my car would be a major job and, providing that parts could be obtained from a wrecker, the cost should not run more than two thousand dollars. Ouch! Not a great way to start the day and trout fishing season! I was left with no choice. Looking at my watch I saw it was now exactly twelve o'clock. I took a deep breath, instructed the chap to proceed with the work as soon as possible, then addressing my patient fishing buddy, I said, "Let's go fishing."

Waders and tackle were quickly transferred into Paul's car and a couple of hours later—exactly 2:00 p.m.—we finally arrived at Denny's Dam[1] on the Saugeen, probably the most popular fishing location on the entire river, expecting to still see dozens of anglers and fishermen plying their skills— and whatever—on the fast flowing water below the dam. Fishing for these migratory rainbow trout, is usually most productive, as is most trout fishing, first thing in the morning. Most of the folks who pursue this wonderful fishery are aware of this and arrive at their favourite hot spots well before

Fishing on the Big Head River upstream from Meaford,
Ontario, in 1954.

sun-up to stake out their desired positions alongside the river. Other than the initial few weeks of the season and the 'bow's spawning run, the majority of these fishermen, tired after standing in ice-cold fast water in their heavy chest waders for hours, seldom remain as long as noon hour and head home to hot showers and possibly even to a warm bed.

Nevertheless, with opening day only hours old, Paul and I were stunned to discover that the river from Denny's Dam downstream as far as we could see was relatively deserted when we arrived at two o'clock. It was discouraging to see that apparently there were few trout in the river, as the weather certainly could not have been a factor in driving the men off the river. It was excellent. But cursing our luck for not having been able to arrive there at the planned time, when whatever fish were still in the river would be most receptive to our offerings, we waded in to the heavy current, firmly anchored our feet on the slippery, rocky bottom and began casting. There were perhaps a half a dozen glum-looking fishermen, here and there, still drifting their roe bags dejectedly with nary a one indicating signals of success, such as a stringer-full of rainbows fastened to their wading belts—or their long rods bowed almost to their breaking points by big fish.

Above the roar of the water cascading over the dam, I shouted to Paul, fishing fifty feet away from me, that we give the area about an hour or so, then head over to Meaford. The proposal was barely out of my mouth when he yelled the expression all anglers appreciate hearing, "Fish on!"

Paul is an expert angler. It was a treat watching him play his catch with the aplomb of a veteran angler, eventually working the silver beauty right by my position so it could be photographed before he casually wrapped his gloved hand around the narrow portion of the trout's body in front of the tail and hoisted it for the *coup de gras* picture, "What do you think, Gord," he asked, "eight pounds?"

"Easily," I yelled back over my shoulder as I resumed my position upstream from him in the river.

With the adrenalin now flowing once again after our initial disappointment upon our arrival, I began working my spinner through the current with renewed vigour and enthusiasm. Several casts later I latched onto another rainbow that performed extraordinary airborne acrobatics in its attempts to shed the foreign object implanted in its jaw. Three, four, five—and possibly even more jumps clear of the water before it began to zigzag all over the place created an exciting show, not only for Paul and me, but several of the remaining fishermen still in the vicinity.

Seeing a couple of big 'bows taken, when apparently their own efforts were proving fruitless was more than the other fellows could endure without comments as one by one they surrendered their positions in the river to gradually close in on us. "What in hell are you guys using for bait, anyhow?" one of them shouted in our direction.

Paul and I simultaneously held our ultra-light spinning rods aloft to display them along with the silver spinners that were our chosen lures. Then, completely disdaining our light tackle, the other fellows simply snorted and went back to their fifteen-foot long rods and drowning their roe bags. At almost four o'clock, only a couple of hours after we had first arrived, we triumphantly marched back to the parking lot area, each carrying our limit of three beautiful rainbow trout, all between five and eight pounds. Why we were able to do so well when it had appeared that our chances were close to nil has always remained a puzzle. Possibly the only answer is that the "angling gods" were taking pity on us after the trials and tribulations we had endured in our earlier efforts to simply go fishing and catch a couple of trout.

We fishermen are a weird lot! A look back over our shoulders when we reached the crest of the hill put the finishing touches on this particular magical memory for me. It was obvious that most of the remaining fishermen, vying for the best spot, had already closed in on our former positions in the river.

Chapter 21
The Mighty Broadback River

The Broadback! The mighty Broadback River! No other body of water has ever created more incredible memories for me.

We first became enamoured with the Broadback in 1961 after learning that an eleven-pound speckled trout, or brookie if you prefer, was captured in Assinica Lake, a portion of the enormous Broadback River watershed. We have since had the pleasure of wetting a line in its magical waters twenty-one times over the years, a number of the fellows returning several times to again toss feathers or lures at the river's remarkable brook trout.

All those enjoyable hours spent in pursuit of Dr. John Cook's[1] magnificent world-record fourteen-pound plus brookie produced many trophy trout for our crew. Over that forty-odd year period, the trout probably averaged just a shade below two feet in length and close to four pounds, but alas, Dr. Cook's record still stands. However, another world record was established in 1961 when I was lucky enough to land the largest speckled trout ever taken on a fly.

Our initial exploration of the Broadback's mighty resources was almost halted before it began. We ran into many obstacles, such as, "You *must* go through an outfitter,"—"You *must* have a fire permit,"—You *must* have a guide"—and a number of other "musts" that happily have long since faded from memory. We could neither afford to, nor wanted to, go through an outfitter, much preferring to do our own thing, camping, cooking, fishing and so on. We finally convinced the powers that if given permission to camp, we would locate well away from the two outfitters who had rapidly established camps on the Broadback after the eleven-pound speckled trout caught in Assinica Lake by a prospector's guide, Bruno Moisin, was reported in *Field and Stream* magazine.

Assinica is one of the territory's largest lakes, with portions of the Broadback flowing both into and out of it. The Demers' camp, established by the colourful Rene Demers, was given the right to establish the first outfitter's camp on the lake and it was through Rene that we eventually received permission to pitch our own camp on the Broadback, provided it was not within thirty miles of his operation. Another camp on Lake Opatica, run by a woman whose name escapes me, had also been in operation for a while. Once we had made up our minds that we would head for northern Quebec and the Broadback River system the following summer, a friend and I spent hours poring over the maps of the area and discovered that there were literally dozens of lakes whose waters drained into the Broadback River system. It seemed obvious that if Assinica Lake could produce a gigantic brook trout like Moisin's, then some of the other headwater lakes with similar ecological features might also harbour record-size brook trout.

We could probably have placed the map on the wall and while wearing blindfolds stuck a pin anywhere in the system and come up with a good chance of getting what we were seeking, huge brookies and maybe a record to boot. Regardless, we settled on an area that appeared geologically similar to Assinica Lake and its nearby rapids, and began a furious exchange of correspondence with the Quebec Tourism, Fish and Game Department to determine the viability of our plans to camp on our own on the Broadback the following summer.

Ultimately, we wore down our opposition, or perhaps they simply tired of our persistence and decided *que sera sera*. They said that if we were able to get permission from one of the outfitters, obtain all the necessary papers and permits and hire a guide, then we would receive their blessing. With the light at the end of the tunnel opening at last, our planning accelerated. We would leave Toronto in mid-summer, make the horrendous, tire-devouring trek through northwest Quebec on roads, hundreds of miles of which were still under their construction. Our destination was the end of the line, Chibougamau, a town of less than five thousand. A typical mining town, it was growing by leaps and bounds in the fifties and sixties when copper and other valuable ores were being discovered almost daily throughout the area. A few months later when we eventually completed the two-day odyssey, which included a blown radiator, two tires destroyed, a broken fan belt and a cracked windshield, the dusty little mining town became a mighty welcome sight for "the two sports with the two boats," the nickname we were known by in town. I believe the translation was, *Les deux sportifs avec les deux bateaux*, or something along those lines.

We had driven to and arrived in Chibougamau with a car-top boat on the roof and a canoe lashed down on top of it. Not quite knowing what to expect, we hedged our bet with a plan to drive as far north of the town as we could on the twenty-odd-mile trail heading to Lac Waconichi. We would then pick our way along a route as far as we could using the car-top and small motor, with the canoe in tow, yet making sure that we had enough fuel remaining to make the return trip. Then, if necessary, we would paddle and portage until we reached one of the headwater tributaries of the Broadback River.

At least that was our plan, but first we had to locate a guide. This was more than forty years ago and there was no e-mail or local tourist bureau to contact from Toronto. Basically we were flying by the seat of our pants, while hoping that we would find a guide among the Natives who lived in a camp near town. That turned out to be a mistake. In town we discovered that the outfitters in the newly created Mistassini Reservation, where our destination lay, had previously recruited the only licensed guides in the area.

In the hopes of hiring one of his guides, we made a frantic short-wave radio call from the local air base (Fecteau Airways) to Rene Demers, the gentleman who had sort of given us his blessing. It proved futile, except he did happen to mention that he had heard that one of the guides working for the camp on Lake Opatica had recently been dismissed. The fellow's name was Maxim Moisim, the brother of the guide responsible for our being there, Bruno Moisim. It was he who had caught the eleven-pound speckled trout to begin the Broadback River and Assinica Lake craze.

Maxim's firing proved to be a stroke of luck, as it appeared he was the only licensed guide not tied up by the outfitters. In the local beverage room in the Waconichi Hotel, referred to by the locals as the "Itchy Scratchy," we learned that Maxim had been released because of his excessive drinking while on the job. We were not concerned with that possible problem however. It was Maxim's licensed qualifications that we required. He could stay in town if he wished as long as it was being recorded that he was our guide. The problem was locating the fellow, but our friendly waiter came to the rescue again, informing us that Monsieur Moisim would most likely be by for a drink or two before long. "Before long" turned out to be a couple of days. On our third day in Chibougamau, after garnering all the necessary permits and spending every spare moment studying the more detailed maps in the tiny Fecteau air base on Lac Cache, our buddy in the beverage room told us that we had just missed our man the day before. He assured us though that he had made him promise to show up the next afternoon.

"Here he comes now," the waiter said, pointing to the dishevelled fellow who had just ambled into the beverage room. We had been awaiting his arrival with trepidation, but that feeling disappeared the moment we first saw him. As long as his guide's licence was still valid we felt that getting this chap to join us for several days and make a few bucks at the same time should surely not be a problem.

Our initial assessment proved correct, but with the assistance of our waiter friend doing the translating, our original plan to take a northwest marine route using both boats had to be abandoned. When the plan was described to Maxim, with the route outlined on our topographical map, he was adamant that a journey of that nature would take more than a month to reach the desired destination and be extremely difficult. He suggested that we tone down the entire proposal, including the duration in the bush by chartering a Beaver float plane from Fecteau Airways and flying in. A close-by lake would make an ideal spot to put down, leaving us with only a mile or two to reach the big red asterisk sketched on the map. When we asked if he had ever been to that precise spot, he replied that he had not. He then added the government mantra about the fishing potential in the entire Assinica and Broadback area—*Beaucoup brochet et dore, monsieurs, mais pas de truit!* Nevertheless, our minds were made up and his suggestion that there were lots of pike and pickerel in the area—but no trout—did not dampen our enthusiasm one iota.

After initial inquiries, tentative arrangements were made with Fecteau. As they had informed us previously that they would not be allowed to fly us in to anywhere in the reserve unless we had a licensed guide along with us, we made a proposition to him. He would not be required to do any of the chores normally assigned to the guide, but simply join our party as one of the "sports." I explained that he would merely be along for the ride and that I would do the cooking and so on, while he could fish, rest, or do whatever he wished. For the privilege of having him—and his licence—along with us, we would pay him the princely sum of fifty dollars and I would give him my leather boots when the trip was completed. His were full of holes and nearly useless. We also agreed to his only request that we buy the biggest bottle of his favourite wine that the local store had in stock and take it with us. The result of all that planning, wishing and persistence paid off big time for all three of us. It also provided the biggest magical memory of all time to this day for me.

With the flight and portage completed twenty-four hours later, and the camp set up, it was time to see if our dreams were just that, or would they

*Gord, in 2005, mounting the motor on the boat, as the Cessna float
plane is about to take its leave from the Broadback River.*

become reality. While our guide stretched out with his bottle in the tent,
we tossed a coin to determine who would fish above the little falls we had
chosen off the top maps and who would work the churning rapids below. I
should have saved that coin and had it framed to place alongside the trophy
of my life that subsequently rested on the wall in my recreation room for
years, before disintegrating for some reason or another.

Taking only a few moments to suck in the majesty of the scene before me,
I broke through the bush near the foot of the falls. I studied the waters carefully in order to select the most appropriate place to place my fly on the first
cast I was to make of many thousands on the Broadback over the next forty
years. Fishing countless streams back home since my youth had already
convinced me of the importance of that first cast. With a turgid and awesome flow running down the middle of the river, the choices were pretty
well limited to the pools and back currents on the side of the river where
I stood, or across the sixty or seventy feet of fast waters to the other side
where similar conditions prevailed. There was a bit of a whirlpool caused by
an enormous boulder near the opposite shore, however, that seemed to call
out to me to try and make the tricky cast.

As has been mentioned several times, we fishermen always seem to believe
in the old adage, "far fields look greener." Trout fishermen are the worst
of the lot. We also believe that if it looks too easy, it probably is not worth
the effort. To place the fly in the heart of that dark and inviting pool from
my perch on a slippery rock would require a double-haul cast with the line
travelling high on the back cast to avoid the scraggly and threatening black

The view of the Broadback River as seen from the "throne" at the camp.

spruces that lined the shores. But if the fly was to pause in the water long enough for a trout to see the thing before the rapids whisked it away, then the final forward cast would have to be mended in a series of "Lazy Ss"[2] to allow the fly to hold and sink momentarily while the current worked on the slack created by the "S" cast. Being so eager to present my offering, to what I felt could be the biggest brook trout of my career, I did not take enough time to assess how I would play the fish if one were to attack it right away. All those years of tournament casting paid off as the cast was perfect, sailing completely across the fast water, then settling in several large "Ss" on the other side before the leader rolled over and deposited the #6 Despair nymph[3] right on target. The following is a scene that I shall never forget.

The Despair barely touched base when the water erupted and the most spectacular moment and memory of the thousands that I have enjoyed over all these years occurred! The biggest speckled trout I have ever seen—before or since—alive or dead and on a wall—other than Dr. Cook's world-record fourteen-pounder that I had been pursuing since I was a youngster, rolled completely out of the water. With my Despair firmly implanted in its jaw, it charged into the middle of the fast water and cartwheeled clear of the white water like an Atlantic salmon. It was a mind-boggling scene!

All I could do as the huge trout shot downstream, with the rapids aiding in its attempt to escape, was hold the fly rod high to alleviate the pressure on the line with its frail leader and tippet while muttering a silent prayer. I glanced at my watch. It was exactly half-past eleven in the morning. Then, after its exhaustive, mad dash downstream as the line rocketed off my reel and into the backing, I could feel the pressure on the nine-foot rod ease a little when the big brookie reached the foot of the rapids and moved into the back current to rest.

Fifty-five minutes later it was tired enough that I was finally able to work the trout in close to the rock where I was perched, then cautiously ease it, head first, into the awaiting mesh just as I became aware that my friend was filming the final moments with the movie camera. "I didn't say anything," he shouted over the roar of the falls where he stood, "because I thought you'd be able to concentrate better if you weren't disturbed. That's one monster trout!"

In order to maintain its weight, I kept the brookie alive at the side of the falls on a stringer in a rocky cairn. That would also serve to prevent any mink wishing a meal of trout from attacking her. When weighed in town four days later in the Bay post store, that record brookie weighed eleven-and-a-quarter pounds and was twenty-nine-and-a-half inches long. That tale is easily number one on my list of all-time magical memories.

There is one other easily recalled exceptional memory from that first trip to the waters of the Broadback River—another adventure with a huge brookie. The day after I caught the eleven-pounder, my friend and I switched locations. I scrambled through the brush and climbed to the crest at the top of the falls. From there it was easy to make out the profile of a fish that was just as big and possibly even bigger than the elusive target presented to us all those years by Dr. Cook's record speckled trout. My initial reaction was that a fish that size had to be a pike. We had already caught several of the brutish fish that triggered the pocket scales to their maximum reading, twenty pounds. The fish, lying in a depression with its tail inches from the very crest of the falls, made precise observation difficult with the current racing over its holding spot. Continuing to study the scene though, I suddenly remembered my Polaroid glasses buried somewhere in my fishing vest.

I almost fainted when they were put to work. It was obvious that this was another huge brook trout, probably just lying on a redd waiting to deposit her eggs. Obviously she had not been there the day before when my friend was working the upstream waters, or I would have heard about her. There was one startling difference between that fish and the "biggie" caught below the falls previously. Although the trout we had safely ensconced in the rocky cairn below the falls was big, the biggest I had ever seen, this fish was even bigger, much bigger—possibly even larger than Dr. Cook's record trout. I estimated it to be close to a yard in length. It seemed ridiculous standing there after all those years staring at what was potentially a world-record speckled trout. *"Must be a lake trout,"* I thought, *"or else I'm just dreaming or something!"* As I watched, the enormous fish rolled on to its side for a moment and was forced to use its great square-tail to right itself and avoid being swept over the crest. Knowing that only brookies have tails like that, with the help of the Polaroids I detected the telltale coloured markings that only brook trout and Arctic char possess. I was momentarily frozen on the spot, but there are no Artic char this far south I reminded myself.

I realized that, if hooked, my only chance to land the huge trout would be in somehow being able to prevent her from turning tail and plunging over the falls. Although the current above the crest where she was holding was obviously powerful, it did not look deep. Remembering that a trout hooked in a stream or river will almost always make its initial attempt to escape in an upstream run, I thought to myself, *"If she takes the Despair, the same fly that worked for me below the falls then, using my wading staff I'll wade out to the middle and try to deter her if she comes back downstream by slapping the fly rod on the surface in front of her. Then, hopefully, I'll be able to get back to shore and play her successfully upstream."*

It seemed like a reasonable plan at the time. However, the huge and possible overall world-record speckled trout was not buying into the theory. The cast was placed twenty feet up current from the big hen brookie to allow a natural drift presentation right into her field of view. As the Despair tumbled in the current towards her, she only had to move forward a few inches to take the fly.

That was a most exhilarating magical moment! I struck and, as anticipated, the great fish, almost ignoring the sensation of the hook being buried in its jaw, casually moved off the redd and swam forty or fifty feet as I awaited her next move with trepidation. For a few moments it appeared that we would be able to do battle with her on my terms then she rolled once on the surface and promptly swam back directly towards where I stood, a short distance from her former position on the redd. I stripped line furiously to remove the slack then readied myself as she rushed towards me, preparing to slap the water as planned. If the fish had been able to, I am sure she would have been laughing as she ignored the sight of me standing, waist high in the heavy current, slapping the water with my fragile, cane fly rod, before she slid over the crest of the falls behind me.

Pivoting precariously to avoid the rod's being broken, I came close to losing my balance and joining her in the plunge over the slippery precipice. I held the rod as high as I could attempting to keep the fly line from snagging on rocks as the trout tumbled down through the rushing water. Somehow, the leader managed to hold and the huge fish stayed hooked right to the bottom of the falls where I had taken the eleven-pounder earlier. While maintaining the rod's position I scrambled ashore as quickly as possible, thinking that if the line could be prevented from snagging on its plunge, then the trout could be played downstream as had successfully been done with my first "biggie." With thoughts of Dr. Cook's record possibly being bettered, I was able to clear the fly line from several large boulders. But it was firmly trapped beneath one large, craggy chunk of granite and held there securely by the current. Freeing it proved to be impossible even though I could sense that the trout was still on and resting in the pool at the foot of the falls.

My brain was initiating possible solutions to the dilemma, but none of the suggestions seemed feasible. It would have been far too dangerous to attempt to breach the current in that area to try to free the line. Sadly, there was only one alternative: scream for my friend or the guide to see if they could somehow cast over the line, pull it in, then hang on while I scrambled down to take over the job of landing the fish. To become an official record, the trout would have to be landed by me. The odds of that being successful were prohibitive at the best, but other than jumping in and following the fish's path over the falls, there was no other choice.

Unfortunately, neither one could hear my shouts above the roar of the falls and eventually, feeling the pressure on the line slackening, I realized the trout had departed with my Despair—and potential world record at the same time, leaving Dr. Cook's status still intact. I felt then, though, that it would only be a matter of time before I, or others in my party fishing the waters of the Broadback, would eclipse the fourteen-pound standard he had established more than a half a century earlier on Ontario's Nipigon River.

The well-stocked kitchen at the Broadback camp in 1998.

Different fishing buddies and I continued to return to the Broadback over the next few years, with its waters producing a number of other large specimens of *Salvelinus fontinalis* (brookies), fish up to eight-and-a-half pounds, but eventually the wanderlust factor began to overtake us again. We still had hopes that an even bigger trout than our own biggest, and Dr. Cook's overall record fish, could be swimming somewhere in the Broadback.

In 1967, one of those dreams that are so vivid that they seem to have been delivered from another unworldly realm came to pass. Gathering my coterie of angling aficionados for an evening of ogling our fishing movies and some chit-chat, I brought out a blackboard and chalk from my son's room. After sketching a crude map of the proposed area, I proceeded to illustrate for them what had been revealed to me in that dream. Using a ruler as a pointer, I indicated a place where a plane with floats could land. From there it appeared to be a four or five-mile canoe trip up the river, then around a sharp bend and right there was the spot of my dreams.

"Doesn't look like much though on a map," I added, "but if it's even close to what was revealed to me in my dream, it'll be perfect."

Continuing, I explained that what I saw in that dream was a huge falls, with a cluster of tiny islands at the foot of it. There was even an excellent place to pitch camp. I shut up and simply waited for their questions and remarks. Eyebrows raised, they looked quizzically at each other for a few moments, each waiting for the other to say something. Finally, Larry Sykes who had been to the river with me once, spoke up indicating that it had to be the Broadback River. He had an eight-pound brookie to prove it, and he reminded the fellows of the eleven-pounder I had also caught there. He was in. Subsequently, Gary Benson and John Smith cast aside their uneasiness about the "dream" and indicated that they, too, would be willing to explore new territory, "Just in case there is reality in that vision that he had," Gary said.

At the end of August 1968, the four of us motored down the river from an old Indian camp where we had been deposited by Fecteau's big amphibious Beaver aircraft. I held my breath as we approached the bend in the river where I was certain the falls and its magical waters lay around the corner. The bush, mostly black spruce, was so dense that there was no sound to indicate that we were indeed on the right track until the moment we broke into the clear around the bend.

It was spectacular! Exactly as it had appeared in the "dream!" The fellows looked at each other in disbelief as I mopped up a stream of emotional tears rolling down my cheeks while making futile attempts to rid my entire body of goose bumps. There it was, the enormous falls, the rapids surging from its base and the cluster of five mini-islands slightly to one side with the currents indicating their respective perimeters. The roar of the powerful waterfall would have drowned out any conversation if there had been any, but there was none, just utter silence in the big canoe while we all stared in disbelief—all, that is, but me. Grinning at the total ambience of the spectacular panorama, I found my brain spinning as it attempted to deal with the whole incredible situation, until Gary finally broke the spell, asking, "Okay, Gord, now where do we set-up camp?"

French toast and sausage anyone? Gord always does the cooking.

There were so many highlights on that first trip to the area that eventually, even at the air base and local government offices, it became known as the "Deval Territory." Old buddy, Gary Benson, figured prominently in two exceptional happenings there that I shall never forget.

The first took place on our first full day in camp after taking the better part of the previous day getting everything organized and shipshape. While John and Larry were still buried in their down sleeping bags and I was busy preparing breakfast, Gary emerged from the tent, wearing long johns, his toque perched perkily on his head, stretched, scratched his belly and said, "Coffee smells good. Can't sleep any longer. Too damn noisy in there!"

That noise is why I have always chosen to sleep beneath the kitchen shelter outside, preferring the exhilarating roar of the falls to the raucous rumbling sounds inside the tent. My camera was still perched on the tripod where it had been left the day before after filming the day's activities in setting up the camp and kitchen shelter. Near it was my little spinning rod. Tied to the line was a number eighteen Rapala,[4] an enormous plug designed to attract large muskie and pike. I had put it on attempting to get a pike that had already stolen several of our smaller lures when its razor sharp teeth sliced through the six-pound monofilament line like a hot knife through butter. The ten-inch long balsa wood plug would give us a better chance to take out the pike and retrieve the lures it stole earlier. However, it was not to be.

Gary asked if he could take a couple of shots with it, then lobbed the big lure forty feet out, just as John emerged from the tent, fists rubbing both eyes.

"Heh, John," I yelled, "do me a favour, please. When you're through beating up on your eyes, would you shoot a few feet of Benson in his slippers and long underwear fishing on the Broadback."

At that moment Larry stumbled out the unzipped door of the old Woods nine-by-twelve canvas abode. He was just in time to hear Gary yell, "Fish on! Big pike, I think."

The fish boiled on the surface twenty-five feet in front of where he was standing, a short distance from the front of the tent. I saw the big tail break the surface just before it dove and took off for parts unknown. It was a square-tail, a brook trout and a big one! I put John on stove detail while I dove for the camera to get this one on film.

Gary was suddenly hit with "muskie fever," the well-known temporary ailment that often overcomes an angler when they tie in to one of those toothy fellows. Only this was not a muskie, nor a pike. It was a damn big brook trout. While the camera was recording the entire scene, there was Gary, walking out in the river, clad only in underwear and slippers. I guess somewhere in his subconsciousness he felt he would have a better chance of subduing the trout if he joined it in its own element. The incident was fodder for some of the most unusual footage that I have ever been lucky enough to obtain, and indelibly etched the scene for me as another all-time memory. After twenty minutes of give and take with his catch, it was eased into the shallows and the awaiting mesh of his landing net. The film of Gary in his sopping wet long johns, toque only slightly askew, holding aloft his biggest brookie ever, ten-and-a-quarter pounds, with the huge Rapala plug firmly embedded crosswise in its cavernous jaw, still draws rave comments whenever shown to other anglers.

Gary's catch from the front of the tent being the obvious incentive, a day or two after his trophy trout was caught we decided that we would take it

Gary Benson with his ten-pounder in front of the camp in 1968.

easy and just do a little fishing close to camp. But he surprised us with the announcement that if we didn't mind he wanted to try something different after lunch. According to him, he just wanted to try fishing the river the same way we fish the streams back home. He wanted to walk the shoreline above the falls as far as he could, then make casts wherever it looked as though there might be a little action. He figured, with luck, he might find a hot spot or a spawning bed or something worth investigating.

Larry said, "Better take a lot of lures with you then, because you'll be donating a pile of them to the snags along the way, as well as the fucking pike."

That startled the rest of us because Larry seldom swore, certainly nothing beyond a simple, "Darn." A few days in the bush with his "foul-mouthed" fishing buddies though had somehow left an obtuse impression on him. He, too, had begun using some of the more explosive epithets and expletives, usually in their proper context, but occasionally, in a completely meaningless phrase. By the end of our fifteen-day trip Larry was swearing like a trooper.

There was plenty of advice and suggestions offered by the rest of the crew as Gary prepared for his solo adventure, including to try to get back to camp before dark. That last one was a "biggie!"

Later, while John, Larry and I worked the waters on both sides of our falls all afternoon, we worried about Gary's decision to take off upstream—and on his own. Supper was delayed until well into the evening, hoping he would return in time to eat with us, but as darkness closed in we eventually cooked and ate the pickerel dinner with hardly a word being spoken—and without him.

Camped on first island with three pairs of eyes hoping to spot the beam of Gary's flashlight, we were constantly searching the shoreline and makeshift bridge that had been constructed from a couple of birch trees. Before he had left, the last thing we had agreed upon was that if he did not get back to camp by midnight it would be foolish for us to attempt to track and find him in the blackness of night in the deep and treacherous bush. Instead we would be up and at 'em at first light to begin the search. Although our camp was equipped with an old short-wave radio, it was felt that we should not attempt to send out an SOS to the outside world until we gave it our all in our own search for him. Gary had promised that he would be extremely careful on his trek, but if something unfortunate did happen, he said that he felt sufficiently competent to look after almost any emergency and would simply bed down for the night and wait for his rescuers (us) if necessary the next morning.

Dinner was finished and our respective cots and sleeping bags were being readied, albeit with the concern and gloom that had befallen us in camp there certainly wouldn't be a great deal of sleep, or even rest. Sleeping outside and beneath the big tarp that served as our kitchen shelter, I was usually the last to pack it in, thus I was the first to see a tiny beam of light piercing the darkness from the mainland at the other end of the bridge.

"He's back, guys!" I yelled, then rushed to give him a hand, just as John and Larry also hustled towards the log bridge. I yelled again, this time at the apparition carefully making its way across the bridge in the darkness; the only light now being the dying flickering flames of the campfire, "Are you okay, Gare? Damn, am I ever glad you made it back alright!"

We were so busy tending to him then that none of us noticed the big brookie tied to a cord and tossed over his shoulder. Although he was physically exhausted, Gary was so fired up after the adventure that he had little trouble staying awake to give us all the details of his great trek. But first we had to tend to his multiple cuts and scratches, most likely caused by the black spruce branches that he had to fight his way through for most of the ten-hour hike.

It was close to one o'clock in the morning before the four of us were finally able to hit the sack, Gary had flopped his second great brookie (it eventually tipped the scales at more than eight pounds) down on the ground for us to admire and told us the whole story... "It was tough," he said, "goddamn tough!"

His story was mind-boggling. Apparently he had had to walk miles around bays and swamps for hours before he found any place where he could toss a lure from shore without hanging up on the interminable spruce branches. Slogging through the muck and heavy bush had taken a toll, but when the sun began setting, he rested awhile before beginning the trek back to camp. He said he actually dozed off, but when the sun disappeared he was so cold it luckily woke him up. However, he decided to make one last cast before the task ahead of him in the dark and latched on to the beautiful mountie that he decided to keep, even though he would have to lug it back with him.

John asked an interesting question, "Heh Gare, now that you've got a better idea of what's facing you up there, would you do it again?"

Gary's response surprised me even more than John's remarks, "Are you kidding, John? Of course, I would!"

Nevertheless, neither John and Gary, nor Larry and I, ever followed in Gary's footsteps on that one, all agreeing that with nothing left to prove, discretion was better than valour.

That first trip, 1968, to the Deval Territory on the Broadback, produced another exceptional mountie for our crew, a beautiful ten-and-a-half pound speckled trout. That fish should have been a brook trout trophy for John Smith's recreation room wall, but a fluke of fate intervened and the trophy sits in a glass case on my wall instead. According to the maps that we had studied long and hard, it appeared that with a little effort, portaging, long-lining and paddling the canoe, we could have as many as three or four other sets of rapids and falls to investigate and fish within a few miles of our base camp.

Beginning the second week on the river we decided to work our way right through to the end of our fishable territory. None of us would wet a line until we reached the last rapids that were situated within practical distance of our home base. Although they had looked good on the map and several previous attempts had been made to reach them, we became sidetracked each time with the apparent possibilities along the way. By the time we reached the last portage it always seemed too late to make the final leg, paddling and hiking a mile or so of each. The thought of having to do a "Gary Benson" hike back to camp in the dark was really not very appealing.

John Smith inching his way across the Broadback.

However, we felt that if we could get away from camp early enough, keep our fishing rods encased and ignore the appeal of all that magical water we would have to navigate to get there, maybe the potential of the far rapids could finally be tapped. Once we managed to adhere to the plan, there was only a paddle of perhaps three-quarters of a mile remaining after the final portage. As we approached, lots were drawn to see who wanted to fish where. Benson and Sykes opted to work the edges of the downstream fast waters, while John thought that a house-sized chunk of granite near the beginning of the somewhat slower current looked like a good spot from which to work. There was only one place left for me to fish, upstream above the rest of the guys. I voiced the opinion that a decent holding spot could well be there.

That must have tweaked John's subconscious. When he headed off into the bush, instead of working his way back out to the giant rock at the foot of the rapids that he had selected for his perch, he went fifty yards past it to the area beyond the corner that had been left for me. I thought I might as well try fishing from his rock instead, rather than being in his way upstream. Moving into position to fish from the rock was a little tricky. Once there, however, after taking a few moments to survey the current for likely holding spots, I checked the slipping clutch on my ultra-light spinning reel, then casually flipped the big spinner a few feet in front of the rock to make sure it was working properly. Spinner shafts occasionally do become bent. It must have been doing its job, as an enormously long shadow drifted out from beneath my perch, obviously from an undercut below the rock. It moved towards the flashing spinner, then with a swish of its great square tail abruptly disappeared in a cloud of tiny bubbles.

Although 1968 was the year I quit smoking, I still had not completely bitten the bullet, so quivering like a leaf in the breeze, I managed to quietly sit down and light up while contemplating my next move. It has always been my experience that a fish displaying an interest in the lure, but not taking it on the first pass, can often be brought back for a second look and possible strike—but only if it has been given a few minutes to think about it before a second offering is presented. It seemed to take forever to finish the smoke. Then, being resolute in adhering to my theory about "giving the fish a rest," I rose cautiously so as not to dislodge any moss or debris into the water. A trout doesn't get that large by throwing caution to the wind. I realized that it would not take much to disturb it, or give my position away. *"More than likely,"* I thought, *"the trout's returned to its lie below the rock…it's been relatively undisturbed…didn't touch the lure…and it couldn't have seen me, above and behind it on top of the rock."*

Rather than cast upstream and draw the lure across the face of the rock, presenting the spinner in the same position that had initially attracted the fish, I decided to repeat the flip cast that drew it out for a look-see the first time, but would allow the spinner to sink to the bottom before twitching it into life with the retrieve. I almost passed out when the shadow emerged once again from beneath my perch the moment the lure began its ascent. The brookie casually swam up toward it, then with no sensation of a strike or planned kill of the thing intruding its territory, it merely opened its cavernous maw and engulfed the spinner. Another of my fabulous memories stored away to be enjoyed again in a future recollection!

I let out a yelp that I felt certain was loud enough to bring one of the fellows on the run to record the battle on film, only I had completely forgotten that it's impossible to run through the black spruce forest. For the most part, the bush is as close to being impassable as anywhere I have ever fished. Fortunately the trout was firmly hooked and the great rock proved to be an ideal place to play the big fellow. By keeping it from reaching the main flow and rapids each time it tried, a healthy back current worked in my favour, whereas it most likely would have been "game over" for me, not the fish, if it had prevailed. Gary arrived from downstream just as it was landed and did manage to capture the trout's denouement on film.

The mountie, ten-and-a quarter pounds, twenty-nine inches long, a twin to Gary's trophy trout caught back at camp, was a gorgeous male specimen. Obviously, I was elated at the catch, but at the same time felt disappointed that fate had put me in position to capture the huge brook trout, when more than likely that one would have ended up gracing John Smith's wall, if only he had adhered to his wishes and fished from the giant rock instead of going completely by it.

As was mentioned earlier, good friend Larry Sykes was having a problem maintaining his reputation as a gentleman who never swore, that is beyond a "gosh darn," "phooey" and an occasional "bloody." Nevertheless hearing Gary, John and me use almost every four-letter expletive ever invented over a couple of weeks when losing a trout or forfeiting a favourite lure to a big pike, unfortunately rubbed off on him. Even the most colourful terms eventually became part of his repertoire of cuss words as well. On the final evening of our wonderful fifteen-day sojourn while relaxing around the evening campfire, someone questioned Larry as to whether he was going to be able to return to his former status as one who never swore after spending a couple of weeks in the bush with his foul-mouthed friends.

He looked somewhat apprehensive as I suggested that I make a bow with a piece of red wool from our fly-tying kit and fasten it to his middle finger. It should act as a reminder and warning to him to watch his tongue when he got home. He agreed to the suggestion, and the "caution reminder" was put in place on his middle digit as described.

Almost forty-eight hours later, his being the first stop back in Toronto, we pulled into the Sykes driveway to drop him off and unload his gear. His wife, Bev, came out to greet us as we were unpacking his equipment and immediately noticed the red bow fastened to her husband's middle finger. Unfortunately, by then Larry had become accustomed to its presence and when Bev inquired about the odd little bow on his finger, he replied, "Oh that! I guess I forgot to take the fucking thing off!"

A couple of years later we returned with a somewhat different crew. Gary Benson and I went back for another go, this time with fishing buddy, Don Petican, and great friend, Tony Whittingham. That is not to infer that my fishing buddies are not all great friends, too, but Tony will always hold a special place in my heart. Although that was his first trip to the Broadback River, in all he has accompanied us on seven occasions, more than any of the others.

A highlight of that 1970 trip and one of my most significant memories, involved another giant chunk of granite and Tony. It took place at the first set of rapids upriver from our main camp. As usual, we chose our respective places from which to begin fishing when we approached the foot of the rapids. Although we do move around a little when fishing the Broadback, we have learned that it is usually most productive to work one particular location thoroughly before exploring another.

Don and Gary had chosen to work the west side of the river while Tony and I selected the east. Tony liked the look of the great rock a hundred yards up the shore above the foot of the rapids, leaving me at another cluster of boulders near where I had dropped him off before beaching the canoe.

A gleeful Don Petican in 1978.

Because we were collecting as much footage as possible for a movie we were putting together, while he worked his way up the shoreline and figured out how to scale the rock that he had chosen to fish from I busied myself taking shots of Don and Gary fishing on the other side.

Satisfied, I began laying a fly out and working the waters in front of my position. Both Gary and Don were into fish rather quickly and their battles with the trout across the river were duly recorded, using the telephoto lens on the tripod-mounted camera. I had just surrendered another streamer fly to a pike's nasty teeth when I happened to glance in Tony's direction and noticed his spinning rod almost bent in two.

To the best of my knowledge, Tony has never suffered from hypertension, but even from that distance it was easy to perceive that his blood pressure had risen dangerously enough to redden his face. I cranked in my line, laid the rod down, then hustled to the tripod and began filming him from a distance for a moment or two before picking it up and moving as smartly as I could to a shallow inshore area. It was just short of where he was playing what appeared to be another huge brookie.

Tony fought that fish properly, giving only enough line to maintain control of the trout's antics, then pumping it in carefully when the fish tired from fighting the current and constant pressure exerted by the graphite spinning rod. However, he made no effort to descend from his rocky perch, but with the rod held sideways to the main flow, was able anyway to convince the trout that it would be easier going for it in the shallow rocky area where I stood with the camera. The brookie was now only a few feet from me. I could clearly see that my old buddy, Tony Whittingham, was into a huge fish—one even larger than Dr. Cook's world-record speckled trout! Tony's trout was almost a yard long and, unbelievably, at least fifteen pounds. Ogling the fish from where I stood in the ankle-deep water, I was so excited that I ignored the whirr of the camera with its lens pointing at the sky, capturing lovely pictures of fleecy, white clouds instead of his giant brook trout.

He refused to get down from the rock and instead suggested, as the brute was now wallowing in the shallows with its dorsal fin six inches above the surface, that I net it for him. Knowing that, if his catch was to be considered legal as a record, he must land it without help, I deferred. I yelled at him to get down off the rock and finish the job on his own. I think he still must have been in shock at the size of his catch and was unable to move, although he continued to maintain enough rod pressure to keep the trout seemingly pacified and under control.

I kept imploring him, screaming, "Tony, get down off the bloody rock before this thing gets a second wind."

Tony Whittingham on his "famous rock" where he surrendered the world-record brook trout.

He looked like he had been hypnotized, so finally remembering the movie camera, I shot a few feet of him for the record, with his rod bent double, just as the great fish began to stir. It began to slowly move from the shallows back towards the current. I knew that if a fish of that size, or anything of that size for that matter, reached the main flow and rapids, that it would be well nigh impossible to prevent its being carried downstream in mere moments. I yelled again, but he just stared, eyes bulging, as the fish began to display signs that it had indeed found its second wind. Tony, normally a calm and skilled angler, lost it completely at that point. Instead of remaining patient, as he had done earlier with the big brookie when he saw the trout casually heading towards the heavy flow and rapids, he tightened the slipping clutch, a feature in spinning reels to help prevent line breakage.

A scene in one of our trout-fishing films that always brings a tear to my eye when viewed, as it has been hundreds of times since, recorded the final moments of that sequence: Tony, frozen on the spot, rod dangerously bowed, clamping down on the reel's slipping clutch—then there is that awful sound that at that moment could clearly be discerned above the sound of the rapids—"Pingggg!"

The six-pound monofilament line that had performed so admirably finally broke. Tony immediately came back to earth from wherever he had been, plunked down on the rock, then while shedding a few tears, raised his arms and rod to the sky in a salute to the angling gods. A little of the pain at forfeiting the world record that was his for the taking was later erased when he subsequently caught several other lovely brook trout, in the six to seven-pound class, fish still larger than those ever seen by ninety-nine per cent of anglers—except in pictures.

The next Broadback River jaunt also provided an unforgettable memory for our entire 1974 crew at the same first upstream rapids from our camp below the falls. We use Hi-D (hi-density) fly lines when fishing in and around rapids and heavy currents in order to get our flies down quickly where most trout lie in the lee of rocks scattered on the bottom of the river. Unfortunately, these lines retain a high degree of memory from being tightly coiled on the reel spools. It becomes necessary to stretch them to remove as much of this memory as possible before proceeding to cast, in order to prevent the coiling interfering with line handling. That can be done, either between your hands

Rick Matusiak and Paul Kennedy lining the canoe through the rapids on the Broadback River.

or as in our case when on the river, by feeding the line out behind the canoe when going up the river. The current, along with the fast-moving canoe will do the job for you.

On this particular occasion I opted to rest my shrinking store of Despairs and fasten a big, brightly coloured Muscarovitch streamer fly[5] to the six-pound leader tippet. About a quarter of a mile from the foot of the rapids where we normally slow down to paddle to where the canoe is beached, the motor was cut to allow for a cautious approach to avoid spooking trout. The moment that the canoe slowed and the line sank a foot or so, I thought it had picked up a gob of weeds, but as the line was brought in to clear the fly we discovered that a small pike had grabbed the gaudy streamer. The "hammer-handle," as they are often disdainfully referred to, rolled up on the leader, badly chafing the fragile two-foot leader tippet with its razor-sharp gill covers. The fly was removed from its toothy maw and the pike pitched on its way, none too sympathetically. Once Don and Gary had been dropped off on the opposite side, Tony paddled us across and into our customary landing spot.

It was taken for granted, of course, that Tony would wish to work from the big rock where he had experienced an adventure with a potential world-record brookie of his own a couple of years earlier. While he picked his way through the bush and boulders along the shore I briefly checked the frayed leader tippet. Not wishing to lose time replacing and retying the fly and leader, I decided to gamble that it would be able to do its job without problems. That decision was probably the biggest faux pas I have ever made.

When I climbed the rock that was to be my spot, I stripped about fifty feet of line from the fly reel, hanging it in my left hand to avoid its tangling if dropped in the water at my feet. A firm double-haul, a casting procedure that utilizes all the power of the rod when the caster is after distance, and a tight loop would allow the line to flow unobstructed from my hand to its intended target. As is my practice though, a few feet were stripped off and fed through the guides in order to move line beyond the rod tip because the leader that I use is considerably longer than the rod. The fly line must be beyond the rod tip to prevent its weight simply drawing the leader backwards through the guides. After that was done and before an actual cast was made, the Muscarovitch that I lazily had not bothered to change, riding along on the frayed leader tippet, settled about ten feet in front of where I stood on the rock. From somewhere beneath my feet an enormous speckled trout emerged.

Perhaps, "emerged" is the wrong verb. That 1968 mountie simply drifted out then engulfed my Mepps spinner.[6] This fish barrelled out from its cover like a racehorse from the starting gate and smashed the fly with its momentum, carrying it several feet in the air. Then, without hesitation, it cartwheeled immediately, once, twice and a third time as the previously frayed leader parted. Flaunting the gaudy Muscarovitch stuck in its lip, snared from the careless and lazy angler up there on the rock, the brookie (a male almost as big as the record fish that Tony had lost upriver and like his fish also probably weighing more than Dr. Cook's trout) continued to cavort all over the surface of the river.

With tears flowing and frustrated at my stupidity, I watched, along with Don and Gary on the other side, as the huge trout continued to perform its impressive show. We agreed that that brookie, too, would have weighed in at more than fifteen pounds if the leader had not parted and, of course, if it had been landed. That was the third excellent opportunity on the waters of the Broadback River that my fishing buddies and I have had to break Dr. Cook's world record. Magical memories indeed! But there would be more to come, and each time we experience these frenetic situations we learn to appreciate more and more the stature of the good doctor's reputation and the enormity of the task ahead if we are ever to top his feat.

There must be something about that first rapids, upriver from our campsite that draws us to it repeatedly to fish its waters, or perhaps it's simply because it also seems to attract a disproportionate amount of our territory's total stock of huge brook trout. Probably more than half the mounties resting on my buddies' walls have been taken from its environs since that 1968 trip, with many other adventures and unusual incidents having occurred there as well.

There are a couple of other occurrences that took place at the first rapids that are worthy of recalling. One that continues to bring a smile to my face was when my son, Randy (the younger of my two boys) joined us for the first time to fish the Broadback River. He was nineteen, the resident fishing tackle expert in a sporting goods store, and unlike his year-older brother Ron who was already playing professional hockey, he had more time to go fishing with his old man.

Randy was already an accomplished fisherman. Hell, he was much more than that! He was a skilled angler who could take a limit of trout from pretty well any stream or lake that he had a chance to wet a line in. On his second or third day in camp in the late seventies on a trip along with Bob Corbett, Tony Whittingham and me, after a morning of wonderful *fishing* but

Gord's son Randy on the Broadback with his speckled trout in 1978.

fruitless *catching* at the first rapids, we decided to head upriver. Once there, we would make the portage around "no-fish" falls to a lovely, quarter-mile long gravel bar, which was labelled "the fly-fishing shoal" when we discovered it back in 1968. It was such an excellent place to wade and fly fish that it had always been deemed by our crews to be off limits to spinning tackle until the final days of the various trips to its waters.

However, we always hedged our bets on the upriver trips, even though fly fishing was almost always our preference, by carting our spinning outfits with us to fish its surrounding waters. While Bob, Tony and I were flailing away on the fly-fishing shoal, my adventurous son decided to explore previously unfished territory upriver from us and around a bend in the river. It was a difficult stretch of water to work with rapids and white water fraught with lure-snatching logs along the shore and craggy boulders jutting out of the main flow. Getting a lure to the reachable holding spots up there would necessitate difficult wading and negotiating deadfalls along its shallows. Nevertheless if any of us could fish it efficiently it would have to be Randy, with his youthful vigour and his accuracy with his spinning tackle.

An hour or two later, engrossed in our own wand-waving on the gravel bar, we barely noticed a sopping-wet apparition emerging from the bush near the tied-up canoe. Dragging a five-pound speck on a stringer with a forlorn look on his face, he explained that he had kept it as he thought we might need it for supper. His net had fouled on a branch and he fell in but managed to get hold of a tree and pull himself out without losing the fish. His camera, however, was on a cord around his neck; it was still dripping water from its insides.

Fortunately, it was un unusually warm day for the end of August in northern Quebec. By the time we had retreated back downriver to the first rapids, his clothes, still somewhat damp, had stopped steaming, but he declined the offer to call it a day and opted for a little fly fishing. He chose to cast from a spot immediately below the clump of boulders that I normally occupied. Proceeding to show off what a nice loop he could throw with his fly rod, casting half-way across and upstream, then allowing his fly to sink in the current, he twitched it along with a dexterous hand retrieve. Meanwhile, Tony and Bob, fishing a hundred yards up from us had caught and released a couple of smaller trout, while Randy and I remained fishless. I decided to just squat for a few moments and watch my son beautifully working the waters before him then I did a double take when he asked if he could use the beat-up old steamer fly in my cap.[7]

He had recognized it and had a hunch that the rusty and beat-up old streamer would produce something special for him. Believing that his intuition might work, the movie camera that had been idle for much of the day was set up on the tripod. On only his second cast with the ancient streamer he was fast to a big brookie. The battle was short-lived as he expertly applied sufficient leverage to prevent its escape into the white water and worked it towards him through the inshore back currents.

The entire scene was filmed, including an exciting moment when the net somehow slipped from his grasp just as he was about to land his catch and began to quickly drift out into the main flow. Without releasing the tension on his rod, necessary to maintain the pressure on the trout, he calmly waded out, then extending the fly rod as far as he could, drew the net slowly back using the rod's tip guide to snag the mesh. A fine demonstration of angling expertise and patience, recorded on film and proudly shown by his father ever since to hundreds of other anglers! The mountie, a fine twenty-six-incher and six-and a half pounds rests magnificently on Randy's wall, the streamer fly still embedded in its jaw.

There was an eleven-year hiatus between 1984 and 1995, due to a personal situation, before we were able to fish the Broadback River again. The 1995 crew included, old buddy, Gary Benson (his fourth trip), Paul Quarrington and Paulo Conceicao (their first) and me.

Things had returned to normal in my life and Paul Quarrington, one of Canada's premier novelists and a member of our fishing club, had begun accumulating detail on my casting and angling history with the idea that it might provide sufficient material to produce a somewhat different type of fishing book. Paul had heard many of the stories about our past trips to the Broadback and seen hours of my old films and asked if it would be feasible to put together another visit to the river. Discussions with his publisher lead to the idea to use the proposed trip as a catalyst for the book that he had been planning for some time. He was paid an advance and told to go for it. The result was *Fishing With My Old Guy,*[8] a book that moved off the shelves quite rapidly.

Unfortunately, due to forest fire restrictions in the area we were not allowed to go to the Deval Territory. The area that we did select from the few that were available, along with terrible weather conditions, created an

Sporting his favourite Tilley fishing hat, Paul Quarrington strikes a pose on the Broadback River.

intolerable situation that only a Paul Quarrington could turn into a best-selling book.

Two years after the "horror trip" (Quarrington's name for it) with the restrictions partially lifted, we were able to go back to the "old spot" as Paulo Conceicao repeatedly referred to it in 1995. For much of our time there we were huddling under the canvas bemoaning the weather and the fates that had contrived to place us where we were. Along with Paul and me for this repeat venture were Paul Kennedy and Rick Matusiak on their first Broadback River trip. Both had been fishing buddies of mine for a number of years and would make several more journeys with us over the next few years.

The 1997 return trip was a great one, the exact opposite of Paul's "horror trip." Although there were no world-record trout caught, there was one record established when one of our crew, who shall remain un-named, did manage to successfully land a world-record "minnow." It was the largest member of the minnow family, something called a fallfish and was more than three pounds heavier than the listed world-record fish. I cannot imagine that anyone would like to be designated as the fellow who caught the world's biggest minnow. Paul achieved his objective in catching his largest pickerel ever, while Rick and Paul caught mounties, brook trout in the five and six-pound class.

Subsequent trips over the next few years continued to produce sensational fishing for our crews, but it wasn't until this century, forty-three years after we first wet a line in the magical waters of the Broadback that we once again experienced the sublime thrill of witnessing possible world-record speckled trout in the river.

Rick Matusiak is an expert angler, perhaps the best that I have had the pleasure of fishing with, but that is not all he has going for him. He is also a superb photographer and filmmaker. A few years ago he designed and built an underwater housing for his video camera. The whole thing sits inside a simulated rock, so as not to alarm fish in its field of view. Its umbilical cord relays the picture to a small television set on the surface, allowing him to monitor the camera's work. His invention worked so well that it caught the fancy of Bob Izumi[9] who hired him to film underwater sequences for his popular fishing television show.

Two years ago Rick, Paul Kennedy, my son Ron and I were impatiently waiting while he set up his equipment, using a twelve-foot long, extendable glass pole to lower its business end in an area that had been tagged as the "Glory Hole" on the previous day. On that occasion, on a hunch, we had decided to explore an unlikely looking bay that to all appearances should have had nothing in it but weeds and a few big pike. Certainly not brook

Rick Matusiak, photographer and angler.

Ron Deval in 2001, at the "far falls" on the Broadback.

trout, we felt, as they seldom stray far from the main flow and variable river currents. Nevertheless, the specks had not studied the same manuals that we had and what followed was one of the most exciting days of fishing in the Broadback that we have ever experienced. Rick exhausted his video-cassettes shooting film of first, Ron latching into a mountie, then Paul following suit with another, closely followed by both of them playing big brookies simultaneously. It was crazy! Rick would put the camera down for a moment, make a cast and hook another mountie which Paul would then gleefully record on film for him.

During most of that hectic afternoon's fishing I merely sat back in the canoe that had been pulled up on shore to enjoy the shenanigans, with first one, then another, then all three of the fellows playing fish at the same time. Lines were crossing and expletives flying as lines were broken, lures lost and fish released right and left after being filmed in close-up action. We counted twenty-five trout caught, in a space of three or four hours and all were five and six-pounders, between twenty-four and twenty-seven inches long. All but one, kept for dinner, were successfully returned to the water.

In the evening back in camp we had an opportunity to review most of the unedited film shot that afternoon and eagerly anticipated returning to the same spot the next day, armed with Rick's underwater paraphernalia to see what else was on the bottom. He suggested that we wait a few minutes before casting to give the trout a chance to get used to the foreign rock's presence. Itching to get our lines in the water we soon discovered that, once again, there was plenty of fine action, but although Rick had assured us that the camera, hidden inside the fake rock, would not be spooking the trout, it was not the furious fishing that we had encountered on the previous day. However, back in camp that evening, while Paul and I were tying up Despairs, a shout came from behind the tent where Rick was reviewing the underwater film that had been shot in the afternoon, "You ain't never seen nothing like this before, I guarantee you!"

He reran the video and we stood there, each with our own thoughts and full of anticipation as the underwater action appeared on the small screen. It should be mentioned here that we have a tiny Honda Generator in camp that Rick uses to charge his camera batteries and run the television set. "Oh my God! My God!" I said, "Did you see that?"

It was mind-boggling! Paul Kennedy, perhaps the most laid-back fellow in my extensive coterie of fishing buddies was speechless. He just stood there with his mouth and eyes as wide open as was physically possible until

Gord catching a trout at the "Glory Hole."

finally he regained his composure a little. At that point, Rick hit the rewind button and played the film again to a number of exclamations from his captive audience—or should that be *captivated*. What we were seeing would have been unbelievable if we had not seen it with our own eyes. The camera in the underwater "rock" was clearly picking out trout after trout cruising back and forth in front of the lens, all of them in the same size range, a little more than two feet long, as the brookies we had been catching in the "Glory Hole" during the two days of fishing there.

What knocked us off our complacency though was that every few moments a huge brook trout would mosey into the picture, seeming to take forever before its tail disappeared from view. Then more mounties would scurry back and forth as another giant speckled trout eased into the picture, looking as if it were from a different planet or something. We estimated that there were three of four of these enormous brookies residing in the same magical waters as the mounties we had been catching—and all were almost a foot longer— speckled trout capable of smashing Dr. Cook's almost one hundred year old world-record brookie!

It was decided that our best chance to catch one of these lunkers was to rest the Glory Hole for a couple of days, if we could restrain ourselves accordingly. After all, it was agreed, there is no shortage of fine places to fish nearby and who knows, perhaps there are other Glory Holes just waiting to be discovered. I can not be certain about the other fellows, but I can honestly say that my dreams that night and the next were full of sequences where either my son, Ronnie, or I was fast to one of those magnificent brookies and gently working it into the shallow to be measured and photographed before being ushered back out into the current.

The "angling gods" intervened again though, as the barometer plummeted and we were hit with a fierce storm. With only a couple of days left before our scheduled departure it would have been foolhardy to venture far from camp. Even a world-record trout is not worth a potentially deadly canoe accident trying to negotiate heavy rapids in gale force winds and heavy rain coming at us sideways. It was all we could do just to keep our tent and kitchen shelter stabilized until the storm blew over then there were only a few hours left to work the waters around camp before it was time to begin packing for the next day's departure. We could only hope that the storm did not return and the plane would be able to fly in without problems. Our satellite phone seemed to confirm that our barometer was reading accurately and weather should not be a problem.

It was difficult to restrain our enthusiasm the next day when the pilot assigned to pick us up asked the customary questions about the fishing after inquiring about our camp's ability to weather the storm. We had agreed that we would take an oath of silence about what we had discovered and merely reply that the fishing had been fair and that we caught enough to eat.

"Yeah," the pilot replied, "it's been like that everywhere this year, up in these parts, not bad, but nothing much to write home about either."

We resisted the urge to grin and simply glanced at each other with closed mouth, smiles.

Chapter 22
Other Magical Memories

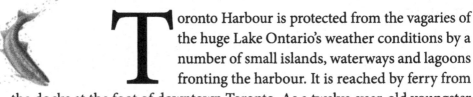

Toronto Harbour is protected from the vagaries of the huge Lake Ontario's weather conditions by a number of small islands, waterways and lagoons fronting the harbour. It is reached by ferry from the docks at the foot of downtown Toronto. As a twelve-year-old youngster living in the east end of the city, it was a simple matter to either bicycle or take the streetcar to the ferry docks and for fifteen cents enjoy the trip across in order to wander the islands while fishing their various interconnecting waters.

I was fishing an area called Long Pond on one of those days and had managed to catch a small pike, which was released and several perch which were kept, when I saw an eruption on the far side of the bay. There was a family of merganser ducks, mother and about a dozen ducklings poking along the far shore. What appeared to be a huge pike was picking off the chicks, one by one.

Fascinated with the nature lesson that was occurring I failed to notice a gentleman working along the shore towards where I was now sitting on a log and watching the big pike consume his dinner. I then heard another splashing commotion down the shore from me, followed by the singing of the fisherman's reel as another pike ripped the line from his fly reel.

Shyly, I retreated back into the bush behind us, worked my way along until I was right behind him. Being unobserved, I could watch the fun and action he was having with the big fish, at least I thought I had been unobserved. The pike that was causing quite a handful for the fisherman got away, either breaking the frail leader tippet or possibly the fly simply pulled out of the fish's bony mouth. At that time, I still did not own fly-fishing tackle, only steel rod and bait-casting reel.

I sat there agog, enjoying the entire scene. Looking like one of the covers I had seen on what was then the number one outdoor magazine of its day, *Field and Stream*. The man was wearing chest waders, a fishing vest with bulging pockets and an old Houndstooth pattern tweed hat, ringed with a band of fleece and a zillion colourful flies. When the pike escaped, he continued to fly cast, creating long graceful loops and a moment later brought in a fat perch and netted it with a small wooden-handled net. After removing the streamer fly from its jaw, he carefully placed it back in the swim. It was a scene I had dreamt of many times since I had first read and seen the lovely fly-fishing pictures in magazines.

Apparently the gentleman knew I was watching and studying him, as after releasing the perch and wiping his hands on the small towel fastened to his belt, he turned in my direction and summoning me with a smile and wave of his hand, said, "Why don't you come a bit closer. I know you've been back there watching for a bit now."

When I hesitantly approached, he continued talking to me, asking what I had caught, then offered to show me how to clean them. "Can I ask you your name, son....mine's Dave Reddick."[1]

Before we parted, he invited me to come to a fun competition his club was staging for its members as a chicken shoot. Thus began my life-long obsession with the competitive side of tournament fly and bait casting. The "chicken shoot" winners would all take home chickens as prizes. The club was the original Toronto Anglers and Hunters Association and I was to be his guest.

I somehow managed to win first prize in the Junior division of the plug casting event and proudly took home a frozen chicken to give to my mom. That was the first ever of well over thousands of awards that have come my way in the sixty-odd years since then. I often wonder if I had not experienced

Dave Reddick, as he was known to many, was an advertising man by day and an ardent fisherman in his leisure time. A much respected author and an expert on the muskie, he was admired by many. Photo taken from The Outdoorsman, *1963. Courtesy of Barry Penhale.*

that magical interlude on Long Pond when I ogled, then met that memorable gentleman, Mr Dave Reddick, if fly and bait casting would actually have become my lifelong passion.

My father was not an outdoors enthusiast, but would hire a guide in the Kawartha Lakes district for a week of muskie fishing once a year. That was the extent of his fishing pursuits until one year he came up with a hare-brained scheme to catch fish—a lot of fish. He had rented a cottage on the Otonabee River, near Peterborough, Ontario. It flows for about twenty miles or so before emptying into Rice Lake.

Dad had been told that there was good fishing in the river for pickerel, bass and possibly muskies near the cottage, so using the boat that came with the cottage we rowed around and fished for several hours each of our first few days there. The sum total of our catch, however, was one small bass, a couple of perch and a handful of sunfish and rock bass. The perch and rock bass were cleaned and the minuscule fillets fried for lunch. Although delicious, they barely appeased all our appetites.

Mom, my sister Barbara, Dad and I all enjoyed eating fried fish so the ridiculous plan that my father had hatched before we even left for the cottage was being put into place. At home in Toronto, we had a ping-pong table in the unfinished basement of our house and Dad and I would often engage in friendly matches of table tennis. The basement, however, like most unfinished basements, was cluttered with hazards and all sorts of flotsam and jetsam that had been moved downstairs to simply be out of the way. There was also the huge, old coal-burning furnace with its melange of pipes branching out in all directions like an enormous octopus and, of course, the washing machine and clothes line, usually half-filled with laundry. It all added up to a frustrating obstacle course for our table-tennis games, especially when a shot was missed and the errant ball had to be retrieved. We lost balls in the basement litter by the dozens.

One day in downtown Toronto, my father had spotted a large commercial fishing net that was being used in a department store window display. That gave him the idea that one of these nets draped around our ping-pong table area would save us the nuisance of trying to track down the stray balls, and we could spend more time actually playing table tennis with them than we had been doing searching for them. The net worked wonderfully well.

My father had to return to Toronto for a day during the middle of our holiday on the Otonabee for business reasons and when he returned the following day, he could hardly wait to put his "brainwave" into practice. He had taken the net down from its moorings around our ping-pong table and brought it back with him to the cottage.

"Now we'll get us some fish, Gordon," he said.

His idea was to drag the net behind the boat while we rowed up and down the river. He figured it shouldn't take long to get enough for a real feed at the cottage, along with a pile to take home. Once cleaned, the fish should keep all right in the icebox. My father actually hated cleaning fish. The task was usually left up to me.

The next morning we rowed down the river a little way to get out of sight of the cottages and Dad began playing out the net. The wooden floats and lead weights had never been removed so the drag of the rapidly filling net soon became too great for me to continue rowing. We discovered that the problem was a huge mountain of weeds piling up in the net. We were "fishing" in water that was too shallow and clogged with weed beds. Once the net was dragged on board and the mesh reasonably freed from the weeds, we headed for an apparently deeper section of the river. Once there the net was again played out and we resumed "fishing." I really have no idea at all as to whether my father and I knew then that what we were doing was illegal. Fortunately, however, our illicit activity was not interrupted by a game warden. What did

The earliest fishing picture ever taken of Gord Deval, shown here with his makeshift rod on the Ottonabee River at age seven.

bring us to a halt, however, was the physical effort called for. Rowing, then hauling the net over the side of the old wooden boat to dump its load of fish was rapidly draining whatever strength we had left.

Although the smallest fish were all tossed back, we still had netted enough to almost fill the galvanized metal washtub brought along for the purpose. There was not a single bass or pickerel in the lot, though, only sunfish, rock bass, perch and catfish. Barbara, waiting on the dock when we returned, took one look at the tub full of fish flopping around as it was hoisted on to the dock, then declined the invitation to join me in the "blood and guts" brigade. The unenviable chore of cleaning what seemed at the time to be about ten thousand fish was left up to me.

Realistically, the count was probably fewer than fifty or sixty. Nevertheless it took several hours of work to turn them into about a two or three-pound pile of tasty fillets. We learned later in the day of the illegality of our fishing procedure when a chap from a neighbouring cottage informed my father accordingly in exchange for a handful of fillets.

The net, a little fishy and still smelling of seaweed, was summarily replaced in the basement and relegated to its former stature. Although this episode can hardly be deemed a magical memory, it most definitely is a memorable one.

I had often wondered just how big a "fish" could be successfully played and landed on a fly rod. In Canada's Centennial year of 1967, I was about to find out. When, along with the *Toronto Star's* excellent outdoor writer King Whyte,[2] I was invited to participate in seminars and demonstrations being conducted in Kapuskasing in Northern Ontario during their Centennial celebration and festival. A couple of situations occurred on that occasion that deserve recognition, the first being rather scary, while the second may have answered my query on the viability of landing "fish" weighing hundreds of pounds on ordinary fly-fishing equipment.

King and I were flown into a tiny remote lake in a small float plane with instructions to catch—and keep—as many pickerel as we could. The local conservation officers, without regard to the normal legal possession limits, had given us carte blanche permission. The fish were to be prepared, along with Arctic char for a huge banquet the next day.

We were told that this particular lake, although really quite small, was teeming with pickerel in the two-and-a-half to four-pound size. We could probably fill the plane with them if you wanted to," so they said. And we damn near did! At least the floats! Their parting instructions were that they would require at least a hundred pounds of pickerel for the Centennial banquet.

The lake was small, but the pilot informed us that his plane was equipped with something called a "Stoll Kit," which, along with the windy conditions we were flying in, would allow us to land and get off the little lake with "no trouble at all." Casting off a rocky promontory halfway down the lake, we found that the fishing was exactly as we had been told, fast and furious. King and I would catch the pickerel and toss them over our shoulders to the pilot, sitting on a log that also served as a secure place to moor the plane's floats. He would quickly eviscerate and remove the heads before stuffing them into storage air chambers in the floats.

After a couple of hours the pilot said that there was no more room and it was time to leave. I could not help noticing that the plane sat considerably lower in the water than it did before we began stuffing the

"KING" of the Outdoors
KING WHYTE

Regarded as Canada's foremost outdoor writer and telecaster, KING WHYTE died suddenly last year in Quebec province. He was preparing a film for his television show.

King served as a public relations officer with the Canadian Army overseas during World War II. For several years he wrote an outdoor column for the Toronto Star and was well known for his television show promoting various aspects of outdoor sport. The programme had a large audience in both Canada and the United States.

He was a director and one of the founders of Outdoor Writers of Canada, and probably the recipient of more honorary membership in fish and game and similar associations than any other man in North America. He is missed by those who knew him personally, or through his writings and TV appearances.

A tribute to King Whyte as printed in The Outdoorsman *magazine in 1963. Courtesy of Barry Penhale.*

floats with pickerel. Our gear was quickly stowed on board and we taxied down to the opposite end of the lake that the remaining breeze was coming from. The motor was revved up and the pilot shouted over the roar of the engine, "When I yell at you guys, sit back as far as you can in your seats. Got it?"

These were not exactly words to instil confidence in our minds that the heavily laden floats were going to be able to escape the natural grasp of the lake surface. The plane then tore down the lake. We could see the other end of the lake precariously closing in on us as the pilot yelled, "Lean back NOW!"

King and I were stretched out backwards as flat as our seat belts would allow, just as he cut the engine and settled back in the water a few feet from a sandy beach at the end of the lake. The pilot said to his somewhat shaken passengers, "Not a problem guys! We'll take her back and perform a little trick I learned from a bush pilot in Quebec."

Once we had taxied back we were instructed to help pull the floats up in the sandy-bottomed shallows as far as we could, whereupon he took a length of cord, fastened it somewhere beneath the tail with the other end tied to a big tree on shore about fifteen feet behind the plane.

The engine was revved up almost to the tachometer's red line before the rope broke and the plane lurched forward giving the three of us a bit of whiplash. Watching the shoreline trees whiz by us as we shot down the lake seemed re-assuring enough, then he yelled, "Okay, now, get back!"

Once again we did as instructed as he rocked the plane from side to side to free it from the grip of the water then cut the engine when he realized that he was not going to be able to gain enough height to clear the trees. King and I looked at each other, took a deep breath and raised our eyes skyward as the pilot, rather sheepishly now, agreed to my earlier suggestion to just drop me off to reduce the load, fly to that big lake we passed before, drop King off, come back for me, then pick King up. A magical memory, certainly not! But certainly memorable.

The banquet was an astounding success, but earlier in the day a number of events took place on Remi Lake, a twenty-mile long lake not far from the town. Perhaps the most popular of these was a cross-the-lake marathon swim. The winner of the marathon would get a thousand dollar bond, a trophy and the dubious honour of playing "fish" to my fly-fishing ability.

Given fifteen minutes to catch his breath and drink a mug of hot chocolate, his bathing trunks were fastened at the back to the end of my eight-pound test leader tippet. Over the loudspeaker, after the introductions and congratulating the swimmer, the MC conducting all the ceremonies explained to the swimmer and the crowd what the rules were for the demonstration, "Mr. Deval, here, Gord, will try to keep the 'fish,' our marathon swim champion from breaking his rod or line, while attempting to see if he can actually tire the 'fish' out enough to land him. We don't have a net large enough so the game will be over for the 'fish' if Gord can tire him sufficiently to work him in to the launch ramp on the dock. The 'fish' is not allowed to grab the line or leader, but can try anything else to cross up the fisherman just like any other 'fish' would, such as suddenly reversing or lunging this way or that. There's another five hundred dollar bond in it for the 'fish' if Gord is unable to land him within twenty minutes, or the 'fish' manages to break Gord's tackle."

It is rather amazing how much pressure one can apply with a nine-foot long fly rod equipped with an eight-pound leader tippet. In less than ten minutes, despite a number of resourceful moves by the "fish" and the raucous chants from the crowd of "Go fish go!" he was brought to heel at the boat ramp. For his effort he was given another trophy describing the event, along with an additional cheque for a hundred dollars.

I had a client who had connections with a real estate firm that had taken over the management of a newly constructed senior's residence in Markham, a town less than a half hour from Toronto. The building had a small park on one side that bordered a section of the Rouge River. The firm had an original idea to attract its senior residents. They received permission from the Ontario Waters Resources Commission to divert part of the river's flow into a pond they had constructed with backhoes in their little park and had it stocked with about two hundred two- and three-pound rainbow trout.

It was equipped with several casting platforms and the rules were posted on signboards around the pond. The eager residents were not allowed to go after the trout until the normal May 1 season opener, even though the pond was on normally unregulated private property. Fly-fishing equipment only had to be used and each angler-resident had an annual quota of trout that they could catch and keep. They were given diaries and asked to record all their catches. Fishing would only be allowed between the hours of eight and five o'clock. Many of the folks had spent the spring months prior to the launch, haunting sporting goods stores, buying equipment and, although completely unnecessary, waders and hip boots. I was asked to come to the pond an hour before it was to open to the angler-residents in order to do a seminar and demonstration for the folks on how best to fly cast and fish their pond.

Along with the two hundred eighteen to twenty-inch long fish that the pond had been stocked with, I was told what the others already knew, that one huge rainbow trout weighing about nine pounds was also in the swim for their pleasure—as if they needed any further incentive. The idea was that if and when the big fellow was caught—and kept—it would be replaced with another. I learned that the pond and these fishing incentives had been the reason the building tenancy rate was a hundred per cent, right from its inception.

Keen and obviously impatient to wet their own lines, the men enthusiastically gathered around the dock where I was demonstrating how to handle a fly rod and line and cheered when the trout took my flies. It gave me the opportunity to also show them the correct way to release the fish even though the barbs on my fly had already been flattened by pliers, as theirs had been.

With about ten minutes to go before the bell was to sound to indicate the start, the men began trickling away to take up their chosen positions. I was about to pack up my own tackle when one chap asked, how far I could cast. When I said probably right across the pond, he challenged me to do it. Although I was using one of my handmade little six-foot ultra-light bamboo wands, it was not a difficult cast as the pond was only about eighty feet across and there was a little wind on my back.

I made the cast, then began working the Despair nymph back while demonstrating the correct retrieve in order to maximize the fly's appeal. When it reached the middle, "Moby Dick," as the men had named the nine-pounder, erupted from the water shaking his head from side to side trying to throw the fly back from whence it had come. I did not wish to risk breaking my cane rod with the brute, so kept it pointed almost directly at the trout during its rampage around the pond, while explaining to the men that normally I would hold the rod in a more vertical position in order that it serve as a shock absorber to cushion the lunges of the feisty fish.

The men were now gathering around again to watch the fun and shout remarks, generally hoping I would put it back for another day. Fortunately, the rod and very light leader held up. The fish was played in carefully and as quickly as I could so as not to tire it out any more than necessary. The fly was backed out of its jaw and after working the big male trout back and forth in the pond by the dock for a few moments to move water over its gills, I sent it on its way with a pat on the head, while whispering, "Bon chance, Moby Dick."

Unfortunately, when the building was enlarged a few years ago, the pond became history, but the memory of watching all those older men salivating over the big fellow while he danced around the pond on my tiny split-cane fly rod is permanently etched in place.

Baltimore Creek, one of the hundreds flowing into Lake Ontario, is a pretty stream that meanders through the Northumberland Forest north of

Cobourg, Ontario, eventually emptying into the lake south of that city. As a youth I fished it many times with my Uncle Bob, but the two instances recorded here occurred many years later; the first during a return from a trip to Hastings, Ontario, in the fifties with my wife, Joan, our kids and dogs in the car, while the second took place the following summer.

Joan was an extremely patient woman. She had to be to be able to tolerate my total dedication to trout fishing and a predilection to wet a line on any opportunity that happened to come along. The kids were contentedly engaged with their comic books as was Joan with her novel, when I inquired if she would mind if I pulled off to the shoulder on the side of the highway to give the creek a go. She agreed if I promised not to be too long.

The headwaters of Baltimore Creek were blessed with a bountiful supply of smallish brook trout and the odd good-sized brown. The pool beneath and alongside the bridge where the stream crosses the highway had almost always produced a decent brownie on other occasions. The first cast beneath the bridge was no different this time. A fat fourteen-incher struck the Mepps spinner and was soon dispatched and creeled. The next upstream pool then beckoned and a couple of nice brookies soon lay alongside the brown in the creel. The barometer must have been on a substantial rise as the fish were hitting like crazy. Although most were small, and of course released, a number were kept for the table as our entire family enjoyed nothing better than a couple of feeds of fresh brook trout.

I was so engrossed in the fishing that I completely lost track of time, until almost a concession further north an hour or so later, I heard a gruff voice up ahead a few yards, barking at me, "You Gordon Deval?"

I thought I must have wandered onto private property, but wondered how they knew my name, until I saw their uniforms. They were Ontario Provincial Police officers. When I confirmed my identity, they continued, "Your wife flagged us down back on the highway. Your kids were crying and she figured you must have broken your ankle or something, because apparently you told her you'd only be gone for a few minutes. That was more than two hours ago!"

Luckily, they did not issue a summons or anything, only a stern warning, but it was nothing compared to the reprimand dished out by my wife. I learned my lesson after that episode.

Baltimore Creek holds another memory for me. My wife and I had been invited to spend a couple of days with Rose and Pete McGillen[3] at their lovely cottage on the shore of Rice Lake near the village of Roseneath, Ontario. Pete

Pete McGillen, the outdoor editor for the Toronto Telegram, *was a colourful character who, at a testimonial dinner in his honour hosted by the Outdoor Writers of Canada, said, "It's just my luck to have been born with the face of a pirate and the soul of a poet."*
Photo taken from The Outdoorsman, 1963. Courtesy of Barry Penhale.

was a superb outdoor columnist for the old *Toronto Telegram* newspaper, perhaps the best ever and certainly the best during my years of reading the journalistic ramblings of most of his successors. Pete's columns were always informative, colourful and an interesting read with his take on a wide variety of outdoors topics. He was well loved by his extensive magazine and newspaper readership, as well as the viewers of his television show, *Outdoors with Pete McGillen*. A number of times I had been asked by Pete to contribute titbits on trout fishing or fly and bait casting for his columns, then one day I happened to mention to him that there was a place close to his cottage where I could catch a trout without even having to step out of the car. "Okay," he replied, "that better be true and not just another one of your fish stories, or it's going to cost you, Gordon. I'll have to take your word that you really did catch the trout without getting out of your car, but your wife will be with you so that should not be a problem. Do we have a bet then? Bring the fish and Rose can cook it up for lunch or whatever when you guys arrive." He wagered a couple of bucks that I wouldn't be able to do it on our way up to their cottage. But if I did (my wife would be my witness), I was to bring it so Rose could cook it up for lunch. The other condition was that I'd write about it for his column, without revealing the exact location.

Of course, I accepted the wager and early the following Saturday morning as we approached this magical bit of Baltimore Creek, I slowed the car down a few hundred yards short of the bridge where the stream crossed the highway to pull the car up as close to the side as possible without spooking any trout that were normally in the pool there. Joan already knew about the plan and the bet, but also recognized the spot as the place where I had taken off and left her and the kids "to cook in the hot car" while I wandered around somewhere in the bush. I confirmed that, indeed, it was, but on this occasion I would not even be stepping outside the car.

I merely had to lean out the window then make a little flip cast towards the undercut bend in the shoreline that I felt certain held my anticipated quarry, a trout—any trout—a two-dollar trout, nonetheless. The spinner fell through some long, overhanging grass and was immediately engulfed by the nice brownie. It was carefully eased up over the steel railing then, by awkwardly passing the rod handle past Joan and out the opposite window, I was able to reach out far enough to grasp the two-dollar fish. After the turmoil I had caused the last time we had stopped by the same creek, I did not surrender to the desire to make a second cast. It was rejected for fear of raising my wife's ire again. I tossed the trout into the cooler in the back seat and said, "That should do the trick, dear. One is all we need, right?"

An hour later I happily exchanged a fat, fifteen-inch brown trout for a two-dollar bill (remember them?) with Mr. Pete McGillen.

In the late fifties, Joan, my first wife, selected New York City for our planned second honeymoon trip. She chose that destination believing that with little fishing to be had there we could spend more time together. While there, I happened to come across an outdoors magazine featuring an article about a covered bridge on the Willemoc River, a tributary of the famous Beaverkill. Every trout fisherman has heard or read about the storied Beaverkill River and just in case I was going to be allowed to snatch an hour or two on the way home, I had packed tackle and a couple of sleeping bags in our hatch-back automobile.

When one wishes to utilize verbal subterfuge, it helps to have a captive audience, so after reading the story in our hotel room while waiting for Joan to get ready to go for breakfast, I suggested to her as she finished dressing, that while her idea of using the New York Thruway for the trip coming down here was good, perhaps we could leave a day earlier than planned and take a more scenic route on the way home. Going through the Catskills might even allow an hour or two of fishing. As it turned out, New York was—well—New York! After doing the "tourist thing," the Empire State Building, the museums, 42nd Street, Broadway and so on, Joan was quite happy to leave a day sooner than planned as I had suggested.

The Catskills, an area only a few hours north of the city, is comprised of a number of lakes, streams and of course the Catskill Mountains, a range of large hills and small mountains. It is a favourite retreat for New Yorkers wishing to escape the high pressure, hustle and bustle. It is also home to the Catskill Fly-fishing Centre, Joan and Lee Wulff, their Catskill Fly-fishing Association and a host of fly-fishing centres, such as Roscoe with its tackle shops lining both sides of the town's streets. There are also world-class fly tyers in the Catskills, many of whom operate small shops along the rural roads leading to Roscoe and the Beaverkill River.

Roscoe became our planned destination as the map accompanying the article that had piqued my interest suggested that it was the centre of activity for all things to do with fly-fishing in the area—and the fabled Beaverkill River flowed right through the heart of it. By the time we escaped the hotel and cleared the endless environs of the big city, the "extra" day we were hoping for had dwindled to a half a day, but driving the back roads an hour or so from Roscoe we came a small stream that simply cried out to me to stop and give it a "boo." I knew that fishing without a licence was risky business but decided to chance it anyhow and in short order had a couple of fourteen-inch browns. They were quickly cleaned and popped into our lunch cooler, then we sped on our way feeling a little guilty, a bit fortunate, yet lucky, all at the same time.

It was time to eat. We had just driven by a roadside tackle shop that had caught my eye with a fish and chip store next to it. There was a large sign in its window that read "fresh cut fries," the only way I like French fries. Checking to see if the road was clear, I made an abrupt U turn then drove back, salivating at the prospect of an idea that had been brewing in my head for awhile. Maybe they would fry up the trout we just caught with a large order of their fries. I would even pay the same price as a regular order. Joan thought I was crazy. She predicted they would never do it.

I somehow managed to avoid window shopping in the nearby tackle shop and went directly to the restaurant carrying the two brown trout that I hoped would be our supper. A half hour later we were driving along still devouring our breaded and deep-fried trout, nicely prepared with slices of fresh lemon and well-salted, along with a carton of fresh-cut fries and washed down with a bottle of root beer, as we arrived at Roscoe. An inquiry at the Orvis Fly Shop produced the information as to the exact whereabouts of the covered bridge on the Willemoc, the sales clerk confirming the accuracy of the map. As he completed my application for a three-day non-resident fishing licence, he commented on the number of guys who had already come, having read the same article.

Once we had checked the motel and cabin situation in the village and discovered it was the same story everywhere, "no vacancy" signs all over the place. Not to be denied this fishing opportunity, I reminded Joan that we had a big air mattress and double sleeping bag. We should be able to find a camping spot near the covered bridge I saw.

The directions on the map were excellent and we pulled up just below the covered bridge and beside the pond just as the last rays of sunshine were filtering through the trees. It was getting dark fast as I unrolled the bag on the mattress and fluffed it up for her just as a splash on the pond sounding like the smack of a beaver tail slapping the surface, spurred me into action. Joan, tired and anxious to get tucked in for an early sleep, encouraged me to see if I could catch that thing, whatever it was making the noise.

Another eruption on the pond became the target for my first cast with the little spinning rod, although I could barely see where the disturbance had occurred. It was darkening rapidly now, but nevertheless I worked the spinner with enthusiasm as the splashes continued and soon became convinced that it had to be a big brown trout that was causing all the commotion. I altered the normal erratic retrieve that I usually employ when fishing with a spinner, realizing that the trout was feeding on some sort of insect or whatever on the surface. The casts were no longer made randomly, but aimed in the direction of each splash with the lure being retrieved right along the surface. The strategy had worked quite well in other situations similar to this with surface-feeding fish, but it was the first time I had tried it in the dark. All to no avail.

It had been years since I fished with worms for trout, but I felt the big brownie might succumb to a different sort of wriggling morsel than whatever he was fattening up on.

With a tiny flashlight that I had expediently thrown in my pocket when setting up my tackle, I began to scrounge around the few grassy areas near the bridge looking for a fat night crawler. Meanwhile the big brownie continued to create an adrenaline rush into my heart with its feeding shenanigans as I soon learned there did not seem to a single worm anywhere in the immediate surroundings. Almost ready to surrender to the allure of the big trout and cuddle up next to my wife in the beckoning warmth of the big, double sleeping bag, I idly kicked over a rock in a last desperate effort to locate something with which to tempt my fishy adversary. The flashlight immediately caught a newt in its beam, momentarily freezing it on the spot. I pounced on the little fellow before it realized it was in danger. At that point I was willing to try anything short of dynamite to get the brownie for another fish and chip supper the next day.

Back at the Willemoc with my tiny prize, not even bothering to replace the Mepps spinner with a single hook, the newt was hooked through its lower lip with the spinner's hook. The entire package was carefully lobbed out into the darkness. The momentum of an ordinary cast would have sent the bait flying off the hook, giving the trout a free meal. It struck the water with a resounding smack in the middle of the pond and I did not have long to wait to determine its effectiveness. The lure and its passenger salamander were immediately assaulted in a slashing strike, which, if the reel's slipping clutch had not previously been carefully adjusted, would probably have broken the rod or, at least, the line. I had not had the foresight to have a net at the ready, hence it was necessary to play the big brownie cautiously so it could be gradually worked in to a shallow area up the shoreline a little where it could be landed easily.

A few minutes later, my wife did not take too kindly to being awakened by the beam of the little, pocket flashlight, as I proudly showed off our next day's supper, a twenty-two-inch-long, three-and-a-half-pound brown trout. That miniature lizard-like creature, salamander, newt, or whatever it was, retrieved from beneath a rock alongside the Willemoc River and its famous covered bridge, produced a permanent addition to my incredible store of memories.

I did not have the pleasure of returning to the Catskills in New York until 1986, some thirty years later, when I was invited by Lee Wulff's[4] wife, Joan, to participate in the summerfest staged by the Catskill Fly-fishing Center. It was the first time that they included fly-casting competition in their annual fly-fishing festival. The competition was, of course, open to the public, but several tournament casters were specifically invited in order that the club members could gauge the level of their own skills and proficiency in the fly accuracy and distance disciplines. I was also expected to do seminars on the correct tournament procedures for all the folks attending, many of whom who were from New York City.

I offered to waive my rights to any of the lovely awards they had obtained to present to the winners of the various games, but Joan refused, as it was be a real competition. Her husband Lee would be out to throw the Anglers' Fly Distance, but she, herself, was too busy running the thing to complete. She did insist, however, that should I be lucky enough to capture the "all-round title" in their casting event that the corresponding award would be presented to me accordingly.

Disappointed at not having Joan, one of the best fly casters in the world as a competitor, I nevertheless was excited at the prospect of meeting her husband, Lee, whom I had not seen since my youth. Some thirty or forty years earlier I had attended several of his movie presentations and seminars in Toronto. The prospect of actually going head to head against this mighty "King of Trout and Salmon" anglers in a casting competition had me almost salivating.

As a lifelong devotee of trout fishing, with a pursuit of Dr. Cook's world-record speckled trout always in the back of my mind, Lee Wulff had long since been my idol in the angling world. His movies, slide shows, his books and articles I had repeatedly read, all have been sources of inspiration. I felt then as I do today, that Lee never wrote a word about fly fishing just for the sake of writing something different about the sport, as unfortunately, too many others do.

It was a fun couple of days, but the excitement was peaking on the second day when Joan reported that she had just heard from her husband that he would be flying his famous little airplane in to join us and throw in the final game, the distance discipline. She reminded me, that despite my success this far, I would have my hands full trying to beat her "old man" in the distance fly. Although he was more than twenty years older than I, he could still throw a mean line when he wanted to. Despite her conjecture, I believed that all my years of tournament practice and competition, regardless of the age difference, should certainly provide me with a tremendous advantage, at least in this particular category, over my idol, Lee. With less than half an hour left before the event was to begin, he still had not arrived. Suddenly a roar over the trees at the far end of the field indicated his airborne approach as the tiny plane soared low over the field causing us all to scatter.

I asked if his and my name could be placed near the end of the competition so we could go head to head as well as against the other competitors. She concurred, but cautioned me. There were quite a few other guys I would have to beat as well as Lee to win the thing. One of our newest club members, Leon Schwartz and my wife, Sheila, had also come along on this trip, with Leon also casting the fly games, while Sheila, a plug caster, relaxed and watched. There were perhaps a dozen or so competitors in the game and most of them cast quite well, much better than the average fellows we see occasionally on trout streams, however their scores were all in the hundred to a hundred and twenty feet category with Leon's easily topping theirs at close to a hundred and thirty feet.

Only a couple weeks prior to our attending their summerfest, I had managed to set a record in the Anglers' Fly Distance category in the North American Casting Championships with a long cast of 177 feet. Although somewhat embarrassed, I wondered out loud to Joan Wulff that since Lee had been my idol in the angling world all my life, should I lay back and let him win. She was astounded that I would even suggest such a thing.

Lee finally arrived amidst a throng of hand shakers and well-wishers, all, of course, rooting for him to win. With only a couple of casters to go before our turns, I was introduced to him and somehow avoided passing out on the spot with excitement, as he said, "I hear you're supposed to win this thing, Deval. Right? Joan tells me that you're a great fan of mine and used to attend my shows and lectures up in Toronto when you were a kid."

Our discussion led to his deciding to accept my offer. He would use my more powerful rod for the competition.

Then came the magical moment! Unbelievably, he asked, "Do you want to put five bucks on this thing, Deval?"

Lee Wulff, Gord's hero, paying off a bet to Gord at the Catskill Club in New York.

I nearly fainted! The prospect of making a five-dollar bet with my idol on anything to do with fishing was almost more than I could handle and certainly more than anything I had ever contemplated when reading his books and magazine articles.

Feeling bolder when I finally regained my composure, I accepted, but on one condition—that should I win, my friend Leon could take a picture of him paying off the wager. He agreed.

Lee cast marvellously for a man of his age and unaccustomed to tournament tackle and procedure, achieving a long cast of more than 130 feet easily winning second place. More familiar with the fast line and powerful rod than he, I cast about 160 feet and smiled as this giant of a man, grinning from ear to ear strode over towards me, his hand extended with a five-dollar bill clenched between the fingers. The resulting picture of his paying off the bet is one that I am most proud of in the twenty-odd photo albums collecting dust in my recreation room. Alongside it is the actual "fiver" that he handed over.

Sadly, Lee Wulff perished a few years later. Shortly after his eightieth birthday after being feted by the navy on a United States aircraft carrier, he and his beloved and ancient little airplane went down not far from his home in the Catskills. In interviews, Lee had often said that when his time came, that would have been his chosen route.

Another mini-magical memory concerns something I learned just a few years ago and it was a delightful bit of information. In my late teens and early twenties, more than fifty years ago, as a member of the old Toronto Anglers and Hunters Association[5] I decided to participate in the weekly fly-tying classes that were being conducted in a large boardroom above their offices. Gentlemen, whose names are coming back to me one by one, were already famous in angling circles and all things to do with the sport including, of course, fly and bait casting, rod building and fly tying.

Tying flies had been a passion of mine shortly after I got my first fly rod when I was twelve, and thanks to the veritable mountain of available books in the library, I had already achieved a modicum of success with my fur and feather creations. On my sixteenth birthday I was given a wonderful present by my parents, a superb hardwood cabinet filled almost to overflowing with the necessary hardware and every conceivable material used to create one's own flies. I eventually realized that if my ability to construct more complicated patterns was ever to improve that I would need hands-on instruction from a veteran, expert fly-tier. The instructors in the course all fitted that criterion, Johnnie McGhee, Herb Telfer, Norm Telfer, and of course the remarkably talented and patient Carl Atwood.[6] It was he who took my limited, self-taught fly-tying skills to the next level. I have since tied flies alongside Mr. Lee Wulff, perhaps the finest trout and salmon fisherman who ever lived and was once commissioned to tie a presentation set of flies for the then Governor General of Canada, Viscount Alexander, in the early 1950s.

Carl Atwood was a full-time entomologist with the Royal Ontario Museum at the time and eventually made quite a name for himself with the discovery of the spruce budworm and how to control, if not to completely eradicate them. These pests, the bane of Quebec's huge lumbering industry, had been decimating acres of forestation in northern Quebec for years. Mr. Atwood's other very well-known credentials were tied to his reputation as a superb fly fisherman and researcher of trout habitat. He thought nothing of spending days on end camping and canoeing in Northern Ontario and his beloved northern Quebec, an area which I now visit for a couple of weeks most years and have since the early sixties. It was he who helped instil the love of all things fly fishing in me as a youth and who encouraged me to pursue the competitive side of fly casting to the maximum of my ability.

Although I have always been interested in creative writing, and wrote numerous articles and short stories for various magazines and newspapers, I had never written a book until I was well into my fifties when I was asked by a publisher to put together a different kind of a how-to book on angling. The idea was to chronicle some of the most interesting tales in my fishing career and subliminally incorporate the how-to so that the reader was not being instructed, but felt that they were simply discovering on their own, tips and information to enhance their own angling abilities. The result was my first published book, *Fishing Hats*. It was through *Fishing Hats* that I met two of my best long-time fishing buddies, Paul Quarrington, one of the most popular authors in Canada today, and Rick Matusiak, definitely the best trout fisherman I know. My interest in writing grew substantially after meeting Paul, who had contacted me after reading *Hats*. With his encouragement, I continued writing, eventually cranking out more than a dozen other manuscripts and reading about other authors and their various creative works.

I had often wondered if author, Margaret Atwood, whose name was continually popping up in literary journals and newspaper articles was somehow related to my fly-tying mentor, Carl Atwood. It was only recently that I read a lengthy question-and-answer interview that had been done with her. At one point she said that when she was quite young, she loved going on camping and canoeing excursions in Northern Ontario and Quebec with her fly-fishing father, Carl Atwood. It seemed like too much of a coincidence until further into the interview, the magical moment arrived when she mentioned her father's fame in discovering and solving the spruce budworm infestation problem. It had to be he—the very same person. It immediately triggered all the recollections of those moments when I was fumbling around trying to marry feathers of different colours together to tie "Jock Scotts" and "Silver Doctors," two of the more difficult trout flies ever designed and her father would gently illustrate the necessary technique. It is truly amazing how often the old adage, "what goes around, comes around" holds true. There was I in my youth, being taught by a gentleman then more than fifty years later discovering how another author, albeit one with tremendously greater credentials as a writer than myself, is my mentor's daughter.

Epilogue

My work on this book was interrupted for more than three months by a terrible, life-threatening situation that overcame me while getting ready to head up north with a buddy, Jim Lloyd, to go ice fishing on Limit Lake in Haliburton, Ontario. While I was packing my lunch in the kitchen to take for the customary shore dinner, with the Skidoos already loaded on the trailer and Jim waiting for me to pick him up, I was struck with a horrendous pain in my lower, right abdomen. There had been no forewarning whatsoever!

A Tylenol 2 did nothing to ease it. A couple of Tylenol 3s were found to be no better. The pain rapidly worsened to the point where my wife, Sheila, grabbed one of the "house-call doctor magnets" off the fridge. She must have found a good one because he arrived in less than ten minutes. He reacted almost immediately after examining me—an ambulance was to be called for, immediately.

That was the second action that contributed to my being alive today. The first, obviously, was Sheila's telephoning him—actually against my wishes. Apparently, according to her, I kept repeating that I would be OK in a moment or two.

I stubbornly believed that I would still be heading up north as soon as I could get rid of the pain, however, I passed out before the ambulance arrived. The last I remember of that day and for the next ten days, or so was briefly waking up, strapped on a stretcher and being carried down our veranda steps to the ambulance. I've been told that I managed to mumble a few words to my distraught wife at that moment asking her to call Jim and tell him I was going to be a little late. *I was more than thirty days late!*

Apparently my heart stopped several times, first in the ambulance, then in the Intensive Care Unit at the hospital where I spent the next twenty days. What had happened was that a couple of gall stones had broken away from the gall bladder, then lodged in the duct going from the pancreas gland, causing it to burst. The poisons it distributed infected almost every major organ in my body and one by one they shut down while I was in a coma. The doctors then chemically paralysed my entire body to allow the Critical Care Team and surgeons to do their work. Evidently, over the next few weeks I had nine cat-scan evaluations, many ultra-sound examinations and remained plugged into every piece of apparatus and equipment they could pretty well find.

I have since learned that of the doctors who were present when I was initially rushed in to the hospital, only one, Doctor Khoa Le, suggested that there might be a chance of survival. The others, their prognoses similar, told my wife and son that there was little hope. Doctor Le, however, has since said that when he studied my face, he saw a glimmer and decided that he would bring me back to my wife even though the odds were apparently all stacked against my recovery. I have now learned that Doctor Le surpassed all the norms in monitoring my situation, even staying in the adjoining bed to rest on occasion.

With one of the drugs alone with which I was being treated costing five thousand dollars a day, according to the staff of the Intensive Care Unit the total cost for my stay and treatment in the Scarborough Grace Hospital

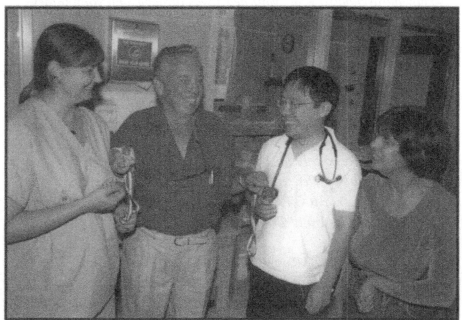

Gord sharing his medals with two members of the Intensive Care Unit at Scarborough Grace Hospital in 2004. Standing between him and his wife, Sheila, is Dr. Le, whom Gord credits with saving his life.

surpassed a million dollars. My wife Sheila, son Ronnie, and dozens of friends from all over the world, some of whom drove up from below the border to personally wish me luck although I was unable to even respond, must, along with the medical staff all take credit for my being here today.

I received e-mail messages from as far away as Europe due to the fact my son put a brief account of what had happened to his father on our club web-site which goes to fishermen and tournament casters all over the world.

With about a week to go before being sent home, Dr. Le hand delivered a letter to me while I sat outside my room in the general ward, saying how wonderful it was to see me up and around. Not knowing, what an immense part he had played in my recovery, I shook his hand, thanked him then sat down to read the letter as he strode away.

With Doctor Le's permission, here is what he had handwritten for me:

April 27, 2004
Dear Mr. Deval:
When you arrived, you were diagnosed with pancreatitis and this caused problems to your heart, lungs and other vital organs. You were on the ventilator for a long time and had to have nutrient fed to your body intravenously, while your heart was unstable and your kidneys threatened to shut down.

The prognoses were all poor and it was thought that you might die. But one day I saw a light at the end of the tunnel when I saw you. Your eyes were half-open and I took the opportunity to tell you that you were going to make it.

I was so happy one day when we were able to take you off the venti-lator. I knew that one day I'd be able to say hello to you on a medical ward and shake your hand.

I'm glad you've pulled through the ordeal,
Khoa Le, M.D., F.R.C.P.C.
Internal Medicine and Critical Care

After reading his letter, I could not contain my emotion and broke into howling wave after wave of wailing and crying. Sounding like a child who had had a car door slammed on a hand, it was impossible for me to stifle my crying. It would momentarily ebb then rise from the depths of my chest into even louder wailing until the racket brought most of the nurses and staff on the ward running to see what was wrong. With a shaky hand I passed the letter to the head nurse who read it out loud for the others then several of them began to display tears of emotion. I have, of course, since suitably replied to Doctor Le's wonderful letter with an appropriate one of my own.

In the hospital's ICU, which I have revisited several times to thank everybody for their part in my being alive, they refer to me as their miracle baby for being reborn again in their unit. The wonderful nurses and attendants there also told me that I was the first person to ever return there to thank them—one of the ladies did say, however, that few actually get the chance. I have since learned on the internet, that there is only a fifteen to twenty chance of survival for people under the age of sixty suffering from pancreatitis and almost none for those my age, seventy-four!

It is now some time since I was discharged from the hospital. As soon as possible I began working out daily at the Fitness Institute to recover my strength, while also writing every spare minute that I can. In August 2004, I attended the North American Fly and Bait Casting Championships in Lexington, Kentucky. I did place in the top half-dozen competitors in five of the twelve disciplines, winning medals in two which I gave to Dr. Le and the gals in the ICU who, along with Dr. Le I believe, were my guardian angels.

Regular visits to keep in touch with the ICU
staff are now part of Gord's routine.

Appendix
Casting Records

The relevance of including information on my casting records, was eventually rationalized using the perspective that personal records have certainly all created magical memories for me. Some of these records have since been topped while others are still in effect.

The only one to do with fishing tops the list—The largest recorded speckled trout ever caught on a fly, twenty-nine inches long, eleven-and-a-quarter pounds, Broadback River, Quebec, in 1961.

- All six Canadian Distance Fly and Bait Casting records, some of which still stand.
- North American Salmon Fly Distance record (fifteen-foot rod) two hundred and forty-eight feet. This record is permanent, as the rules were subsequently altered to allow rods as long as seventeen feet.
- North American Anglers Fly Distance record, one hundred and seventy-one one feet.
- North American Senior, Single Hand 7.5 gram Spinning Distance record, two hundred and sixty-one feet.
- North American Senior, Two Hand 18 gram Spinning Distance record, four hundred and twenty-eight feet.
- North American Senior, Two Hand 30 gram Spinning Distance record, five hundred and twenty-eight feet.

Notes

Chapter 1: The Waters of Uxbridge

1. The Mepps Aglia evolved from a wide variety of weighted spinners being made in Europe after the first stationary spool (spinning) reels came into our hands. Spinners such as the ancient Colorado spinner, a round blade attached to a split ring between two swivels with another split ring and treble hook on its bottom, had been marketed in England and North America for years before that, but required the addition of split shot or a sinker to cast and fish them properly.
2. The "Paramachene Belle trout fly," or the Par-Belle as it is often called, features contrasting red and white colours, making it more easily spotted by trout in roiled or muddy waters.
3. There are many different species of trout. The ones encountered in this book are mainly brook trout, brown trout, lake trout, rainbow trout and speckled trout. For more information on trout, see *Fishing for Brookies, Browns and Bows* (Vancouver: Greystone Books, 2001).
4. The Scarborough Fly and Bait Casting Association occasionally sponsors fishing derbies for eight to twelve-year-old kids, usually in July.

Chapter 2: Fishing on the Ganny

1. Other anglers frequenting the river have also adopted these handles. Obviously, there is a story behind every one of the monikers for the Ganaraska River.
2. Allan Hepburn was the name of the former owner of the land in the area who gave us access rights to fish the stream passing through his property.
3. "Throwing tin" is fisherman's lingo for fishing with a spinning tackle.
4. The term "opening weekend" is applied by anglers to the dates when one can legally fish for a particular species. Obviously, the closing weekend is the end of that species' legal fishing season. These dates are normally set

by the Ministry of Natural Resources to prohibit fishing when the fish are spawning.

Chapter 3: Land O' Lakes and Land O' Fish

1. Shank's mare is an old term for walking, meaning to use one's own legs as a means of conveyance. The term is of British origin, but the source is not known.
2. A "wabler" is a lure, usually metal, that "wables" from side to side when retrieved through the water. This particular one was made in Switzerland.
3. The "Halfwave" is a lure made of brass with ridges on one side to reflect more light to attract fish. The "Despair" is a nymph wet fly, usually fished near the bottom. It somewhat simulates two of the prime foods in the trout larder—stonefly nymphs and dragonfly nymphs. A "bucktail streamer" is a fly, fashioned to look like a minnow, the body of which is made from the hair of a deer's tail.
4. We have yet to discover what the "EGB" in this wabler's name stand for, but it is a tremendous fish catcher. It could be mistaken by trout as any number of things from a crawfish to a minnow, depending on how it is fished. The "Crocodile" originated in Scandinavia and is another wabler designed to swim and look like a minnow. There have been many copies of the original Crocodile and they will all catch fish, but the best of the lot is the "Gord Deval Crocodile," a redesigned version with a number of key refinements. It was on the market a few years ago and should be available again shortly.
5. A "winterkill" occurs when a comparatively shallow and smallish body of water becomes capped with an exceptionally heavy ice and snow load, preventing sunshine from passing through its surface. The resulting gasses, created by decaying vegetation robbed of its life-producing sunshine, mean certain death to trout found in these situations.
6. An esker is a long narrow ridge of earth, sometimes extending many miles. Usually composed of sand and gravel, eskers were "pushed up" during the retreat of the glaciers.
7. A "Mickey Finn streamer fly" is one with alternating red and yellow colours tied to resemble chubs and small perch.

Chapter 4: Muskoka Magic

1. Wablers, those metal lures that wobble from side to side, are occasionally called spoons due to their spoon-like shape. A "Rapala," made in Finland,

is a plastic coated, balsa-wood core lure designed to look and swim like a minnow. These are phenomenal "fish-catchers."

2. In fishing terms. a "series of give and goes" could mean either of two things. During the lure's retrieve, the best lure action is usually achieved by varying the speed that one works the lure through the water. In playing a fish, how ever. it could mean allowing the fish to run to avoid line breakage.

Chapter 5: Up Pefferlaw Way

1. As for fishing lures, there is considerable controversy over the advantage of one colour over another in lure design, however I subscribe to the theory that fish are colour-blind and react to different shades, or contrasts. The colours of lures mean more in terms of catching fishermen, rather than fish. I still believe that silhouette and contrast are the most important factors in a lure's appearance. Many "experts" have recently come to the conclusion that a pale green may be the colour generally most attractive to fish.

Chapter 6: The "Pigeons" of the Kawarthas

1. A "Jitterbug popping plug" is an oval-shaped surface lure, with a metal contrivance on its front that causes the lure to make loud popping noises on the surface when retrieved. It is excellent for bass and other fish that feed in the shallows.

Chapter 7: A Mystery At Tedious Lake

1. *Fishing Hats* (Toronto: Simon and Pierre, 1980).
2. The label "7X" gives the designation of the strength of the tip of a fly leader, the material between the fly line and the fly. It is one of the lightest strengths normally used, usually with very small flies.
3. The Fisherman's Prayer has been passed down through many generations. It's origin is not known.

Chapter 8: Blue Lake of Temiscamingue

1. Fly lines vary considerably in their overall performance. Frequently because of my extensive experience I am asked to be a "tester." Depending on the circumstances, my reports may be given verbally or be written.

2. The Despair fly, designed to imitate a nymph as noted earlier, is, in my opinion, the best artificial fly for trout fishing.
3. The "thermocline" is the middle layer, temperature-wise, of cooler suspended water that develops once the waters in the lake settle down after the spring thaw.

Chapter 9: Sullivan—A "Pot of Gold" Lake?

1. The Fish O' Buzzer is an arrangement of a buzzer fastened to a length of wood with a trigger and wire assembly to which the fishing line is attached. When a fish attacks the bait on the line beneath the ice, the line being pulled activates the buzzer, putting the angler into high gear.

Chapter 10: Poaching Pierce's Pond

1. The Glen Major Club is probably one of the oldest private trout fishing clubs in Canada. It consists of a clubhouse, several cottages and two ponds with docks and boats, the entire property is surrounded by a high fence. The club is very exclusive with, I believe a maximum membership of 25 men. The club is in the hamlet of Glen Major, north of Balsam, Ontario, some fifty plus kilometres east of Toronto.

Chapter 11: The Phenomenal Echo Creek

1. Canada Fishing Tackle and Sports was a wholesale distributor of outdoor equipment, owned and operated by Jack Harris. Originally, the company was called Canada Needle and Fishing Tackle, but as the market for needles diminished, the name was changed. The company had a small factory in Havelock, Ontario, but the head office was in Toronto. Shortly after I left the company as the representative in Eastern Ontario in 1964, Jack sold the company and it soon folded.

Chapter 12: Pleasurable Pursuits on Grenadier Pond

1. The legend, as interesting as it seems, does not stand up to scrutiny. The 1813 Battle of York occurred in late April when there was no ice on the pond. As well, the battle took place further east and all casualties were documented, none of whom disappeared into the pond. In reality, the

name is a Victorian romanticism that arose because soldiers from the Toronto garrison spent time around the pond, both on manoeuvres and during their leisure hours, including officers who fished the pond as guests of John Howard, owner of the property at the time. It was John Howard who bequeathed the land and the pond to the city to be a park for the citizens of Toronto.

2. The "Pflueger Supreme," the best revolving spool fishing reel of its time, was made in Michigan. It is no longer available.

3. In 1974, there were six accuracy games, three of which were fly casting, the other three being spin and bait casting:

i. Dry Fly Casting is performed on five targets placed between twenty and forty-five feet with floating flies and lines, two casts at each 30-inch diameter floating target. Scoring, as it is in all the accuracy games, is on a demerit system, i.e. the caster begins with a perfect score of 100 and loses one point for each foot or fraction thereof that the fly strikes away from the target. Therefore hitting all ten targets results in a perfect score.

ii. Trout Fly Casting combines Dry Fly as above, only five casts, but includes five casts with only one false cast before laying the fly down. That's called "wet fly," then the caster has fifteen tries to it all five targets roll casting. Scoring is also done on a demerit system.

iii. Bass Bug Accuracy requires a heavier fly rod and line and there is an additional target place at 70 feet from the casting box. The Bass Bug is made of cork rather than feathers as is the trout and dry flies.

iv. 1/4 Ounce Spinning Accuracy ten casts are targets from 40 feet to 75 feet using spinning tackle with a 1/4 ounce casting plug.

v. 3/8 Ounce Plug Accuracy as above only using a 3/8 ounce plug and either spinning or revolving spool outfits.

vi. 5/8 Ounce Plug Accuracy as above only a 5/8 ounce plug.

There were six distance casting games, three fly and three plugs:

vii. 5/8 Ounce Unrestricted Revolving Spool Distance is performed with revolving spool reels, mostly custom-made. The object was simply to throw it as you could within a one hundred and eight degree court. The caster had five tries and his three longest were averaged to determine the winner.

viii. Two-Hand Spinning Distance as above, only using a one-ounce casting weight (plug) with stationary spool (spinning) equipment.

ix. Single-Hand Spinning Distance as above, only with a 3/8 ounce plug.

x. Trout Fly Distance casting single-hand with a nine-foot rod and an ounce and a half weight fly line for distance.

xi. Salmon Fly Distance casting double-hand with a fifteen-foot rod and an 1820-grain weight fly line for distance.

xii. Anglers Fly Distance casting single-hand with a nine-foot rod and a #10, 300-grain shooting head fly line.

In 2006, once again there are six accuracy disciplines and six distance games, but with some changes.

Chapter 13: The Magic of Sludge Lake

1. "Rotenone" is a toxic crystalline substance obtained from the roots of the derris and other plants.

Chapter 14: From Novice to Accomplished Angler

1. Barklay's was located in Oshawa. In 2005, it suffered a major fire and I understand is now closed.

2. A Berry Aneurysm is the worst kind of stroke that can hit the brain. It refers to the rupture of arteries and veins, causing massive bleeding in the brain, often necessitating the removal of large sections of brain tissue in order to preserve life. Obviously, this stroke often results in loss of mobility and other neural functions, and occasionally causes death.

3. A "roe bag" is a dime-sized cluster of trout or salmon eggs contained in a silk, nylon or mesh material, tied like a small sack. The roe is a principal food of spawning rainbow trout and salmon. The roe bags are, of course, fastened to a small hook as bait.

4. This stocking program was an experimental program established by the then Department of Lands and Forests. Currently, Kennesis Lake is being massively stocked with brook trout by the Ministry of Natural Resources.

Chapter 15: The Trout of Loughborough Lake

1. This project is currently ongoing in several lakes in Ontario. The intent is to make trout fishing more accessible since access has been denied in many lakes recently. The Ministry is now only stocking waters where there is guaranteed public access, even if on privately owned land.

Chapter 16: Lake Simcoe: A Most Fishable Body of Water

1. A "Deep Diving Heddon River Runt" is a small plastic plug with a metal scoop lip that, when retrieved or trolled, pulls it down deeply.

Chapter 17: I Always Wanted to Fish in a Stream Called Piss Creek

1. Wet flies are fished beneath the surface while "dries" are above.

Chapter 18: A Wonderful Lake With No Name

1. The *Toronto Star* fishing contest ran for a number of years, probably in the 1950s and '60s, but I am not certain of the dates.
2. The stomach contents are checked so we can see what the fish have been eating. Once known, we attempt to duplicate these foodstuffs as closely as possible through the design of our flies and/or lures.
3. A "Handigaff" is a metal device that can be used to grab fish at the surface when ice fishing. It works on the same principal as a pair of ice tongs.
4. The source of this verse is not known.

Chapter 19: More Trout Fishing in Haliburton

1. The "Crocodile" lure" is my favourite for trolling as it is perfectly balanced and won't twist the line.
2. When the barometric pressure falls, all animal life, including humans, becomes less active.
3. A "Rapala jig" is a weighted plastic, minnow-shaped lure worked beneath a hole in the ice. It is weighted and balanced so that it will swim in a wide circle at whatever depth the angler chooses.

Chapter 20: Saugeen Country Booty

1. Denny's Dam is on the Saugeen River, a few miles upstream from the Town of Southampton on Lake Huron. It would be interesting to know who "Denny" was, assuming there was a "Denny."

Chapter 21: The Mighty Broadback River

1. This was Dr. John William Cook of Fort William, Ontario, now part of Thunder Bay. For more information on Dr. Cook, see *Outdoor Canada*, Vol. 32, No. 4 (May 2004).

2. The "Lazy S" cast is performed in a manner to throw slack in the line, allowing the fly to rest momentarily before being swept away by the current.

3. I would choose the #6 Despair in this scenario because the fish are staging deeply and feeding on nymphs; the fly should be presented to them accordingly.

4. A Rapala "plug" is a lure that is either trolled or cast out then retrieved. A Rapala "jig," on the other hand, is fished vertically, simply jigging it up and down vertically through a hole in the ice.

5. A "Muscarovitch streamer fly" is a fly tied with both squirrel and polar bear hair over an orange body.

6. Whether it's Mepps, Vibrax, Cybelle, or a host of lesser copies of the original (the Mepps Aglia), we anglers owe a great deal to the "French" spinner, perhaps the number one producer for fishermen over the past fifty years. The Mepps Aglia evolved from a wide variety of weighted spinners being made in Europe after the first stationary spool (spinning) reels came into our hands. Spinners such as the ancient Colorado spinner, a round blade fixed by a split ring between two swivels with another split ring and treble hook on its bottom, had been marketed in England and North America for years before that, but they required the addition of split shot or a sinker to cast and fish them properly. With the advent of the spinning reel which allowed for long, effortless casts, many new lures were being turned out, initially in Europe then gradually in Canada and the United States. The Mepps Aglia, right from the first day it arrived, proved to be a winner for all concerned. George Breckenridge, a tackle salesman and fisherman in Quebec, foresaw the potential in the lure and immediately applied for the rights to be the sole distributor of the lures in North America. His company was able to retain them for many years as the market for the "French" spinners mushroom exponentially. However, the sheer numbers of the lure's copies hitting the shelves, and wholesalers arguing successfully against the initial trade agreement between Mepps and Breckenridge, gradually lessened his proprietorship and they became available everywhere.

   The Mepps spinners are available in a variety of blade shapes, colours and sizes. The wider blade Aglias can be fished in extremely shallow waters because of the blade's resistance on the retrieve, whereas the narrower blade Comet, with less resistance, is fished in somewhat deeper waters. Both lures should be retrieved with the tip of the rod and the slack retrieved accordingly. Simply reeling the spinners in will, of course, entice the odd fish in to striking, but using the rod tip retrieve is much more productive.

The Mepps Aglia finally received some legitimate competition when the Vibrax Blue Fox spinners hit the market some fifteen or twenty years ago. The Vibrax has a balanced construction system that somewhat offsets the natural twisting of the line and like the Mepps, is a superior lure. Somewhat heavier than the Mepps, it is of course sturdier and runs deeper, whereas the spinner blade on the Mepps will gradually lose its shape, therefore also losing its ability to function correctly.

None of the French spinners should be trolled unless necessary as they can hopelessly twist the line. Bending down the wire slightly at the front of the lure can help avoid the problem but also diminishes the lure's action a little. Of course a weighted keel a short distance up the line will also alleviate the trolling problem, but the fact is the "French" spinner remains primarily a casting lure and, in my book, one of the greatest ever.

7. Some four or five years earlier, Gary Benson had accidentally hooked young Randy in the nose while we were fly fishing on Mosque Lake. Afterwards I stuck it on a hat as a memento.

8. Paul Quarrington, *Fishing With My Old Guy* (Vancouver: Greystone Books, 2000).

9. The show is called "Bob Izumi's Real Fishing Show" and is still running. Bob is a tournament fisherman and now one of the best. He also has a magazine called *Real Fishing*. An entire line of hats and other merchandise bearing his name is available.

Chapter 22: Other Magical Memories

1. Dave Reddick was the president of the Toronto Anglers and Hunters when it was a strong and viable association in the 1940s. He was Canada's muskie expert and chaired the important Nogies Creek Muskellunge Research Project sponsored by the Canadian National Sportsmen's Show, of which he was a director. An accomplished angler and talented writer, he authored a number of books, including *Fishing Is A Cinch* and the very popular *Ma-Kee: The Life and Death of a Muskellunge*.

2. King Whyte was an exceptional *Toronto Star* outdoor columnist. He was one of the pioneers of televised fishing shows.

3. Leo "Pete" McGillen, a descendant of Otonabee pioneers, was a noted newspaper man. A former city editor of the *Peterborough Examiner*, he held the position of "Outdoors Editor" at the *Toronto Telegram* for many years. He wrote numerous articles for other journals and magazines as well. His television show filled the time frame between the end of the Saturday night hockey games and the late news. I appeared as a guest on it several times.

   Pete was involved in the naming of the Land O' Lakes tourist region and, with his wife Rose, operated a fishing lodge on Rice Lake.

4. Lee Wulff, of New York, was a prolific writer and the world's best trout and salmon fisherman in almost every trout fisherman's eyes. His films and lectures were legion. He married Joan Salvato, a professional caster for the old Shakespeare Fishing Tackle Company, which had plants in Kalamazoo, Michigan, and in Toronto, and the two were like bread and butter until he died in his plane crash about eight years ago.

5. When Dr. Francis Kortright was president of the Toronto Anglers and Hunters, the association was instrumental in establishing the first Toronto Sportsman Show in 1947, which eventually became a separate entity of its own. In its earlier years, the association had great instructors in all phases of angling. A recent e-mail was received informing me that because the group has so few casters now, they are merging with another small association, the Westhill Anglers.

6. Carl Atwood (1906-1993) was born in Clyde River, Nova Scotia. A forest entomologist by training, he was an avid outdoorsman and frequently took his family on annual trips to northern Ontario and Quebec. In 1998, the Canadian Museum of Nature, with the participation of Dr. Atwood's daughter, Canadian author Margaret Atwood, launched the Nature Discovery Fund (NDF). The NDF is a not-for-profit fund designed to encourage public support for systematics—the science of classification and a cornerstone of the study of our natural world.

Index

About the Author

Gord Deval holds, or has held, over one hundred records both nationally and internationally, including several world records during more than six decades of tournament casting. He won the North American All-Round Senior Championship fourteen times. He was the president of the Ontario Fly and Bait Casting Association in the fifties, while organizing the first Canadian Casting Association and acting as its president. Deval has also competed thirty-seven times in the North American Championships, winning many titles and awards. He has been the recipient of Ontario's Athletic Achievement Award every year since this special recognition became available.

Deval has been a qualified casting instructor since 1949, beginning with the old Toronto Anglers and Hunters Association and at present with his Scarborough Fly and Bait Casting Association. He estimates that he has personally taught over a thousand anglers and tournament casters the finer points of the sport. In 1995, Deval and his club hosted the North American

Gord Deval

In 1996, Gord Deval received an award from the City of Scarborough as part of the city's Bicentennial celebrations. The award recognized the top 200 individuals who had brought honour to Scarborough over the past 200 years. Here, Gord is being congratulated by Mayor Frank Faubert.

Championships in the City of Scarborough. It was agreed by most of the participants to have been one of the best of these events ever held. He has qualified for the select All American team numerous times over the years after being the first Canadian to ever win that honour.

In addition to his casting, fishing and cooking seminars, Deval also teaches rod building and fly tying. A collection of his personally tied trout flies was presented to Viscount Alexander, the then Governor General of Canada, on behalf of the Toronto Anglers and Hunters Association back in the fifties and he has since taught many hundreds of others the intricacies of fly tying.

Of course, there have been many radio and television appearances along the way, with casting, fishing, fish-cookery demonstrations and seminars. He has also written many magazine articles and a number of books.

Deval was honoured in 1992 by the City of Scarborough with a special award for his service and dedication to his sport and the city over the years. As already mentioned, in 1995 Deval and his club hosted the North American Fly and Bait Casting championships, attended by over eighty competitors. Despite the rigours of running this event, he managed to establish a new record in the two-hand distance spinning event—428 feet. Deval believes that the biggest honour he has had to date was being selected to receive the Bi-Centennial Award of Merit and Medal presented to him by the Mayor of the City, His Worship Frank Faubert, in 1996. This was recognition as one of a very exclusive group, the top 200 Scarborough citizens to have brought honour to the city over its history during the past 200 years.

Other Books by Gord Deval

Fishin' Hats: A Collection of True Fish Stories
(Toronto: Simon & Pierre, 1983)

Fishin' Tales: A Collection of True Fish Stories
(Toronto: Simon & Pierre, 1984)

Life (and Death) in the Yoonited States of Uhmurica: A Montage of Media Items
(Toronto: Simon & Pierre, 1984)

Take Me Fishin' Too, Daddy, Please
(Toronto: Simon & Pierre, 1985)

Fishing for Brookies, Browns and Bows:
The Old Guy's Complete Guide to Catching Trout
(Vancouver: Greystone Books, 2001)

CPSIA information can be obtained
at www.ICGtesting.com
Printed in the USA
LVOW03s1518171117
556616LV00010B/82/P